PopEnomics

12 RELATABLE
(AND NOT BORING)
POP CULTURE INSIGHTS
FOR RETIREMENT
SUCCESS

JESSE W HURST,
CEO, CFP

Spur Circle Publishing
www.spurcirclepublishing.com

ISBN: 979-8-9987314-0-2 (paperback)
ISBN: 979-8-9987314-1-9 (ebook)
ISBN: 979-8-9987314-2-6 (hardcover)

Contents

Introducing PopEnomics

What is PopEnomics? It is a unique lens through which to view the economic and investment world. You may be surprised to find that there are many financial topics and lessons that have parallels to things seen or heard in television shows, movies, and popular music. As a fan of all three, I use these unique illustrations to create a narrative that allows me to share complex topics in a much more fun and engaging way. This is what I call PopEnomics! I invite you to come along for an entertaining and interesting exploration of the social security challenges, stocks, bonds, low birth rates, and how they can impact your retirement.

I began writing blog posts for my clients in 2010. My goal was to explain complex topics in a way that would be relatable and understandable. When I started, I generally wrote one or two blog posts per month. That eventually ramped up to a weekly cadence until early 2020, when the COVID-19 pandemic shut down—at least on a temporary basis—much of my face-to-face interaction with clients. At that time, to help keep clients in the loop during what was an unprecedented set of economic and financial circumstances, I doubled down on this strategy and began posting at least twice a week. Early in the pandemic, economic and political issues were coming up that most people would not have believed could have occurred just a few short years before. I started to see more analogies and life lessons from pop culture showing up in everyday life. I regularly used these to try to explain things to my clients and other readers. Based on the significant feedback I received, this was a wildly popular and fun way to explore the world. I was encouraged to continue to share future topics through the PopEnomics lens!

Your Retirement Puzzle: Opening the Box and Examining Your Unique Puzzle Pieces

I am going to frame the 12 topics we will cover in this book as the pieces you will need to create your unique retirement puzzle. When was the last time you did a jigsaw puzzle? If you are like most adults, it has been a while. I have a few clients for whom putting together large and complex puzzles is a hobby that they share with their spouses. However, for most of us, the last time we put together a puzzle was with our kids or grandkids. For a few of us, it may even date back to when we were children.

If you think about the process of putting together a puzzle, how do you start? When asked this question, many people think about laying all the pieces out on a table. Often, people think about turning all the puzzle pieces over so they can see the picture side of each one. Some even respond that they find the four corner pieces first so they can build out their puzzles from there.

[1]

However, the most important thing you must do when putting together a puzzle is to look at the picture on the box. You need to have a picture in your mind of what you are trying to complete before you start. Planning for a successful retirement is exactly the same. If you don't have a fully defined picture in your head of where you want to go, it is hard to know what steps to take to get there.

I am not talking about vague generalities like "Someday, I would like to be able to retire comfortably" or "When I retire, I would like to be able to travel." While those statements may feel good, they are very fuzzy and undefined. They do not lead you toward a clear vision and the action steps needed to get there.

I am talking about developing a *highly detailed and highly personal* picture of what you want from life when you retire. You need to know what the picture on the box looks like before you start putting together the puzzle. This level of detail brings clarity and focus, reassuring you that you are on the right track.

Some of you who have worked in corporate America may have heard the acronym SMAC when it comes to goal planning. It stands for specific, measurable, achievable, and compatible. Your retirement goals should be defined according to this thought process as well.

Instead of giving vague goals like "retiring comfortably" or "traveling," we could say, "I would like to be able to retire at age sixty-five, be debt-free, and have an income of $7,500 per month or $90,000 per year, which would allow me and my spouse to take two significant vacations each year!" That meets our criteria. It presents a well-defined mental picture, like the picture on the puzzle box. It also allows us to determine what steps we need to take to achieve that goal and vision.

I will use the analogy of putting together a puzzle to frame the issues and challenges you will have to work through to complete your retirement puzzle. Along the way, I will use lessons and illustrations from pop culture, and sometimes history, to illustrate many of the points in this book—hence the name PopEnomics.

What does pop culture have to do with economic and investment principles? Great question. First, I believe you can draw many parallels between things you observe in movies, music, and television and what's going on in real life—if you pay attention. Second, I think that the last thing the world needs is another dry, boring economics- and statistics-based book about planning for a successful retirement. Finally, I believe that people will remember lessons better if they associate them with media that really resonates with them.

For example, have you ever thought about what steps you should take to plan for your retirement and wished you could be watching reruns of your favorite television show instead? Have you ever wondered whether lyrics from a classic rock song could help answer your investment and asset allocation questions? Have you ever wondered whether—or feared that—you could learn real-life family or business lessons from the way that

Don Corleone managed his complex world in *The Godfather*? If this sounds unique and fun, PopEnomics is for you!

Introducing Your Financial Narrator

Many memorable movies have narrators who help tell the story. These include *Forrest Gump*, *A Christmas Story*, and *The Sandlot*. However, due to the financial nature of this book, I am going to use the example from the 2015 movie *The Big Short*, based on the book written in 2010 by Michael Lewis, which tells the story of the 2008 subprime mortgage crisis. A number of the film's characters break the fourth wall to explain important financial concepts to the audience; this is most frequently done by Ryan Gosling, who plays Jared Vennett and serves as the film's narrator. I won't be breaking the fourth wall in this book, but I will be explaining financial concepts throughout the book using a number of movie, music and other pop culture references. In doing so, I hope to make them as fun and accessible as Vennett and his celebrity assistants do in *The Big Short*. I invite you to join me on this journey as we examine the various pieces you will need to successfully solve your own retirement puzzle.

2

Since I will be serving as the narrator of this book, let me start by introducing myself. I want you to get to know the person who is sharing these economic and investment principles with you through a pop culture lens.

I have more than 35 years of experience in the financial planning industry and am a Certified Financial Planner® (CFP®) and an Accredited Investment Fiduciary®.

I began my career as a financial advisor in August 1987, just a few weeks before the Black Monday stock market crash in October of that year. In 1997, two other CFPs and I became the founding partners of Millennial Group. The firm focused on helping people successfully pursue their retirement goals and aspirations.

I founded Impel Wealth Management in 2017 to help individuals and families continue "moving life forward" (our tagline) through meaningful conversations, comprehensive planning, and sound financial advice. Since then, I have had the honor of being named to *Forbes*/Shook Research's "Best-in-State Wealth Advisors" list for the state of Ohio six times. A more detailed list of industry recognition and accomplishments is included in the "Your Narrator's Story" section at the end of the book.

The Importance of Client Stories in Our PopEnomics Journey

As an advisor, when I understand the meaning and purpose that money holds in a client's life, it allows me to help guide them in using their income and asset resources to accomplish the things that make life meaningful to them. At the end of the day, money is simply a means, not an end. Whoever dies with the most does not win. The relevant question then becomes "What is your money and wealth a means to for you and your family?"

This is a deep question, and it's easier to explore such issues within a trusted advisor relationship. Throughout our PopEnomics journey, I will share a number of real-life client examples with you to illustrate the various principles we are exploring. My wife, Rachel, pointed out to me that many people may be surprised to see the level of personal knowledge and intimacy explored in these client scenarios. Most people might think that a book about investment principles and retirement success would be mostly focused on numbers and finances. They could not be more off base. People largely make family-based, emotional decisions that are later justified by logic, not the other way around.

Rachel, whom I will often reference, is my best friend and trusted advisor. She runs her own very successful HR consulting and recruiting firm. She has been my biggest cheerleader and has encouraged me throughout my career endeavors, including the writing of this book. By the way, her name is pronounced Rachelle, like in the *Seinfeld* episode where Jerry and his friends try to see the movie *Rochelle, Rochelle*.[3]

In order to identify what you are trying to accomplish with your financial resources, you need to ask yourself deep questions and be open and honest with yourself about what is truly important in your life. You can then take the necessary steps to accumulate the means necessary to do the things that truly make life meaningful for you and your family. This process allows you to align your dreams with your financial resources.

I trust that you will enjoy the client stories, as they will illustrate the issues we are exploring in each of the chapters—or puzzle pieces—of the book. My hope is to make each principle outlined come to life and feel more authentic in the context of real-life scenarios. To clarify, all names and certain personal and family details have been changed to protect the identities of my trusted and valued clients, many of whom I have worked with for 20 to 30 years or more.

Kicking Off Our PopEnomics Journey with the Good Doctor

Before we move on to the first puzzle piece, I would like to explore some wisdom from one of my favorite authors and artists, Theodor Geisel. Most people are more familiar with him through his pen name, Dr. Seuss. He was an amazing author who wrote a lot about life, success, the environment, workers' rights, and racism. You just had to pay attention and get past the fact that these lessons were conveyed via children's books.

Did you ever think that you could address life's financial challenges by turning the pages of Dr. Seuss's unique and insightful writings? Let's give it a shot with a lesson from one of my favorite Dr. Seuss books, *Oh, the Places You'll Go!* I give it to almost every person I know who is graduating from high school or college.

According to Wikipedia, *Oh, the Places You'll Go!* "was first published by Random House on January 22, 1990." It was the last book Dr. Seuss published during his lifetime before he passed in September 1991 at 87.[4] The book highlights the ups and downs of life's journey, emphasizing that challenges and setbacks are a natural part of the process. It encourages readers to keep moving forward, even when faced with difficulties. This is a helpful mindset as you address both life and planning for retirement.

One of my favorite quotes from the book points out that where you end up in life—and on your journey toward a successful retirement—is largely based on yourself and on the steps you take as you go forward: "You have brains in your head. You have feet in your shoes. You can steer yourself any direction you choose."[5]

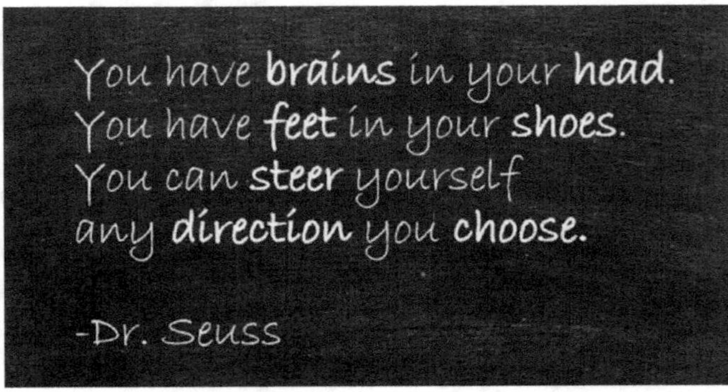

[6]

This is the perfect sentiment to launch us on our PopEnomics journey! What direction will you choose, and where do you want to end up? I look forward to leading you through a thoughtful and meaningful exploration of the issues we need to address and the steps we need to take to move you toward a retirement that you will be excited about. I invite you to come along with me as we begin by looking at "Puzzle Piece #1: Determining Where You Are Financially."

PUZZLE PIECE

#1

Determining Where You Are Financially

Have you ever had to make a connecting flight in a large unfamiliar airport? For those of us who travel regularly, this is not an unusual occurrence. If you have ever been on a tight schedule while trying to get to your next gate in a city like Chicago, Atlanta, or Denver, you know how daunting this task can be. How did you figure out how to get from where you were to where you wanted to go?

If you are like most people, you looked for the concourse map and then found the dot that said "You Are Here."

7

Once you locate yourself on the map, you can chart a course to get from where you are to where you want to go. Depending on how much time you have before your connecting flight, you may even be able to stop at the restroom and then go get yourself a latte.

Without having a proper map, you may never get where you want to be. This is especially true if you are a man and don't like asking for directions. Please remember that Yogi Berra once said, "If you don't know where you're going, you might not get there."[8]

The same is true for your financial life. You must know where you are before you can begin charting a course toward where you want to go. This has become much more difficult over the last few years. To put things in context, since early 2020, we have experienced a pandemic, government-mandated shutdowns, enhanced stimulus checks and unemployment benefits, and rapidly rising inflation—followed by rapidly rising interest rates, geopolitical uncertainty, and multiple wars.

These waves of economic and investment uncertainty have knocked many people off course. They no longer know where they are financially, let alone how to chart a path to get where they would like to go. If this describes your situation, you have come to the right book.

Let me begin by sharing an example of how I helped two clients determine where they were, define what their ideal retirement looked like, and begin assessing whether the financial resources they had accumulated would allow them to reach their future goals.

Jack and Diane: Trying to Determine Whether They Could Still Retire After COVID

Let's begin with a "little ditty" about a different Jack and Diane. Jack and Diane are actual clients with whom I have worked since 1992. Over the years, they have both been employed in different areas of the medical field. They did what many of my Midwestern millionaire-next-door-type clients have done. They worked hard, spent less than what they made, paid down debt diligently, and saved money in their employer-sponsored retirement plans and their home-state college education plans for many years.

In other words, they had good financial habits and were very disciplined in applying those habits in their daily lives. As a result, they were able to provide college education for all three of their children, who are now in their 30s and 40s. They were also able to build up substantial future Social Security benefits, and retirement assets in their 401(k) and 403(b) plans.

They were planning to transition from their work lives to what they hoped would be a retirement of significance in 2022. However, they became very concerned that the economic lockdowns caused by the COVID-19 pandemic, along with the resulting stock market volatility and steadily rising inflation, were making their retirement dreams less certain or attainable.

Luckily, the wealth management and financial planning processes that we discussed provided the economic road map they needed to get from where they were to where they wanted to be financially. We began by assessing their current financial resources and reconfirming their lifestyle goals for their retirement years. This meant we had to begin the process by knowing where they were financially.

This included looking at their base living expenses that were covered by their regular take-home pay from their salaries. We looked at what expenses might decrease in retirement, such as debt payments that might be paid off by the time they retired, automobile expenses for commuting, work-related clothing, and meals away from home. We also reviewed what expenses might increase during their retirement years. These included additional money for travel and hobbies and health-care costs that would no longer be covered by their employers.

In my more than 35 years of helping clients plan their retirement income needs, I have found that there are consistently five areas that tend to drain financial resources from the typical retiree, whether a client has $500,000 or $5 million of retirement savings. They are as follows:

1. Unreimbursed medical, dental, and prescription-drug-related costs
2. House projects and repairs
3. Automobile repair and replacement
4. Travel, hobby, and lifestyle expenses
5. Gifts to kids, grandkids, and charities

I meet with my clients every six months like clockwork. In fact, before clients leave the office, we schedule their next semiannual investment review, and tax and cash flow planning meetings. One of my clients noted that it is just like going to the dentist, except the dentist gives them Novocain.

Whenever we discuss clients' cash needs that are outside of their normal monthly budgeted expenses, it inevitably comes down to one of the five categories outlined above. This is normal and to be expected. It helps to have a process to ensure that the money being spent on these unique or unplanned expenses will not knock clients off track from reaching their other goals and objectives.

We used this process to determine that Jack and Diane could indeed still plan to retire in 2022. I reminded them that even though inflation had spiked significantly higher that year, based on economic history and the Fed's actions, we would expect price pressures to migrate back toward historical norms in the future.

We reviewed the income resources they would be receiving from Social Security benefits they would be initiating (Jack's at age 68, Diane's at age 65). I was pleased to share with them that the combination of their regular monthly income and the significant retirement plan savings they had accumulated, along with their relatively conservative lifestyle and low level of debt, still had them on track to reach their retirement goals as they hoped.

Armed with this updated financial road map, they confidently retired in mid-2022. I am happy to report that they are enjoying life, traveling more than they ever have before, and using their time to create shared experiences and memories with their children and grandchildren. I often remind clients that time with family is one of the best investments they can make. Years from now, their family will still value the cherished memories of the times they shared together.

Without the financial planning process, Jack and Diane might still be working due to the fear and uncertainty that accompanied the years leading up to their retirement transition. Financial planning gave them confidence instead of just hope. Unfortunately, many people rely on hope alone to achieve their retirement dreams. As we will explore, this strategy does not typically lead to success.

Hope Is Not a Strategy

In 2023, a study conducted by Escalent (a top research, data analytics, and advisory firm) found that 40% of retirement plan participants were guessing when asked how much money they needed to have saved for their retirement goals.[9] It seems that rather than putting time and effort into carefully planning for a successful transition from work life to retirement life, retirement plan participants were simply speculating about how much money they would need to accumulate to retire comfortably, then hoping for the best.

The survey was conducted among 4,000 401(k) plan participants who actively contributed to their plans and had balances of at least $5,000 in their accounts. To give us a little more optimism, the survey found that approximately 30% of the respondents used some sort of online savings calculator to create a plan to help guide their savings habits and achieve their future goals.

[10]

When asked how much they believed they would need to save to be able to live comfortably in retirement, the average savings goal was $946,000. Younger employees were more likely to guess they would need $500,000 or less, while employees in the baby boomer generation, heading toward retirement in the next few years, generally responded in the neighborhood of $1.2 million or higher.

It also seems that the older the respondents were, the more confident they were that they would be able to meet their future retirement income goals. While nearly half of baby boomers were confident about meeting their retirement goals, only 10% of Gen Xers shared a similar level of confidence.[11] Gen X is the generation that comes after the baby boomers, born between 1965 and 1980. Anecdotal evidence shows that people in the Gen X and millennial generations have been heavily influenced by the major events since the turn of the millennium. These include the significant recessions, periods of job loss, and stock market drops of 30%–50% associated with the dot-com bubble, 9/11, and the Global Financial

Crisis (which coincided with the failure of AIG and Lehman Brothers), as well as the COVID-19 pandemic and economic shutdowns.[12]

As you would probably guess, those of us who are CFPs do not believe that hope is a great strategy when planning for your retirement, a.k.a. your *Permanent Vacation* (an intentional nod to Aerosmith's 1987 album).

I believe that an intentional approach to planning for this significant life event makes much more sense. Many people seem to spend way more time planning a two-week vacation than planning a retirement that may last 20 to 30 years or longer—their permanent vacation.

Unfortunately, only 25% of survey respondents had relationships with trusted advisors, such as CFPs, to help them understand and define their goals.[13] As I stated at the beginning of this chapter, the first and most important thing that you need to do when contemplating your retirement is to determine where you are now. If you don't know where you are, it is hard to create goals and action plans to get where you want to go. Please remember, it is never too early or too late to start this process. We can always make progress toward a more successful tomorrow.

When building a customized retirement income plan, there are two main resource pillars that need to be examined. The first pillar is your family's income resources, such as Social Security, government pensions, and even defined benefit pensions, for the lucky few who will still receive them.

The second pillar is the asset resources you have worked hard to save and accumulate during your working years. These include personal savings, 401(k)s, IRAs, and stock and mutual fund investments, to name a few. We will invest significant time exploring both of these resource pillars in "Puzzle Piece #3: Determining How Much You Need to Retire (What's Your Number?)."

Building strategies that increase confidence as you move toward a successful transition from work life to retirement life is complex. Many variables that influence your plan can be affected by employment changes, economic and market volatility, health issues, and even changes in the tax law.

Please remember that planning is not a static one-time process. Once your retirement income plan is created, it is important to update it regularly to ensure that you are still on course to reach your desired destination. You simply cannot review all these dynamic and interrelated factors one time, shove your plan in the drawer, and think everything will work out all right. Your plan must be updated regularly. You can then compare the assumptions you made to the economic and investment reality you experienced and make midcourse adjustments if and when necessary.

Let me give you a travel-based analogy. You wouldn't want to get on an airplane leaving from Cleveland and flying to Los Angeles without your pilot having a flight plan. However, it seems that's what many people are doing today financially. They are up in the air. They have not determined where they want to land, and therefore, they have no idea whether they have enough fuel in the tank to get there. Remember what Yogi Berra said: "If you don't know where you're going, you might not get there."[14]

In addition, you want your pilot to continuously monitor the progress of your plane on its route to its destination. It is way easier to make a minor midcourse correction over Chicago than to wait until you are out over the Rockies and find that you are hundreds of miles off course. The same principle applies to carefully monitoring and updating a retirement plan that is unique to your family's resources and goals.

Navigating these uncertain economic waters by yourself can be lonely and dangerous. Enlisting the help of a trusted advisor can give you more confidence in your retirement journey. I firmly believe that hope is not a strategy that will lead to the successful outcomes you and your family aim to achieve.

People Get Ready

Curtis Mayfield, lead singer for the Impressions, wrote the song "People Get Ready," which was released in 1965. *Rolling Stone* named the gospel-influenced track the 24th greatest song of all time.[15] The song has a deep sense of both spirituality and community. In a 1997 interview, Mayfield stated, "It doesn't matter what color you are or what faith you have. I am pleased the lyrics can be of value to anybody."[16]

The song has been covered by dozens of performers through the years, including Bob Dylan and Bob Marley. One of my favorite versions was released by Jeff Beck and Rod Stewart in 1985 and reached #5 on the U.S. *Billboard* Hot 100 chart. If you need a reminder, please go to YouTube and play one of the many, many versions of this incredible song.

In our world, people are trying to get ready for a confident transition from their work lives to their retirement lives. Each year, the Employee Benefit Research Institute (EBRI) releases its annual retirement confidence survey.[17] While the 2021 report showed that seven out of 10 retirement plan participants felt they were on track to retire with the lifestyles they wanted, *there were a number of disparities across gender and income levels.*

The survey shows that women are nearly 20% less likely to report that they are on track for retirement than men. They are more concerned about outliving their savings due to generally lower Social Security benefits and longer life expectancies than their male counterparts.[18]

Working for a company that offers a retirement plan dramatically influences the perception of future retirement success. Eighty-seven percent of people who earned over $75,000 a year had access to an employer-sponsored retirement plan. For those making less than $35,000 a year, the number dropped to 45%.[19] This means that lower-income and part-time workers, as well as those who are part of the gig economy, such as DoorDash and Uber drivers, are left to figure out how to save for retirement on their own.

Two other issues seem to be influencing people's confidence levels about their future retirement income. The first is not having enough short-term emergency savings.[20] This leaves people feeling less secure about allocating income to a long-term retirement plan that they may not be able to tap prior to age 59½. It also leaves them more vulnerable to current setbacks such as housing, vehicle, or medical expenses.

In fact, the 2022 *Economic Well-Being of U.S. Households* report released by the Federal Reserve in May 2023 showed that just 63% of adults said they could cover a hypothetical $400 emergency expense "exclusively using cash or its equivalent [such as tapping their savings or charging a credit card that they could pay off the following month], down from a high of 68% in 2021."[21]

This leads us to a second great concern revealed in the EBRI report: having a high level of debt.[22] The combination of credit card, auto loan, and student loan debt totals more than $17 trillion nationally.[23] Paying on this debt can create obstacles to saving for retirement. This appears to be a bigger problem for people in lower-income groups. (Although, anecdotally, I have seen low-income people who are amazing savers and high-income earners who are head over heels in debt.)

Whether tendencies to fall behind in retirement planning are caused by fear of outliving savings, too much debt keeping people from participating in retirement plans, lack of access to plans for lower-paid workers, or lack of emphasis put on financial education in our school systems, we must do better as a society if we truly want to give everyone a chance to get on the train. These younger workers need to learn good habits from an early age so they can get on board.

I also want to address the reality of family dynamics. Many of our clients are dealing with extenuating circumstances within their own families, which can create challenges or strains on both financial resources and quality of life. Let me share a real-life client example with you to illustrate.

Steven and Elyse: Sandwiched in the Middle of Parents and Kids

To illustrate my next client story, I will use Steven and Elyse, the parents of Alex P., Mallory, Jennifer, and Andy Keaton, from one of my favorite TV shows, *Family Ties*. For those of you who know me, it should come as no surprise that Alex P. Keaton was one of my high school heroes.

Steven and Elyse's situation differs from Jack and Diane's scenario, which we reviewed earlier. In addition to all the financial considerations most couples have to deal with as they move toward retirement, Steven and Elyse also had several family issues that had to be addressed. Although their situation initially looks somewhat overwhelming, don't worry, things work out for them in the end.

Much like Jack and Diane, Steven and Elyse took their financial responsibilities seriously and developed good savings habits early on in their married lives. They both worked in corporate America. Steven was an engineer for a local utility company, while Elyse did marketing and public relations for a manufacturing firm.

They had reasonable salaries that grew over time. They diligently saved money for their retirement in their 401(k) plans. Each year, when they got their annual reviews and raises, they increased the amount that went into their retirement plans. That way, they still got to enjoy some of the additional cash flow from their raises each year while also continuing to save more for their future needs. However, as you will see, Steven and Elyse were dealing with real-life issues with both parents and children, and this initially impeded their ability to enjoy the resources they accumulated for the retirement life they imagined.

Steven and Elyse have two children, a son and a daughter. They systematically saved so that both of their children could attend college, but only their daughter took advantage of the opportunity. Unfortunately, both of their children worked for small employers, each making less than $50,000 annually. Worse yet, neither of them participated in a retirement savings plan such as a 401(k). Their son's employer did not provide one, and their daughter did not feel like she had the resources to be able to save money for the future. Inflation and debt payments had created financial hardships that required her to use all her earned income just to make ends meet.

In addition, Elyse's mom, who was in her late 80s and struggling with declining health, lived in Bluffton, South Carolina, inland off the coast of Hilton Head. She wanted to continue living independently. However, Steven and Elyse worried that it was not safe for her to live alone. They were also very concerned every time she got behind the wheel of her car, even if it was to drive to a doctor's appointment or the grocery store. She promised them that she would never drive at night.

Steven and Elyse are typical of what is known as the sandwich generation. They are stuck between parents who need ongoing help in their later years and children who lack the education, income, financial resources, or all three to build wealth independently as their parents had.

This combination can create a great deal of stress for couples looking to retire to their own dreams and aspirations. Steven and Elyse had worked hard and saved money for several decades to get to this point in life. Unfortunately, life and family responsibilities initially left their retirement years looking very different from what they had hoped for or imagined.

Steven and Elyse sold their home in Northeast Ohio and moved to South Carolina so that they could be available to help care for Elyse's mom. This was a worthy and noble gesture. However, as Elyse's mom's health continued to decline, she became increasingly dependent on Steven and Elyse's assistance. What started out as checking in on Elyse's mom two to three times a week and occasionally taking her to the grocery store or a doctor's appointment became a daily ritual.

Thankfully, Elyse had financial and health-care durable powers of attorney to handle matters as they arose for her mom. She ended up paying her mom's bills and balancing her checkbook. This also required her to talk to her mom's stockbroker about her investment account and IRA. These assets had largely been accumulated and previously handled by Elyse's dad, who had passed away nearly 10 years before. Elyse also talked to the people at her mom's bank about her savings and CD accounts there. Luckily, Elyse's mom had enough financial resources to provide for her own income and care needs, but she became dependent on Elyse to manage those assets.

All of this did not allow Steven and Elyse to pursue the travel and lifestyle plans they had had for their retirement years. Even if they enlisted their adult children or one of Elyse's mom's friends to check in on her, they found it difficult to be gone for more than a few days. They did get a couple of brief respites, though, allowing them to do a few short driving trips to explore the areas around their new home in South Carolina. However, going to Europe or taking an Alaskan cruise, both of which were on their retirement bucket list, were put on hold while they took care of Elyse's mom.

Ultimately, Elyse's mom passed away two years after Steven and Elyse moved to South Carolina to help care for her. While they missed her, they knew that she was not suffering anymore. This also gave them a major wake-up call to make the most of the time, health, and resources they had worked so hard to accumulate.

In addition, Steven and Elyse watched their adult children struggle financially. They were acutely aware that their children were not actively saving money in their 401(k) plans like they had. They also knew that neither of their children would receive a monthly defined benefit pension check like Steven was receiving from his employer. Unfortunately, unless you are a government or education system employee, defined benefit pensions are largely a thing of the past. This means it is each individual's responsibility to save for their own future retirement needs.

At first, this knowledge made Steven and Elyse reluctant to spend more money than necessary to maintain their base standard of living. They were aware that if they did not leave a significant inheritance to their adult children, their children would likely lead very sparse and difficult financial lives after their parents were gone.

Steven and Elyse have been my clients for more than 25 years. I have watched them work hard, pay down debt quickly, and save diligently. Most CFPs would say they are ideal clients who have done everything they were supposed to do to have successful retirements. However, despite these good habits and even though they had accumulated significant financial resources for their retirement aspirations, family pressures from Elyse's mom and their adult children did not initially allow them to enjoy the fruits of their diligence and hard work.

Fortunately, we were able to introduce a service offering to help coach Steven and Elyse's children to start developing good financial habits. The CFPs of Impel Wealth Management and our partners at Horizon Advisor Network developed a subscription-based financial client service known as Simplifynance® to help our clients' younger family members (typically in the 25–40-year-old age range). One of the problems that younger workers have today is getting access to qualified financial advice in a cost-effective manner.

There are some banks and brokerage firms that will not talk to younger investors unless they have at least $250,000—and sometimes as much as $500,000—to invest. If they don't meet these very high standards, they are relegated to websites or call centers where, each time they have a question, they are forced to talk or chat with someone they've never met before who does not know their personal or financial situation.

This is the antithesis of what a relationship with a CFP should look like. When working closely with a smaller number of clients, an advisor gets to know not only a client's financial resources but also what makes life meaningful to them. It has been my experience that in the best financial planning firms, this extends beyond the advisor to the entire service team. This makes each client interaction feel like you walked into the bar in *Cheers*, where everyone knows your name.

[24]

Simplifynance marries a financial planning technology platform with personalized advice from a CFP. By introducing their son and daughter to this service and even offering to pay for the first year's monthly subscription fee, Steven and Elyse were able to set their adult children on a path toward good financial habits. It was also interesting to see that their kids took advice from a CFP more seriously than they took advice from "just Mom and Dad" (trust me, we all go through this) and actually began to implement it.

Steven and Elyse are now more confident that their children will make good financial decisions and start to develop their own resources. Their children are both now saving a small amount of money for retirement each month. Their son is putting money away each month in a Roth IRA, and their daughter is starting to defer some of her income to her company's 401(k) plan, where at least a small amount gets a company match as well.

This process is also grooming their children for whatever future inheritances they may receive. Steven and Elyse had previously worried that if their kids got a large sum of money at their passing, they would not know what to do with it or they would be vulnerable to bad decisions or bad influences.

The changes they have made allow Steven and Elyse to start using the resources they accumulated for the purposes they had originally intended. They are traveling regularly now that they are no longer tied to caring for Elyse's mom in South Carolina. And now that their kids are showing real steps toward financial maturity and wisdom, Steven and Elyse are starting to get more comfortable with the idea of spending some of the money they accumulated to create joy and meaningful moments together.

This is why I strongly advocate for starting the financial planning process as early as possible. Once we know where we are and how much of our current resources we need to allocate to achieve our future goals, we gain the freedom and the confidence to use the rest to enjoy life along the way. I tell clients regularly that there is a window of time when they can enjoy the gift of health, the gift of time, and the gift of resources to do what makes life meaningful for them and their families.

This is a theme that we are going to explore in more detail next. Many people work in career fields that they don't necessarily enjoy. They can't wait to retire from the daily grind. However, I have learned from watching clients for more than 35 years that the ones who are really happy in the next phase of life are the ones who are not just trying to get away from jobs they don't like but are looking forward to what the future holds with excitement.

You see, accumulating a certain amount of financial resources or achieving a nominal rate of return on your investment assets should not be your financial goal or measuring stick. Money should always be viewed as a means, not an end. Having enough to pursue the things you want to do is what makes life enjoyable. We are going to explore these ideas in detail in the next chapter, "Puzzle Piece #2: Retiring to Something vs. Retiring from Something."

PUZZLE PIECE

#2

Retiring to Something vs. Retiring from Something

In the whole history of mankind, we have only figured out three things that you can do with money: *save it*, *spend it*, or *give it away*. And if you don't give it away while you're living, you are going to give it away when you die because you can't take it with you!

This piece of wisdom and advice was shared with dozens of my clients over nearly three decades by my very good friend and mentor, estate planning attorney John Rasnick.

John usually shared this perspective when helping clients create their wills or trusts. Many times, this discussion was driven by how much money a client wanted to leave to their heirs versus how much money they felt they would need for their own retirement lifestyle goals. Unfortunately, John passed away in 2021 at the age of 63, far too young. My clients and I miss him every day and speak about him often.

I honor John by continuing these same conversations with my clients. However, they are usually in the context of developing a retirement income strategy. A significant part of that strategy is understanding how much money you need to cover basic living expenses such as groceries, insurance, utilities, and so on. We often like to have fixed-income resources such as Social Security or pensions or lower-risk income streams from investment portfolios to cover these necessary costs. The idea is to have fixed income available to help cover fixed expenses, providing a foundation of security and confidence in your retirement years.

Once we have established a budget for basic life needs, we can then delve into the more enjoyable part of retirement planning. This involves envisioning time spent traveling, pursuing hobbies, and enjoying activities with friends and family. As you start to consider what kind of financial resources will be necessary to support these more fun and fulfilling aspects of retirement, your CFP's goal will be to inspire you to dream big about what you are going to *retire to*!

Follow That Dream

According to Wikipedia, "'Follow That Dream' is a song first recorded by Elvis Presley as part of the soundtrack for his 1962 motion picture *Follow That Dream*...Bruce Springsteen said 'Follow That Dream' was one of his favorite Elvis songs...[He] recorded the song during the *Born in the U.S.A.* sessions, although it remained unreleased. He performed the song in July 1988 in Switzerland, and many times in succeeding decades."[25]

I have often encouraged clients who are moving toward retirement in the next few years to do as Elvis suggested in his iconic song and begin dreaming about their visions for their ideal retirement lives. Remember, you have to define your dreams before you can follow them. To do this, you can use an exercise that I call "Dream Big for Retirement."

Start by taking a sheet of paper and writing at the top, "My Retirement Dreams Look Like..."

Then write the following categories down the left side of the page:

1. Health and Wellness Activities
2. Educational and Lifelong Learning Pursuits
3. Bucket List Travel Destinations
4. Family Time and Activities
5. Hobby and Leisure Activities
6. Volunteer Activities
7. Spiritual and Charitable Endeavors

This is the time to think and dream big! I want you to develop your own list of future activities that inspire you. This process is kind of like getting a custom-made suit. It doesn't have to fit anybody else; it just has to fit you perfectly.

As each person has their own goals and their own vision for things that excite them about the future, I often encourage couples to start this process separately and then share their results with each other. This gives each of them the opportunity to get their initial thoughts down on paper without the more verbal partner dominating the process.

I speak from experience. I happen to be a very external thinker. I think things through by talking out loud. On the other hand, my wife, Rachel, is an internal thinker. Whenever we have a big life decision to make or a problem to tackle, I have found that there is wisdom in giving her time and space to organize her very valuable thoughts. Then we can come together and have a meaningful and collaborative discussion about what to do next.

This inevitably results in a better and more constructive outcome than if I had just started jabbering and not given Rachel space or time to contribute. If you are going to live life together, it helps to be able to create common dreams and common goals that you both want to achieve.

Most of my clients are over 50. Many of them first came to me when they were in their 40s or early 50s and were starting to seriously think about their future retirement. They were uncertain whether they were on track to retire successfully. Many of them had not developed firm goals for when they wanted to retire and what they wanted to do during their retirement years.

As we discussed in the previous chapter, if you don't know where you are going, you will not have any idea what proportion of your financial resources you need to set aside to achieve your long-term retirement goals. Beyond this, you will always be nervous about spending any additional dollars you have for current lifestyle aspirations if you are not confident that you have set aside enough to provide for yourself as you move toward a future retirement.

Recent evidence, as well as multiple conversations the CFPs of Impel Wealth have had with clients in that age group, seems to confirm that Gen X is feeling this stress and anxiety at particularly heightened levels.[26] They are the generation that comes after the baby boomers and before the millennials. They are smaller in number than the generations that preceded and followed them. This sometimes leads to them being known as the "middle child" generation and the "baby bust" generation.

Gen Xers, those born between 1965 and 1980, were alive to see the invention of personal computers, cell phones, the internet, and social media. In contrast, millennials, who were born between 1981 and 1997, grew up with these things as regular parts of daily life. However, despite all these advancements in technology and quality of life, many Gen Xers are struggling to save for retirement in the face of higher costs and higher debt levels.

(Not) Going in Style

According to Wikipedia, "*Going in Style*" is a 1979 American heist comedy/drama film written and directed by Martin Brest and starring George

Burns, Art Carney, Lee Strasberg (in his final film role) and Charles Hallahan. It was Brest's first commercial feature film."[27]

The movie tells the story of Joe, Al, and Willie, "three senior citizens who share a small apartment in Queens, New York City."[28]" In the midst of the late 1970s inflation spike, the three do not have much in the way of financial resources or opportunity to enjoy the finer things during their retirement years, and their days are mostly spent on a park bench.

[29]

One day Joe suggests that they go on a "stick-up." They have no experience as criminals, but after some reluctance, the two others agree.

Al surreptitiously borrows three pistols from the gun collection of his nephew, Pete, who lives with his wife and children a few miles away. The trio, disguised with novelty glasses, pulls off the heist, netting $35,000 [which was a significant amount of money for three seniors in 1979].[30]

A 2023 survey conducted by New York Life Wealth Watch found that many people in their 40s and 50s are having the same financial struggles and limitations that Joe, Al, and Willie had in *Going in Style.* The survey found that Gen Xers reported the highest levels of anxiety and lowest levels of hope compared to the generations coming before or after them. Nearly 40% of them feel that they will not be able to reach the financial goals necessary to achieve a successful and independent retirement.[31]

One of their biggest concerns is high levels of debt. The combination of the high cost of homes and cars and financing either their own or their children's college education is forcing them to use their financial resources to pay down debt rather than save for their future retirement. The report stated that 53% of Gen Xers do not have any retirement savings or a strategy for their future transition from work life to retirement life.[32]

As a result, many Gen Xers are planning to work longer and retire later than they had initially hoped. A large percentage expect that they will have to continue working part time in the early years of retirement just to cover their financial shortfalls.

Even though there has been much written about their parents amassing large amounts of wealth that the next generation will ultimately inherit, only 12% of Gen Xers expect that a future inheritance will help fill the retirement gap.

Many clients have shared stories with me about friends or family members who are facing this type of anxiety and stress. As we discussed in Puzzle Piece #1, the first thing that people in this situation need to do is assess their current financial position to give them a better understanding of their future potential income and asset resources. Once this has been completed, they can then develop plans and concrete steps to start creating the funds they will need to enter their retirement years *Going in Style.*

While Joe, Al, and Willie resorted to crime to give them the money they needed to break out of their lives of retirement boredom and financial repression, I would like to suggest a more constructive—*and legal*—route. As our clients know, your financial plan should be your North Star and should guide your future financial decisions.

Once you are armed with your financial plan and know what steps you need to take to move toward your preferred future, you can begin executing your plan in small increments over the coming months and years. One of the great things about the financial planning process is that when you know how much you need to save to reach your goals, it should give you the freedom and confidence to spend the balance on things that make life meaningful now.

However, as we will explore next, some people become so focused on accumulating resources for the future that they have a hard time giving themselves permission to spend and enjoy life in the present.

Should I Save or Should I Spend Now?

I often refer to the 1996 book *The Millionaire Next Door* by authors Thomas Stanley and William Danko. I usually draw analogies between the people outlined in this book and my clients. Oftentimes, my clients have been surprised to find themselves approaching retirement with net worths well in excess of $1 million. This is typically due to the compounded effect of good habits over long periods of time.

I have found that people who spend less than what they earn, save and invest the difference, do not make flashy lifestyle purchases on credit, intentionally pay down debt, and do not make speculative investment decisions based on hot tips (whether from the golf course or social media pages) tend to build financial resources over time.

I call this the cumulative effect of days. The results of these good decisions, habits, and behaviors generate a growth effect that inevitably leads toward wealth creation. However, in an unusual corollary to this thought process, the very habits that lead to wealth creation often prevent people from enjoying the wealth they worked so hard to create once they reach retirement.

To help illustrate, let's divide our financial lives into two phases. The first is the accumulation phase, which starts when we begin our working careers. The second is the distribution phase, which starts on the day you retire and lasts until the day you pass away. We will explore these two distinct phases of your financial life in more detail in the next chapter.

According to a study published December 2023 by BlackRock research (in conjunction with EBRI), many retirees hardly touched their retirement savings. The study found that, across all levels of wealth, most retirees still had 80% of their preretirement savings remaining after almost 20 years of retirement.[33]

There are several factors that could lead to this outcome. I will touch on a couple of them here. First of all, most retirees feel better having financial security than using their wealth to live it up during retirement. In short, they have built and gotten used to a large financial security blanket. They do not want to spend too much too quickly and risk seeing that security blanket pulled out from under them.[34]

Many retirees also have a hard time breaking out of the accumulation and saving mindset. They feel like they created financial security through a certain set of habits. They have a hard time flipping the switch and spending resources as they move into retirement. Many also fear that long life expectancy and high potential health-care costs could cause them to deplete their assets. Therefore, they are unwilling to spend resources in the early days of retirement when they are younger and healthier and have the gift of time to pursue bucket list activities.

The study also found that men and women approach retirement finances differently. Many retired women report having a higher level of financial anxiety and tend to be more risk averse than men. A number of these fears "are well-founded, as [women] often live longer and typically enter retirement with lower asset balances" than their male counterparts.[35] Women also realize that the survivor benefits payable to them from pensions or Social Security will be reduced after a spouse passes away.

My goal is to help people successfully transition from work life to retirement life, confident that they have saved enough. This means that they will have the resources necessary to create a life of meaning, purpose, and value throughout their retirement years with the freedom to know not only how much they can spend but also what surplus they can give away to bless others.

In full deference to Joe Strummer, Mick Jones, and the rest of the Clash, "Should I save or should I spend now?" is a question that financial planning can help you answer. I would like to give you a couple of real-life examples of how the planning process has successfully helped guide the lives of my clients.

Mike and Carol: Enjoying Life and Helping Others

Running for just five seasons starting in 1969, *The Brady Bunch* is an enduring and beloved sitcom. It tells the story of Mike, Carol, and their six kids. I was referred to my own Mike by his coworkers, who had been my clients for a number of years. Mike was an extremely successful corporate executive with a local utility company. He and his wife, Carol, were in their early 50s when they were referred to me. They were starting to think more seriously about their future retirement. They wanted to develop a relationship with a CFP who could help them determine whether they were on track to meet their goals.

In addition to Social Security benefits, Mike was going to get a defined benefit pension plan from his company. On top of that, before entering the corporate world, Mike had served 20 years in the military as an army officer, and he was also going to be eligible for a military pension. Carol was also going to receive a small defined benefit pension from her years of service at the local library. This meant that Mike and Carol were going to have significant income resources that would more than meet their base living expenses.

It seems the book *The Millionaire Next Door* could have been based on Mike and Carol. They had always been diligent savers, both personally and in company retirement plans. They had aggressively paid down debt. In fact, when I met them, they had not had a mortgage or a car payment in more than 10 years. The cumulative effect of their good habits, along with Mike's executive benefits, like company stock options and deferred compensation plans, had allowed them to accumulate significant asset resources as well.

Unlike the Bradys, Mike and Carol had only one son, who married early in life and unfortunately divorced a few years later. Their son's marriage had resulted in the birth of Mike and Carol's only grandchild, which meant that they only had two heirs to leave their significant resources to. Mike and Carol had always lived a conservative lifestyle, well below their means. Now that they had accumulated financial assets far beyond their needs, they approached me to begin to use some of those funds to help others.

Mike shared with me that even though they had previously had charitable intentions, they had never felt confident giving away meaningful amounts of money. This was largely because they were uncertain whether they had enough to provide for themselves in retirement. Even though I was confident they had accumulated more than enough resources to do everything they wanted to do during their retirement years, we still developed a formal retirement income plan projection for them, and the projection confirmed this.

Armed with this information, Mike and Carol were finally able to start making concrete plans to help others. Mike shared that they had never given more than $4,000 to charity in any year previously. Knowing that they had more than $2 million of investment assets, they wanted to start doing something more significant going forward.

As we will address in the next chapter, numerous studies and financial planning history shows us that clients can withdraw up to 4% a year from their investment portfolios, adjusted annually for inflation, and confidently fund a 30-year retirement life expectancy.

Four percent of $2 million meant that they had $80,000 a year that they could spend or give away. Since Mike and Carol had such significant Social Security and pension income that already covered the bulk of their needs, I was having a hard time getting them to spend much of their asset resources on additional travel and lifestyle goals. They traveled when they wanted to, and Mike, who was an avid outdoorsman, enjoyed activities such as biking, skiing, and fishing.

This meant that Mike and Carol could give away a significant amount of money to charities each year and still have plenty in reserve to live their ideal lifestyle. They set an initial goal of giving $25,000 a year to various churches and charitable organizations they wanted to help. While this was an admirable goal, long-held habits that had allowed them to accumulate significant wealth made it hard to write those first few large checks.

I remember Mike calling to tell me that the local volunteer fire department was trying to raise money to buy a new fire engine. He wanted to know whether it was OK for him to send them a check for $2,000. Mike was not used to writing four-figure checks to charitable organizations—yet. I assured him that he and Carol had plenty of money to be able to help this worthwhile community organization. Furthermore, I told Mike that unless he was planning to write a check for more than $10,000 to any one organization, he should never call me again to ask permission—he should *just do it.*

I am happy to report that as Mike and Carol's assets continued to grow over time, so did their charitable giving. Eventually, their annual charitable gifts grew to $40,000 per year. They enjoyed vetting and exploring new opportunities to help people through the various 501(c)(3) charitable organizations they gave money to. They also decided to make several charitable organizations beneficiaries of some of their IRA monies. That way, they could give money they never paid taxes on to charities that will never have to pay taxes on the funds either.

Unfortunately, Mike passed away several years ago. Like so many of my clients, he was a great man who I enjoyed spending time with. Carol is continuing the legacy that she and Mike began together. She is now giving away more than $60,000 a year to help others.

I recently shared with her that over the years we have been pursuing these charitable gift strategies, she and Mike have cumulatively given away more than $750,000. What's more amazing to her is that she still has more assets available today than they did when they started their charitable journey. This is a testament to what good planning and compounding interest can allow you to accomplish over time.

Now that we have seen an example of how someone has successfully used their excess financial resources to help others, I would also like you to begin to think about how you can use those same resources to enjoy your next phase of life. My clients who enjoy their retirement years the most are those who *joyfully anticipate the future.* They look forward to the activities that they want to pursue during their retirement years. They want to make the most of the gift of health, the gift of time, and the gift of financial resources. In short, they are the people who are retiring *to* something and not just retiring *from* something.

What Are You Retiring To?

[36]

A few years ago, I stopped at a local coffee shop to pick up a cup of green tea before heading to an early morning meeting. A couple who had been clients of mine for many years was sitting at a table enjoying coffee and the morning newspaper. They were both recently retired schoolteachers. They stated that even though that day was Tuesday, for them, it was Saturday—the seventh Saturday that week. They were clearly enjoying the newfound freedom of retired life.

After 35 years of helping people successfully transition from work life to retirement life, I have observed that my clients who are happiest are those who have meaning, purpose, activities, and social interactions in their lives that make retirement life fulfilling for them. In other words, they did not just retire *from* something; they had something to retire *to*!

You may be surprised to find that some people enjoy consulting or continuing to work part time during their retirement years. Anecdotal evidence seems to confirm this thought process. More baby boomers and Gen Xers seem open to working postretirement than previous generations.[37] However, their reasons for pursuing work are not driven wholly by financial needs or the recent spike in inflation.

Recent studies show that nearly 41% of retirees who go back into the job market do so to seek personal fulfillment and social interaction. Another 37% are looking for a sense of purpose, and working during their retirement years helps them maintain a daily calendar and social structure. A similar number states that working helps them stay physically and emotionally healthy, as it keeps both their minds and their bodies active.[38]

I have often encouraged married clients to start talking with each other about what retirement life will look like three to five years before it happens. If they create a vision together for what they would like to do to keep themselves healthy and active, it can help make the transition to their retirement years much easier. Let's explore how this played out in real life for several of my clients over the years.

Fred and Ethel: A Bumpy Start on the Road to a New Normal

Fred and Ethel were Ricky and Lucy's close friends and landlords on the TV show *I Love Lucy.* William Frawley and Vivian Vance, who played Fred and Ethel, were known to bicker off-screen, much like my real-life Fred and Ethel did when they came in to my office for their semiannual meetings. I first began working with them in 1994, and they quickly helped me realize how difficult the transition to retirement could be. At the time, my firm had been hired to do retirement planning workshops for a local publicly traded corporation. The corporation was giving early retirement incentive packages to their salaried employees aged 55 and over. The additional pension benefits, payout of unused vacation time, and employer-paid health insurance until age 65 (when they were eligible for Medicare) proved enticing enough that many employees who had originally been planning to work several more years decided to take advantage of the extra benefits and retire over the next 30 to 60 days.

However, this did not give them or their spouses much time to adjust psychologically to the idea of retirement. The best example I can remember from that time is Fred and Ethel. Fred was 58 and had been planning to work for at least another four to five years. Less than a month later, he found himself retired. This led to a massive period of adjustment for both him and Ethel.

About a month after Fred's retirement, Fred and Ethel came in to meet with me. They wanted to review the rollover of Fred's 401(k) and plan cash flow once his severance benefits ran out. We met at 10 a.m. at my office. About 30 minutes into the meeting, Fred mentioned that he had had too much coffee and that he was going to run to the restroom. As the door to my office closed, Ethel looked at me and bluntly stated, *"He is driving me crazy!"*

You see, prior to Fred's early and unplanned retirement, Ethel had her own daily schedule and plans. This included reading the newspaper on the deck each morning after Fred left for work. She used to love listening to the birds and having some quiet time for herself. Now Fred sat next to her every morning and told her every detail of the sports page. She didn't have a desire to know the box score for every baseball game from the night before. She explained that when she would go to the grocery store, Fred now went with her, and he would put things in the grocery cart that they didn't need or would never use.

It took Fred and Ethel a good six months or so to develop new routines and habits that made each of them happy now that Fred was retired. They did many things together. However, they also needed some time to do things they enjoyed on their own or with their friends. I am happy to report that no counseling was necessary. They enjoyed many years of happiness during their retirement.

When people are used to working 40 to 50 hours a week and traveling to and from work, they often find it daunting to fill their retirement calendars with new activities. When going to 0 mph overnight after 40+ years of working at 60 mph, people who have not properly planned for this transition can experience stress, boredom, and anxiety. Let's examine this through the lens of two different clients, both trying to retire and happily pursue the next phase of life.

Ross and Chandler: Two Paths to the Same Retirement Destination

Let's use the examples of Ross and Chandler. Even though they are not *Friends* in real life, their stories illustrate two very different experiences with the "pivot" from work life to retirement life. Ross experienced a more difficult retirement transition compared to Chandler, whose transition was smoother. Unfortunately, Ross's transition represents a very typical retirement transition experience. Some of the ease of Chandler's transition was due to Chandler's company's thoughtful policies as he looked toward his future retirement.

Ross spent 42 years working for the same publicly traded manufacturing company. He started off as a mid-level engineer and worked his way up the corporate ladder to the executive level. Ross's unique skill set caused his employer to want to make the most of his abilities and keep him employed as long as possible. This led to many years of long hours, significant responsibilities, and high levels of stress. It also did not give him much time to develop hobbies and social activities outside of work, beyond his family and his church.

When Ross finally retired at age 67, the first six to 12 months were difficult for both him and his wife, Rachel. Much like Fred and Ethel above, it took a full year of practicing retirement before Ross finally started to get good at—and enjoy—this new phase of life.

On the other hand, Chandler's company allowed him the option, with manager approval, to work half time for half pay for up to two years before his planned retirement date. Very importantly, that option also allowed him to keep his full-time benefits, such as his health insurance and 401(k) plan. After discussing that option with me and updating his retirement plan projection to account for his reduced pay for two years, Chandler and his wife, Monica, decided to give it a try.

That option had great benefits for everybody involved. Chandler got to practice retirement two and a half days a week. He worked full days on Monday and Tuesday, worked Wednesday until noon, and then was off until the following Monday. This gave Chandler and Monica the opportunity to envision what retired life would look like in the future. It gave them time to try to get involved with different activities and community groups. It also gave Chandler's employer a chance to transition Chandler's significant institutional and client knowledge and history to his successor. It was a win for everybody! I don't know why more companies don't provide this option for their long-time employees approaching retirement.

For people who derive much of their personal identity and self-worth from their work personas, retirement can be difficult. At home, you do not have direct reports. Nobody asks you for your opinion or approval multiple times a day. My wife loves to tell the story of when her former boss, an executive of a very successful company, retired and was told in no uncertain terms by his wife that he was not the CEO of their household! I can tell you from more than three decades of experience that the more planning you can do in advance of this transition, the easier it will be—for everyone.

Here is a great exercise to start the wheels turning. I call it My Ideal Retirement Schedule. Try taking a weekly calendar and mapping out your time from 7 a.m. to 10 p.m. daily, thinking through what your new schedule or routines will look like in your future retirement. This can be a helpful exercise. You may be surprised by the number of blank spaces in the calendar, or you may be excited by your newfound flexibility. Married couples may want to try doing this separately and then discussing their separate goals and ideas for the future together so they can create a cohesive vision.

My clients who are happiest in retirement also tend to be active and busy. They may be looking forward to future travel or exploring hobbies and activities they didn't have time for during their working years. Many are also pursuing part-time work and volunteer activities during their early years of retirement to help them transition and maintain some sense of structure and social interaction as they seek fulfillment. However, you get to decide how to create your ideal new life schedule. Retirement should be a time of joy where you can now make use of the gifts of time, health, and financial resources to do what makes you happy!

I want you to be confident that you have the resources you need to dream big and retire to something. In our next chapter, we will review how to determine how much you really need to pursue your unique retirement dreams. We will look at your income and asset resources to determine whether they are sufficient to help you attain your retirement goals and dreams. Please turn the page as we begin to explore "Puzzle Piece #3: Determining How Much You Need to Retire (What's Your Number?)."

PUZZLE PIECE

#3

Determining How Much You Need to Retire (What's Your Number?)

How do you know how much money you will need to do everything you want to do during your retirement years? This is a great question and one that is very common when starting the financial planning process. In discussing the first two pieces of the retirement success puzzle, we first reviewed how to determine where you are today financially. Next, we examined what you want to retire to—your unique vision for what will make life meaningful for you and your family during your retirement lifetime.

Planning for retirement can seem like a big task. The numbers are so large that it can be overwhelming. So, I thought it would make sense to go back to one of the first *Schoolhouse Rock!* episodes, one that aired in January 1973: "My Hero Zero." In the episode, a young boy dresses up as a superhero to show his older sister, Maggie, the importance of the number 0. Most people assume that they will need a lot of zeros at the end of their investment accounts to retire successfully. (It should be noted that this song was voted #11 of the 65 *Schoolhouse Rock!* episodes on its 30th Anniversary DVD.[39])

40

This chapter will help you determine whether you have enough fuel in your financial tank to get to your preferred future. Much to my wife Rachel's dismay, to do this, we have to use math! Rachel had aspirations of working as an accountant when she was in high school. However, she realized that this meant she would live her life surrounded by numbers and calculations. She quickly determined that a career in human resources would be much better aligned with her abilities and temperament. Luckily for the rest of the world (especially for the countless employees she has helped through the years), strategic HR consulting and recruiting is her wheelhouse.

For those of you who have known me over the years, you know that I am probably the least handy person you have ever met. Rachel is very much "the handyman" and "the car guy" in our family. She understands my lack of handiness and tells me that it's OK—I'm good with math and numbers. Being a CFP allows me to work in my areas of strength and giftedness, something I have been blessed to do for more than 35 years.

As I mentioned in the previous chapter, your financial life can be divided into two long-term phases. The first is the accumulation phase of life. This begins the day you start working and earning an income. Hopefully, you are able to (1) spend less than what you make, (2) save and invest the difference, (3) pay down debt, and (4) not make too many of the myriad of investment mistakes that often hamper people in their quests to accumulate financial resources. The accumulation phase lasts until the day you retire and stop earning an income.

This is followed by the distribution phase of life. This is the time when we start using the resources we spent so many decades accumulating to create the income we will need to have fun and enjoy our retirement years. Unfortunately, many people are uncertain whether they have accumulated enough money to retire confidently. This also means they usually struggle with knowing how much they can spend in retirement.

As you may remember from the last chapter, the distribution phase lasts from the day you retire until the day you die. This is probably a longer time frame than most people believe. According to recent statistics, for a healthy couple aged 65, there is a greater than 50% probability that at least one will live to age 90. This means that you likely need to plan to have your financial resources last 25 to 30 years or longer. As I will explore further in Puzzle Piece #10, inflation and rising prices over a multidecade retirement can create significant challenges and require you to build sufficient resources.

Before we begin calculating how much you will need to fund your retirement goals, let me introduce you to a couple who have been clients of mine for nearly 30 years and are quickly approaching their transition from working years to retirement. We will use their goals and resources to examine how to determine how much money you may need to retire successfully. We will also review when and how to confidently make critical retirement income decisions.

Paul and Jamie: Seeking to Be Confident They Have Enough Money to Last a Lifetime (Hers)

In the TV show *Mad About You,* Paul and Jamie Buchman offer wit and wisdom about life, work, and relationships as they share life in New York City with their dog, Murray. My clients Paul and Jamie do the same in Northeast Ohio with their cat, Boots. They have been clients since the mid-90s, when we were all in our 30s. Paul, who is 63, works in IT, where he is now a manager for a regional bank headquartered in Ohio. He makes a good income, which has continued growing with annual reviews and promotions. He defers a reasonable amount of his income to his 401(k) plan, where he gets company matching funds. He also receives an additional profit sharing contribution.

Jamie worked as an elementary school teacher in a private parochial school. She is a couple of years older than Paul, and she moved into retirement recently when she turned 65 and was eligible for Medicare benefits. Upon retiring, she rolled her 403(b) plan, which had a balance of approximately $300,000, over to an IRA, which gave her much more in the way of investment options and flexibility.

Paul and Jamie have one son, Murray, who is in his mid-30s. He is a very successful attorney with a large multi-office practice. His wife works for a manufacturing company in their corporate accounting and finance area. They both make six-figure incomes and have made it known that they do not plan on having any children. As a result of their son Murray's success and financial independence, Paul and Jamie can focus on using their retirement resources for their own lifestyle goals and financial security. Murray has told them that he and his wife do not need or expect an inheritance. He wants his parents to use the money they worked so hard to accumulate to enjoy life together.

In addition to her government-provided health care, Jamie also began drawing her Social Security benefits, even though Paul was still working and bringing in a very good income to their household. She wanted to make certain that they had plenty of income to travel in their early days of retirement.

This is a very personal decision that every family will have to work through. Some couples are very comfortable taking a reduced benefit at an earlier age so they can enjoy more income while they are young enough and healthy enough to use that income to do things that make life enjoyable for them.

Other families are more concerned about deferring their Social Security benefits so the benefits can grow to a larger dollar amount in the future. This will provide them with a higher guaranteed income for the rest of their lives. Their priority is making sure that they have enough income to support their lifestyle needs if they live beyond the average life expectancy. These decisions need to be well thought through and vetted carefully, as they are generally irrevocable—once they are made, they can't be changed.

The big question that Paul and Jamie are facing today is how long Paul should continue to work. There are many considerations in determining the right answer to that question. Paul is generally healthy and lives an active lifestyle. However, he does have several preexisting health conditions and does not have great longevity in his family health history. Paul is also not enjoying work as much as he used to. Even though he primarily works remotely, he puts in a lot of hours and does not feel that he is adequately appreciated or compensated for his contributions to the company. He has many hobbies, and—unlike their CFP—he is very handy and likes doing things around the house.

On the other side of the coin, Jamie is very healthy and has a family history of longevity. This includes both her parents, who lived well into their 90s and both ended up in an assisted living facility and then graduated to full-blown nursing care. This was very expensive and depleted the financial resources they had worked so hard to accumulate throughout their careers. It was also very hard on Jamie, as she oversaw her parents' care on a day-to-day basis. This became a greater time burden as their health continued to decline.

As a result, Jamie wants to ensure that she and Paul have accumulated enough income and asset resources that they can enjoy life together. However, she also wants to feel comfortable that if, based on personal and family health history, she ends up a widow, there are enough financial resources to assure her that she can be cared for with dignity and respect. After watching her parents lose their resources and independence, she considers this a very real concern.

Luckily, these are not new questions or concerns for Paul and Jamie. We have been talking about these concerns and planning for them since the turn of the millennium. This brings me to a very important point: *Financial planning is not a static process.* It is something that needs to be reviewed and updated on a regular basis. Changes are made to people's salary and benefit plans. Changes are made to tax laws. Oftentimes, clients change jobs at least once during their working years. All of these changes necessitate updating the resources, goals, and assumptions we use in crafting an individually tailored financial plan.

The important thing is to start as soon as possible. This gives us more time to adjust to the inevitable changes that life and the economy may throw our way over the years. Every time we make a midcourse change or adjustment, it is another baby step toward our ultimate destination. To help illustrate this point, let me introduce you to Bob Wiley.

Baby Steps and the Financial Planning Process

I have been a fan of Bill Murray since he first replaced Chevy Chase on *Saturday Night Live* in 1977 (when I was 12 years old). Murray has always had the ability to create characters that make me want to tune in and laugh, from his earlier silly movies, such as *Meatballs* and *Caddyshack*, to what are now comedy classics, such as *Stripes*, *Ghostbusters*, and *Groundhog Day*.

One of my all-time favorite Bill Murray movies is the 1991 classic *What About Bob?* Murray plays Bob Wiley, a multiphobic and unstable patient who follows his psychotherapist, Dr. Leo Marvin, played by Richard Dreyfuss, on his family vacation because he is afraid he won't be able to survive while he is gone.

[41]

During their first meeting, Dr. Marvin introduces Bob to the concept of baby steps, which happens to be the name of his new book. The basic premise is that instead of trying to tackle all of his many overwhelming fears at once, Bob needs to take small steps each day—baby steps—and continue making progress. Even a small positive step in the right direction can be considered a victory. If you have never seen the movie, or if you want a reason to laugh, you should go to YouTube and search for the *What About Bob?* baby steps scene to fully appreciate what I am talking about.

Why am I sharing this with you? The fact is that many people are struggling and are uncertain of their financial position today. They are often overwhelmed and fearful, not knowing what steps to take to improve their financial position or how to move closer to their preferred future.

The financial planning process can be extremely helpful and freeing in this situation. The process is relatively straightforward, but many people are overwhelmed by trying to figure out where to start. The first step is to determine where you are today. This means taking inventory of your income sources, assets, and liabilities. It also means understanding the benefits that your employer provides. We would typically try to get an inventory of your insurance coverages and estate documents during this initial discovery phase.

Then comes the fun part. You get to share your hopes, dreams, and aspirations for the future. Where would you like to live? What dreams do you have for educating your children or grandchildren? When would you like to retire? What charitable organizations do you want to help?

Then your CFP takes all these inputs and creates a customized plan for you and your family's unique situation and goals. Once this plan is implemented, you can start taking your own baby steps toward the future you envision.

42

As I stated before, financial planning is not a static process. You don't just do it once and say, "Thank goodness that's over," shove your plan in a drawer, and forget about it until the day you retire. It is a dynamic process that must be reviewed and adjusted regularly to reflect updates in your family, work, and goals, as well as the economic and investment backdrop. By regularly reviewing and updating your plan with a CFP, you will see how these baby steps can lead you toward your goals over time.

Contrary to popular opinion, the financial planning process is not restrictive—quite the opposite. Once you have defined your goals and know what proportion of your resources you should allocate to reach them, you can use the rest of your resources to enjoy life today.

Let's Start at the Beginning

So, where do we begin? To answer this, we turn to Maria, "a free-spirited young Austrian woman studying to become a nun" in Salzburg in 1938. The combination of "her youthful enthusiasm and lack of discipline" concerns the sisters in the abbey.[43] Maria is sent to the villa of retired naval officer Captain Georg von Trapp to be governess to his seven children.

Maria decides to teach the von Trapp children, who have been raised in a very strict military fashion since their mother's passing, to sing for the first time. As the classic song "Do-Re-Mi" opens, Maria tells the children that the best way to address an issue is by starting at the beginning.

[44]

The same principle holds true when planning for your income needs in retirement. The first thing you need to do when charting a course toward a successful transition from work life to retirement life is to understand how much income or cash flow you think you will need to live the life you want in the future. A good place to start is by looking at your current net paychecks while you are working.

Let's return to our friends Paul and Jamie. They currently bring home $8,000 per month of net cash income from their paychecks after deductions for taxes, health care, and 401(k) contributions. We know they are living on $96,000 per year of cash flow. If we know they are living comfortably on this amount, we can then make adjustments for other expenses that may or may not be there in retirement.

For example, I know that some of my clients are currently making monthly mortgage payments that will be paid off by the time they retire. Others are still making tuition payments for their children who will be out of college before they stop working. Since these expenses would no longer exist when they retire, the income that is being allocated toward them will no longer be needed.

On the other hand, many people receive employer-subsidized health insurance that ends when they retire. Depending on whether they retire prior to age 65 and are Medicare eligible, we will have to make certain there is money available to cover their health insurance needs.

Also, many clients want to make certain that there is additional money available to help them with the aspirational travel, hobby, and lifestyle goals they did not have time to pursue during their working years. Obviously, we will need to calculate and plan for how much this will cost each year and how much in the way of resources they need to accumulate to fund these objectives.

Paul and Jamie's Retirement Income Goals

As a result of our analysis, we decided that, to fund Paul and Jamie's retirement lifestyle goals adequately, they would require $7,500 per month or $90,000 per year of net cash flow to meet their basic living expenses. As we expect that they will both be 65 by the time they retire, we will only have to cover Medicare Part B and Medicare supplement health insurance costs. Over and above this, they would like to have $20,000 a year for travel and lifestyle expenses during the first 10 years of retirement. We will reduce this expense to $10,000 per year from years 11 through 20 of retirement, as it is common for clients to plan to spend more money in the early days of retirement, when they are younger and healthier.

When you add together the $90,000 per year of net cash flow they will need to cover their basic monthly living expenses, approximately $7,000 per year for Medicare Part B and Medicare supplement health insurance, and $20,000 a year for travel, hobby, and lifestyle expenses, you end up with a total annual income need of $117,000 per year. And it is important to remember that this is net cash flow after all income taxes have been paid. It is even more critical to understand that this number needs to be adjusted annually for inflation for as much as 30 years of retirement life expectancy. This total initially seemed like a large and unattainable number for Paul and Jamie.

The next step is to inventory the income resources and asset resources that will be available to help you fund your retirement goals. Success in retirement is all about having the cash flow you need to do the things you want to do. That income will come from the paychecks you continue to receive during your retirement years and from the income that can be created from your investment assets.

Paul and Jamie's Income Resources

Let's start by identifying the income resources available to people entering retirement. These are continuing monthly payments that will fund some portion of your retirement income needs on an ongoing basis. They are as follows:

- Social Security or government pensions
- Defined benefit pensions

Both of the above are guaranteed sources of income that will continue for the balance of the retiree's life. Many of these also have survivor benefits that will pass on to a spouse if the retiree should pass away first.

Below are additional sources of income that may provide additional income to some retirees.

- Rental income: This will generally continue as long as you own the rental property/properties. We will need to account for the net income after expenses and taxes.

- Part-time work or consulting income: As we discussed in the previous chapter, there are many reasons that people continue working during their retirement years. In preparing your retirement income plan projection, we would need to make assumptions about how much income you would make and for how long you would continue to work.

Neither Paul nor Jamie worked for a company that provided a defined benefit pension plan. They also have no income-producing rental properties. However, Paul has been approached by a friend he has known from his work life. The friend would like Paul to do some part-time IT consulting for his company when he retires from the bank.

Paul likes to keep busy and feel like he is still valued, and this would also provide some additional cash flow to the household. He is planning on working from age 65 to 70. Paul and Jamie believe that he will make approximately $50,000 a year from this part-time, flexible work hours arrangement. This will provide enough cash flow that Paul can wait to claim his Social Security benefits until they max out at age 70. This will also provide an important benefit for Jamie, as Paul's higher Social Security benefits would be available to her as a survivor if Paul were to pass away first.

Jamie's Social Security benefits are currently $2,500 per month or $30,000 per year. Based on Paul's Social Security Wage and Benefits statement—accessed by creating an online account with Social Security at ssa.gov—his benefits at age 70 would be approximately $4,200 per month or just over $50,000 per year. Paul will wait to claim these benefits until age 70 and will use his consulting income of $50,000 per year to bridge the income gap until that time. This means that all together, Paul and Jamie will have approximately $80,000 per year of income to help fund their retirement goals.

Paul and Jamie's Asset Resources

Now that we know how much income Paul and Jamie will bring in from Social Security and part-time work, we need to look at the asset resources they have accumulated. Withdrawals from these investment assets will be used to make up the remaining cash flow and income they require to lead the retirement life they envision.

These assets generally come from some combination of the categories below:

- IRA and Roth IRA accounts
- 401(k) plan or other defined contribution pensions
- Executive benefits such as stock options or deferred compensation
- Nonretirement investment accounts
- Bank account assets, checking, savings, and CD accounts
- Insurance and annuity assets
- Proceeds from a business sale

Paul and Jamie have done well in their quest to save and accumulate resources for their future retirement. After her mom passed away, Jamie and her brother had each received an inheritance of approximately $150,000 from her parents' estate. Given that Jamie's parents' estate had been well over $1 million before they went into nursing care, this had seemed like a small remainder amount.

Paul and Jamie's retirement assets are as follows:

- Paul's 401(k) plan: $800,000
- Jamie's 403(b) plan: $300,000 (this was rolled over to her IRA)
- Paul and Jamie's Roth IRAs: $200,000 each
- Jamie's inheritance: $150,000
- Checking and savings accounts: $100,000
- Gold and silver coins: $50,000

Altogether, this gives Paul and Jamie $1.8 million in investment assets to help fund their retirement income goals. Assuming they take initial withdrawals of approximately 4% per year from their investment portfolio, this would give them $72,000 per year or $6,000 per month over and above the $80,000 per year of income they receive from Social Security and part-time work.

The great news is that $72,000 per year from their investment portfolio plus $80,000 per year from their income sources totals $152,000 per year, or more than $12,600 per month. This means that Paul and Jamie appear to be well on their way to successfully transitioning from work life to retirement life when Paul turns 65.

It is important to remember that these are gross numbers before taxes. As I write this book in 2024, the income tax law that is in effect is the Tax Cuts and Jobs Act, which was signed in late 2017 and went into effect in January 2018.[45] Because the law did not get a supermajority of 60 votes in the Senate, it is not a permanent tax law. Therefore, much of it will expire at the end of 2025. It is very important that you either understand the tax code or work with a qualified tax professional, in addition to your CFP, in order to make smart decisions when planning cash flow and taxes.

Retirement Spending—Take the Money and Run

According to Wikipedia, "Take the Money and Run" is a song recorded in 1976 by the Steve Miller Band. A song about two young (possibly teenage) bandits and the detective pursuing them, it was one of the many hit singles produced by the Steve Miller Band in the 1970s and featured on the 1976 album *Fly Like an Eagle*. The song peaked at number 11 on the U.S. *Billboard* Hot 100 in July 1976."[46]

Many early retirees have considered "taking the money and running" too. It's easy to think, *I worked my whole life to save this money. I delayed gratification and wasn't able to do many of the things I wanted to during my working years. It's now time for me to splurge and enjoy life.* While I agree with that sentiment in theory, we still want to be smart about how we approach spending the resources we worked so many years to accumulate.

I want to address several important topics related to your unique income plan. Retirement income planning is a complex topic with many moving parts, from income sources to asset allocation strategies to income tax ramifications. Below, I will try to address two of the questions I receive most often from clients as they transition to retirement life.

How Much Should Retirees Withdraw Annually, and Which Accounts Should Be Tapped for Income First?

A groundbreaking study authored by Bill Bengen was published in the *Journal of Financial Planning* in 1994. It determined that the sustainable withdrawal rate during retirement years was 4%, adjusted for inflation annually.[47] However, the study was done when interest rates were much higher. Therefore, many financial planners and retirement income specialists believe that the actual sustainable withdrawal rate may be lower today. When stock markets are near all-time highs, it is important to remember that future returns may be more moderate.

The accounts you draw from should be carefully orchestrated based on your income needs and income tax situation. Withdrawals from different buckets of money—such as IRAs, Roth IRAs, annuities, and nonqualified investment accounts—all have different tax ramifications.

Under current income tax law, a married couple age 65 or older can have taxable income of more than $10,000 per month and stay in a low income tax bracket. Careful planning and coordination can help avoid any unnecessary income tax liability. If you do not have an income tax plan as part of your retirement income strategy, you may be paying more tax than you need to be. I don't know anybody who thinks that our elected officials on Capitol Hill are doing such a good job that they want to send them more money than is absolutely necessary.

What Are Some Common Mistakes to Avoid So That I Can Help My Retirement Funds Last?

One of the common mistakes I help retirees correct is having an asset allocation that is not structured to produce an inflation-adjusted income over a 20-to-30-year retirement horizon. Many retirees get too conservative too quickly, which does not allow for the growth of their asset base or income over such a long period of time.

The second mistake I see retirees make is not understanding the *sequence of return risk*. This is the risk that markets might experience a period of sharp decline and negative returns in the early retirement years. Having advised clients for more than 35 years, I can illustrate this by showing you two groups of retirees whom I saw struggle when they retired, as markets had melted up toward all-time highs.

The first group includes those who retired in '99–'00, just as the dot-com/9-11 bubble burst, leading to a two-year 47% decline in the stock market. The second group retired in '07–'08, right before the subprime market crisis and the failure of AIG/Lehman Brothers caused the stock market to drop more than 55%.[48]

With markets nearing all-time highs again today, it would make sense for those nearing retirement to ensure that they had enough cash and short-term liquidity to make it through their first two to three years of retirement. By doing so, they would help mitigate the risk that short-term market volatility or periods of dislocation did not derail their retirement income goals and lifestyle plans.

Remember that these are general guidelines. Your situation's specific details could vary greatly and likely warrant discussion with your financial planning and income tax advisors.

As we conclude our journey through Paul and Jamie's retirement income goals and resources, I am happy to report that they are right on track for Paul to retire in less than two years when he turns 65. The combination of income resources and asset resources should allow them to enjoy life now and give Jamie peace of mind that she can be well cared for in the future.

As we begin to look at the additional pieces that will make up your unique retirement income puzzle, I promise not to put so much emphasis on math and numbers. We will be exploring economic and investment history, we will look at various asset classes and their roles in your retirement income portfolio, and interesting topics such as investor psychology and social media influences and their potential impact on your financial resources.

Let's start by exploring a fundamental piece of most people's retirement income plan: Social Security. There is much confusion and misinformation about how Social Security is funded and what the best strategy is for getting the most out of the system you paid FICA taxes into during your working years. Let's turn the page and begin exploring "Puzzle Piece #4: Maximizing Your Benefits from an Underfunded Social Security System."

PUZZLE PIECE

#4

Maximizing Your Benefits from an Underfunded Social Security System

In the mid-'90s, several local corporations and adult education centers selected me to teach retirement planning workshops. At the time, our curriculum outlined three key components for a successful retirement: a company's defined benefit pension plan, Social Security benefits, and personal savings and investments. These three components were considered to be like the legs of a stool: all were necessary for a secure retirement.

However, over the last 30 years, the private sector has shifted away from defined benefit pension plans and replaced them with defined contribution plans like 401(k) and profit-sharing plans. As a result, today we primarily consider two pillars when creating retirement income plans for our clients: income resources and asset resources. Income resources still include defined benefit pension plans for a chosen few, but for most people, Social Security is their primary source of income during retirement.

Therefore, understanding the Social Security system and how to maximize benefits is even more critical today than it was before. Before getting into Social Security claiming and timing strategies, I would like to begin by discussing the system's creation and funding, as well as its current stress and potential shortfalls.

Are We Really Socially Secure?

President Franklin Roosevelt signed the Social Security Act into law in August 1935. It "created a social insurance program designed to pay retired workers aged 65 or older a continuing income after retirement." Upon signing the act, President Roosevelt stated, "We tried to frame a law which will give some measure of protection to the average citizen, and his family, against the loss of a job and against a poverty-ridden old age."[49]

The first Social Security recipient was Ida May Fuller of Ludlow, Vermont. She began collecting benefit checks on January 31, 1940. Miss Fuller worked as a legal secretary and paid into the Social Security program for three years. The total amount of money that she paid was $24.75. Her initial monthly check was $22.54.[50]

Even though life expectancy at that time barely pushed into the mid-60s for most Americans, Ida May Fuller lived to be 100. Over her lifetime, she collected more than $22,000 of total benefits, more than 800 times the amount of money she paid into the system. This should have sounded the early alarm system for the long-term sustainability of Social Security.

In the Warner Brothers cartoon *Ali Baba Bunny*, Bugs and Daffy end up inside a cave filled with treasures instead of arriving at Pismo Beach. They ended up in the wrong location because they didn't turn left at Albuquerque. All this newfound wealth leads Daffy to believe he is now "comfortably well off." But in contrast to Daffy Duck's assumption of financial well-being, this government backed social safety net program was never meant to make you socially secure on its own. It was meant to be part of a multifaceted strategy that includes company retirement plans and personal savings to provide the income you need over a typical retirement lifespan.

Each year, the Social Security Trustees release a report showing the financial health and solvency of the system. You can review each year's report at the Social Security website (https://www.ssa.gov/oact/trsum/). This report is generally released in the spring of each year (though in 2021 the report was not published until August due to pandemic-related government delays). People look forward to each year's updated outlook, as Social Security's solvency has the potential to significantly affect the retirement plans of millions of U.S. citizens.

The 2021 Social Security Trustees report showed that the Social Security trust fund surplus was now expected to run out of money one year sooner than the previous year's report had projected.[51] This confirmed what many people feared: The trust fund that most Americans rely on to help fund their retirement income is rapidly depleting its surplus funding.

There are two reasons why Social Security is running out of funding at a faster pace than was previously expected. First, each time the economy experiences a financial crisis or significant recession, it causes many people to lose their jobs. As the unemployment rate rises, fewer people will pay FICA taxes into the Social Security system. This reduces the projected surplus.

Secondly, during periods like the bursting of the dot-com bubble, the 9/11 downturn, or the '07–'08 Global Financial Crisis, people who planned to work several more years experienced job loss in their early 60s. Needing income and lacking good job prospects, many of these people retired and started drawing Social Security benefits at an earlier age than anticipated, draining additional funds from the Social Security surplus.

As expected, this one-two punch has again clocked the Social Security trust fund. So, where do we go from here? The closer we get to the trust fund surplus depleting, the more difficult the choices will be and the more dramatic the changes will need to be to keep the system afloat.

According to the same report, Social Security's 75-year projected shortfall has tripled in the last 10 years. In 2011, the shortfall was forecast to be $6.5 trillion in present value between payroll taxes collected and benefits paid out over that time. In the 2021 report, that shortfall's new net present value was projected to be $19.8 trillion.[52]

Many people believe that fixing Social Security is a second-term presidential issue. It is such a hot-button issue and produces such rancor and contention that many presidents avoid addressing it during their first terms for fear of not being reelected.

The last president who tried to address fixing Social Security was George W. Bush. Unfortunately, he failed in his attempt. No other president has seriously addressed the issue since then. In 2005, the Social Security trust fund surplus was projected to last until calendar year 2044, nearly 40 years down the road.[53] After nearly 20 years of government inaction, the trust fund surplus is now set to run dry within the next 10 years, nearly a decade earlier than was projected in 2005.

The remaining runway to solve this problem is getting much shorter. If no changes are made before this fund depletes, benefits being paid to recipients will have to be reduced by 20% or more. Unfortunately, we hear very little from those on Capitol Hill about fixing Social Security. And the closer we get to the end of the runway, the harder it will be to fix this problem.

Due to the challenges outlined above, the United States and governments around the world are exploring options to reduce or eliminate the projected shortfalls in their Social Security and public pension systems.

In 1983, the Greenspan Commission recommended raising the age at which retirees could collect full Social Security benefits from 65 to 67 for people who were 30 years or more away from retirement.[54] The amount of FICA tax that both employees and their employers pay into the Social Security system was also increased. These changes were implemented to help fund the system and keep it solvent for decades to come.

As we consider various options to keep Social Security afloat, the U.S. government desperately needs to create a more sound and sustainable funding formula. We wonder what kind of protests and backlash it will face. It also seems that nobody in the federal government has the political courage to say out loud what they know must be done.

The (Next) French Revolution!

History reminds us that the French people have regularly taken to the streets to protest, overthrow their government, or both, over the last 250 years. According to Peter Jones, a professor of French history at the University of Birmingham in the United Kingdom, "If revolution is a regime change involving collective physical force, then [revolutions took place in France in] 1789, 1830 and 1848."[55]

History books teach that the 1789 revolt was *the* French Revolution. In June of that year, "widespread social distress" led to the creation of a National Assembly. The unrest continued until July 14th, when the storming of the Bastille took place. This "led to a series of radical measures by the Assembly, including the abolition of feudalism, the imposition of state control over the Catholic Church in France, and extension of the right to vote."[56]

The first revolt ultimately ended with King Louis XVI and Marie Antoinette losing their heads via the guillotine.[57] The second revolution, also known as the July Revolution, saw the House of Bourbon dethroned and replaced by the House of Orléans.[58] The third revolution, sometimes known as the Revolution of 1848, ended the reign of the House of Orléans and brought in a period known as the Second Republic.[59]

More recently, a *new* revolution seems to be brewing. Beginning in November 2018, the French people took to the streets weekly. This was known as the Yellow Vests Revolution. It "was initially motivated by rising crude oil and fuel prices, a high cost of living, and economic inequality" and "argued that a disproportionate burden of taxation in France was falling on the working and middle classes, especially in rural and peri-urban areas."[60]

[61]

Protests began again recently when French president Emmanuel Macron unilaterally raised the legal retirement age in the country from 62 to 64. In doing so, he bypassed parliament and potentially set up his government for a vote of no confidence. He stated that this extraordinarily unpopular reform was "necessary to address the financial deficits caused by pandemic spending and the European energy crisis."[62]

Even with the increased age, the people of France still enjoy one of the youngest retirement ages in the Western industrialized world, as the chart below shows.

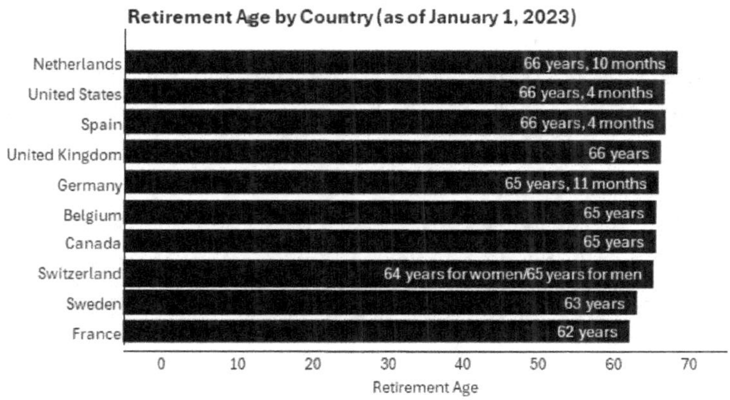

Source: Eurostat and Statista [63]

I believe that U.S. lawmakers should closely monitor this political situation and its fallout. These widespread strikes and marches could not only indicate the potential end of Macron's government but also hint at what U.S. politicians may face in trying to reform our own Social Security system.

As of 2023, the most recent year for which data is available, more than 67 million Americans are currently receiving monthly Social Security benefits.[64] This equates to approximately 20% of our population. We all know that something must change in the coming years to keep Social Security funded as a baseline retirement income social safety net for Americans.

Given the potential for increased life expectancy due to advances in health care, one of the changes under consideration may be raising our retirement age from 67 to as high as 70. However, this would only solve less than half the projected shortfall.

Again, the longer we wait to address this issue, the more difficult it will be to fix. More than a few politicians have tried to wall off the program and make it untouchable. However, if politicians continue to delay creating a real solution, the ultimate measures will need to be more draconian.

Hopefully, legislators from both sides of the aisle can come together to address the Social Security system's funding and benefit payout challenges. Our goal should be to create more palatable solutions sooner rather than later. Maybe the most recent French protests will serve as a wake-up call to those on Capitol Hill.

We now see that the Social Security trust fund surplus is being depleted at a faster rate than originally anticipated. Let's turn our attention to another recent challenge that has come roaring back for the first time in nearly four decades: inflation.

You may wonder why inflation would create additional stress on the solvency of the Social Security system. You see, when inflation rises, so does the cost-of-living adjustment that Social Security pays to current retirees. It also increases the future benefit amounts everyone qualified for social security is eligible for, even if they have not started collecting.

In our post-COVID world, inflation has risen at the fastest pace since the late 1970s and early 1980s.[65] As a result, Social Security had higher cost-of-living adjustments in 2021 and 2022 than we had seen in many years. These increased benefits are reducing the remaining trust fund surplus more quickly than if inflation had remained at the levels we had gotten used to over the previous decade.

The recent run-up in prices has disproportionately affected retirees living on fixed incomes. Retirees allocate a larger portion of their spending to housing, medical costs, and travel expenses, which tend to rise faster than the general inflation rate.

As a result, many retirees face difficult decisions about how to spend their finite resources. When prescription drug and grocery costs are both going through the roof, those at the lower end of the income spectrum are forced to make difficult life choices. Let's explore the policies that some senior advocacy groups are pushing for to help those struggling during retirement.

Please, Sir, I Want Some More

[66]

Charles Dickens's second novel, *Oliver Twist*, was published as a serial beginning in 1837. It tells the story of an orphan who starts his life in a workhouse and then does an apprenticeship with an undertaker. He escapes the apprenticeship and travels to London, where he meets the Artful Dodger, a member of a gang of juvenile thieves.

Early in the novel, it states that Oliver is "desperate with hunger" and "reckless with misery." He rises from the table and walks toward the master, bowl and spoon in hand, and famously says, "Please, sir, I want some more."[67]

As might be expected, this does not go over well with the workhouse master or with Mr. Bumble, the parish official who runs the workhouse where Oliver was raised. To ensure that the other boys are too afraid to ask for more, Oliver is punished badly for asking for additional gruel. Mr. Bumble puts him into solitary confinement and only allows him to wash with cold water.

Today, those living on Social Security also want some more. However, they are unsure whom to ask or how to get additional benefits. Social Security started providing annual cost-of-living adjustments in 1975. Prior to this, adjustments to Social Security were only made through acts of Congress. After massive stimulus was provided by the federal government and the Federal Reserve Bank both during and after the COVID-19 pandemic, inflation, as measured by the Consumer Price Index (CPI), started rising dramatically in late 2021 until it peaked at 9.1% in June 2022.[68]

This led to a 5.9% cost-of-living adjustment (COLA) for Social Security in 2022. In 2023, the COLA rose to 8.7%. As you can see in our chart below, this was the third-largest COLA in Social Security history and the largest one since 1981.

SOCIAL SECURITY COLA HISTORY 1975-2025

Year	COLA	Year	COLA	Year	COLA
1975	8.0%	1992	3.0%	2009	0.0%
1976	6.4%	1993	2.6%	2010	0.0%
1977	5.9%	1994	2.8%	2011	3.6%
1978	6.5%	1995	2.6%	2012	1.7%
1979	9.9%	1996	2.9%	2013	1.5%
1980	14.3%	1997	2.1%	2014	1.7%
1981	11.2%	1998	1.3%	2015	0.0%
1982	7.4%	1999	2.5%	2016	0.3%
1983	3.5%	2000	3.5%	2017	2.0%
1984	3.5%	2001	2.6%	2018	2.8%
1985	3.1%	2002	1.4%	2019	1.6%
1986	1.3%	2003	2.1%	2020	1.3%
1987	4.2%	2004	2.7%	2021	5.9%
1988	4.0%	2005	4.1%	2022	8.7%
1989	4.7%	2006	3.3%	2023	3.2%
1990	5.4%	2007	2.3%	2024	2.5%
1991	3.7%	2008	5.8%	2025	2.5%

Source: Social Security Administration - SSA.GOV [69]

Even though retirees saw their Social Security benefits rising at the fastest rate in four decades during this time, this money was desperately needed to pay for the higher cost of nearly everything seniors buy, such as groceries, gasoline, and medicine. Subsequently, inflation fell to 3% in June 2023.

On October 12, 2023, the government released the September CPI report, the last one for the 2023 fiscal year. Later that morning, the Social Security Administration announced that the 2024 COLA for Social Security would drop to 3.2%.[70] Not surprisingly, this was met with frustration from retirees who were still dealing with the cumulative effects of higher costs. These costs never went down—they are just growing at a slower pace today.

A survey released by the Senior Citizens League (TSCL) shows that eight in 10 retirees think Congress should provide a COLA that more closely reflects the inflation experienced by older adults.[71] As a result, Social Security benefits have lost approximately 36% of their purchasing power since calendar year 2000, according to TSCL.

In December 1982, the government started publishing an additional measurement of inflation known as CPI-E. This index measures price changes specifically based on the spending patterns of the elderly. According to TSCL, the COLA for 2024 would have been 4%, 0.8% higher than the adjustment given, if the alternative measurement had been used.[72] The senior citizen group is backing legislation known as the Social Security 2100 Act, which was introduced in the House of Representatives by John Larson, D-CT. This legislation would require the higher of the two CPI calculations to be given to seniors each year to help them keep up with rising costs during their retirement years.

Of course, the big question is how we pay for all this. In a world where the government is racking up annual budget deficits at a rate normally only seen during times of crisis or war, we hope that somebody on either side of the aisle on Capitol Hill starts taking financial responsibility more seriously. In order to reduce deficits, you need some combination of higher revenue—which primarily comes from taxes—and lower spending, of which entitlement programs such as Social Security, Medicare, and Medicaid are a very big line item.

In the meantime, many people in our country, including seniors, are struggling to make ends meet. Like our friend Oliver, they are looking to our leaders and saying, "I want some more." They are uncertain whether anybody is listening.

We will now turn to the movie *Airplane!* to frame our last topic: how far off course Social Security funding is from the projected benefits our government has promised to pay retirees. We know that Social Security is funded by the FICA taxes we all pay during our working years. Since the '07–'08 Global Financial Crisis, more benefits have been paid out of the Social Security system than have been paid in by taxes. This means we are slowly deflating the funding balloon, and we will eventually run out of air.

Changes will need to be made to make the system solvent in the long term. Several strategies are available that, if applied in some combination, would solve this problem. The big question is whether anybody on Capitol Hill has the political courage to take these steps before we reach a crisis.

In the state of Ohio, the teachers' state pension fund was in a similar situation several years ago. To address future shortfalls that would affect benefits, the funding formula was changed, and both the teachers and the school systems contributed a higher percentage to shore up the shortfall. Teachers had to work more years to qualify for benefits, and those benefits were somewhat reduced based on the funding formula.

At the time, nobody was happy with the compromises. Nobody was comfortable with the pain they were feeling or the extra dollars they were contributing to help solve the problem. However, today, those same teachers are retiring with greater confidence that the benefits that they worked so hard for will be there for them down the road.

Will anybody on Capitol Hill look to this model as a potential solution for the similar issues we are dealing with in our Social Security system?

Surely We Must Be Off Course?

According to Wikipedia:

> *Airplane!* (alternatively titled *Flying High!*) is a 1980 American disaster comedy film written and directed by Jim Abrahams and brothers David and Jerry Zucker in their directorial debuts, and produced by Jon Davison. It stars Robert Hays and Julie Hagerty and features Leslie Nielsen, Robert Stack, Lloyd Bridges, Peter Graves, Kareem Abdul-Jabbar, and Lorna Patterson. It is a parody of the disaster film genre, particularly the 1957 Paramount film *Zero Hour!*...[as well as] *Airport 1975* and other films in the *Airport* series. It is known for its use of surreal humor and fast-paced slapstick comedy, including visual and verbal puns, gags, running jokes, and dark humor.[73]

I was a freshman in high school when the movie was released, and it was immediately a huge hit with me and my friends. Whenever it is on television, I still watch at least a portion of it for a few laughs (much to my wife's chagrin). It appears that I am not the only one who holds the movie in such high regard. The movie has become more appreciated with time. Per Wikipedia, "It ranked sixth on Bravo's 100 Funniest Movies. In a 2007 survey by Channel 4 in the United Kingdom, it was judged the second-greatest comedy of all time, behind *Monty Python's Life of Brian*, and in 2012 was voted #1 on The 50 Funniest Comedies Ever poll. In 2010, it was selected for preservation in the United States National Film Registry by the Library of Congress as being culturally, historically, or aesthetically significant.'"[74] It's in good company—*Life of Brian* is another favorite of mine.

One of the running gags in the movie is "Don't call me Shirley." When Dr. Rumack, hilariously portrayed by Leslie Nielsen, discovers that the fish served during meal service has caused food poisoning that has incapacitated the entire flight crew, he turns to Ted Striker, a former fighter pilot who was traumatized during the war, and asks him to land the plane and save the passengers: "Can you fly this plane and land it?" Ted is surprised by the request and retorts, "Surely you can't be serious." This leads to Dr. Rumack's famous deadpan reply: "I am serious. And don't call me Shirley!"[75]

Throughout the movie, we get scenes from the flight control tower in Chicago, where they are worried that Ted will not be able to land the plane—and, worse, that they could be miles off course due to all the issues that have occurred during the flight.

This brings us to our topic of the day: the upcoming Social Security shortfall. As mentioned above, the last changes made to Social Security occurred in 1983. Those changes allowed us to create a surplus in the Social Security Trust Fund, which will be completely depleted within the next 10 years. As Social Security is a foundational part of most retirees' income, this is an extraordinarily important topic. Yet politicians on both sides of the aisle on Capitol Hill have continued to kick the can down the road instead of fixing the situation.

I referenced earlier that creating a plan for long-term financial stability and viability can be compared to flying a plane. If you were getting on an airplane in Cleveland and flying to Los Angeles, you would expect your pilot and crew to have a flight plan and to make adjustments as necessary. This same logic would hold true in fixing the upcoming shortfall in Social Security. The amount of FICA taxes paid by workers began to fall short of the amount of benefits paid to retirees by Social Security around 2007, despite original projections that this would not happen until approximately 2018.

The initial increase in outlays and the decrease in revenue coincided with the '07–'08 Global Financial Crisis, which was precipitated by the collapse of the subprime mortgage market and the subsequent failures of AIG and Lehman Brothers. This led to a significant recession and major job losses over the next few years. You see, when people lose their jobs, they no longer pay FICA tax into the Social Security system. At the same time, many workers aged 62 and over decided to retire and start drawing benefits earlier than expected. This reduced the reserves in the Social Security trust fund and brought forward the date at which it would run out of money.

As mentioned previously, no president has seriously tried to address this situation since George W. Bush did in 2005. Unfortunately, W's proposal to partially privatize Social Security didn't go very far and was probably misguided at best. However, it would have been much easier to make minor midcourse corrections 30 years before the trust fund ran out than to find ourselves where we are today. Neither subsequent presidents nor Congresses have taken any serious steps to fix the problem. We now find ourselves out over the Rockies, hundreds of miles off course, and the decisions and actions to fix the funding gap are becoming more difficult.

The projected benefits that can be paid from current taxes once the surplus runs out could cause a 20% or greater drop in benefits. This would be devastating to many retirees. There are only a few levers that can be adjusted to fix the situation. This includes raising the age at which Social Security benefits can be collected, raising the FICA tax rate, raising the amount of wages FICA tax is paid on, or reworking the COLA formula. None of these are fun solutions, and the longer we wait, the more drastic the changes will have to be.

In the movie *Airplane!* we learned that the trauma of war led our pilot hero, Ted Striker, to develop a drinking problem where he was unable to get a glass to his mouth Not only was this excessively messy, but Ted ran the risk of severe dehydration.

76

It is our sincere wish that somebody, anybody, on Capitol Hill begins to proactively address the Social Security shortfall that is now only a decade away. We hope that the trauma of the future changes to the Social Security system that will inevitably come does not cause anyone to develop a drinking problem like our hero Ted. Surely, we are *not* joking about this!

Throughout this chapter, we have reviewed the history and formation of Social Security, the current structural and financial challenges it faces, how other countries and even state pension systems are attempting to solve similar situations, the unique cost of living pressures being faced by many retirees, and the potential options available to fix our Social Security system.

Now I want to move to the topic you have been waiting for: What does all this mean to you, and how do you make the best decisions about when and how to claim your Social Security benefits? In this concluding section,

I will share the stories of two client couples who took different approaches based on their goals and unique family situations.

Danny and Sandy: Maximizing Long-Term Social Security Benefits to Reduce Market Volatility and Longevity Risk

Danny Zuko and Sandy Olsson, of *Grease* movie fame, began dating in high school. This strongly resembles my clients—who also happen to have been my friends since high school—Danny and Sandy. Currently, Danny and Sandy are trying to accomplish two goals: maximize their guaranteed cash flow during their early retirement years and reduce the potential impact of market volatility and downturns. Danny clearly remembers his parents retiring around the peak of the dot-com bubble and seeing them struggle as the stock market went through a two-year downturn of more than 45%.

Sandy is a 58-year-old schoolteacher who will soon be retiring and will have state teacher pension benefits. These will be $5,500 per month gross, or $4,500 per month net after federal and state income tax and deductions for health insurance benefits. Danny will be turning 60 but does not want to collect his Social Security benefits until at least age 67, which is his full retirement age under current law. He may wait until age 70, the maximum benefit-claiming age.

Danny's Social Security benefits at age 67 would be approximately $3,500 per month, and they could rise to as much as $4,400 per month if he waited until age 70 to collect his maximum benefits. There is generally wisdom in having at least one retired spouse wait to take benefits until a later date. This gives that spouse a permanently higher benefit. It also generally gives the spouse a higher survivor benefit if they should pass away first.

To provide guaranteed income until full Social Security benefits kick in, Danny and Sandy have decided to use the assets in Danny's nonqualified annuity, which they purchased more than a decade ago, to create an additional income stream for the next seven years.

They will do this by annuitizing the contract, which had been funded with a $150,000 deposit that they have already paid tax on. The current account value is approximately $260,000, which will be paid out monthly over a seven-year period. In essence, they are exchanging an asset for a guaranteed income stream.

The monthly income stream of approximately $3,500 will also be tax-advantaged, as the $150,000 cost basis will be spread over seven years. This means that approximately 52% of every payment they receive will be tax-free. The remaining 48% will be taxable.

This means that Danny and Sandy will receive approximately $3,000 per month after taxes from the annuity. When this is added to Sandy's net teacher pension of $4,500 per month, their total guaranteed income will be $7,500 per month for the first seven years of retirement.

Danny and Sandy's retirement income goal is $10,000 per month of net cash flow. This means they only need to rely on their investment portfolio for approximately $2,500 per month or $30,000 per year of income to make up the differential. Given that their investment resources—even after converting the annuity to an income stream—currently total approximately $2.5 million, this is well within their means.

By allocating approximately 6%, or $150,000, of their investment assets to lower-risk assets, such as Treasury bills and short-term bonds, they can provide for this income shortfall for at least five years. This gives them time to live through the market's inevitable ups and downs. Our typical goal would be to use market upturns and dividends from the portfolio to continue filling the cash and short-term bond reserves for future withdrawals. This would allow them to not worry about short-term volatility. Over a typical market cycle, we should have several opportunities to sell during upturns and refill the cash and short-term bond assets they will need for the next several years. In using this strategy, the objective is to never have to sell when markets are down.

During my more than 30 years as a CFP, I have watched two groups of clients struggle during their early years of retirement. First were those who retired in late 1999 or early 2000 at the height of the dot-com bubble. Those clients were faced with a two-year stock market downturn. The second group were those who retired in late 2007 or early 2008, as we entered the subprime mortgage crisis and the failure of AIG and Lehman Brothers. This led to an ultimate peak-to-trough decline of 57% in the stock market.

Our ultimate goal should be to make certain that we have sufficient liquidity to live through the inevitable ups and downs of the market. Doing so gives us the ability to be patient and take advantage of upturns in the market to fund our future cash flow needs. More importantly, it also gives us the ability to turn off the news and noise screaming that the sky is falling, which can be more of a problem than ever these days thanks to our 24-hour cable news and social media platforms. It also allows us to create confidence in our retirement income plan so that we can focus on doing the things that are most important in life.

Rob and Laura: Maximizing Current Income and Resources to Enjoy Retirement Now

The Dick Van Dyke Show, one of television's early comedic classics, centers on the lives of Rob and Laura Petrie. Rob is a writer on a fictional TV show, and Laura is a devoted housewife and mother to their son. This is very similar to our next client couple, Rob and Laura. During his working years, Rob was a mid-level executive at a local manufacturing company. When he retired, he had been earning more than $100,000 a year. He had accumulated 401(k) and other retirement plan assets totaling approximately $1.2 million. Laura had been a homemaker for most of their married life. Therefore, she would be eligible for Social Security benefits equal to one-half of Rob's.

When they retired, Rob and Laura had a different goal than Danny and Sandy. They wanted to maximize cash flow during their early retirement days, when they hoped to be young and healthy enough to enjoy an active life together. Also, because of their personal and family health histories, they did not have a strong belief that they would have life expectancies beyond their late '70s or early '80s. This led them to want to maximize benefits right away instead of being overly concerned about longevity issues.

As I have discussed throughout the book, a successful retirement income plan is largely built by maximizing both income and asset resources. For Rob and Laura, their income resources would only consist of their Social Security benefits.

When Rob retired, Rob and Laura were both 63. At that time, their full Social Security benefit age was 66. Rob and Laura asked us to help them analyze the best Social Security strategy for them to create the income needed to reach their life goals.

To do so, we ran retirement income projections, one showing them taking reduced Social Security benefits at age 63 and a second showing them taking full Social Security benefits at age 66.

Beyond this, the rest of their retirement income would be funded with withdrawals from the $1.2 million of investment assets that had accumulated during Jim's working years. Historically, multiple studies, including Bill Bengen's original study from nearly 30 years ago, have shown that people can take a 4% withdrawal from their investments, adjusted for inflation, over a 30-year retirement life expectancy.[77] This means we would start with withdrawals of approximately $48,000 annually. We would then increase this over time so that their standard of living could keep up with the rising cost of living during retirement.

Luckily, Rob and Laura, like many of my clients, are debt-free and live a modest lifestyle. They would like to be involved with charitable activities at their church, be active and engaged with their children and grandchildren, and travel from time to time.

If Rob and Laura took their Social Security benefits at age 63, they would bring in approximately $3,600 per month of combined income. This would consist of Rob's benefit of $2,400 per month and Laura's benefit of $1,200 per month. The combined benefit, along with approximately $4,000 per month of gross income available from their investment portfolio, would be more than sufficient to meet their income goal of $6,500 per month or $78,000 per year.

Alternatively, Rob and Laura could wait until age 66 to claim full Social Security benefits. Doing so would increase their combined benefits to approximately $4,800 per month. This would be $3,200 monthly for Rob and $1,600 for Laura. However—and this is the big issue—if they waited to take Social Security benefits for three years, their entire standard of living would have to come from withdrawals from their investment assets in the meantime.

In turn, this would cause their investment assets to be depleted much more significantly than if they drew Social Security immediately. Interestingly, the higher Social Security benefits they would eventually receive at age 66 would allow their future withdrawals from that point forward to be much lower. The lower future withdrawals would eventually allow their investment assets to compound and grow to a greater amount than if they took Social Security at a younger age.

The crossover point for most of my clients for whom we have done similar analyses is between the ages of 78 and 80. After that, the compounded growth and lower withdrawals allow the asset base to grow and exceed the amount they would have if they had taken benefits at a younger age.

In reviewing the two scenarios, Rob asked me, "What do I care if I have more money when I am eighty-five?" Based on Rob and Laura's goals and the factors outlined above, they wanted to have more money when they were younger and healthier. As stated earlier, they were not overly concerned about planning for longevity based on their personal and family health histories.

Therefore, in this particular case, Rob and Laura took Social Security at a younger age to maximize cash flow during their early retirement years. They fully understood the implications of doing so. They knew that they were giving up some longevity benefits to maximize their lifestyle during the younger days of their retirement life.

By the way, it is not my job to tell clients what they should feel most comfortable doing. My job is to make sure they understand the potential financial and family implications of their various options so they can make the decision that allows them to sleep best at night.

Ultimately, retirement success is about having enough cash flow to do the things that make life meaningful for you and your family. These two scenarios give you a window into some of the issues that need to be considered in your unique situation. There is no one-size-fits-all solution that will work for every family.

Now that you have a better grasp of the many personal, health, cash flow, and longevity issues that may affect your Social Security claiming and timing decision, you are in a much better place to develop a strategy that makes sense for you and your family's needs.

If, on the other hand, you look at all these factors and say, "Now what should I do?" then you may be among the many people who would benefit from consulting with a CFP who specializes in helping people transition from work life to retirement life. They will be equipped to help guide you through this maze and create a retirement income plan that gives you a higher probability of success.

As we turn the page to Puzzle Piece #5, we will begin to look at another factor potentially wreaking havoc on current and future retirees as they are looking to create retirement success. The psychological impact of both 24-hour cable news and social media can be extraordinarily negative. In our next two chapters, we will first explore the damage that these inputs can create on our emotional health. We will then look to help you recognize and manage your response to this so you don't do something hazardous to your wealth!

PUZZLE PIECE

#5

Navigating the Negative 24-Hour News and Social Media Spin Cycle

Cable news and social media should come with a warning label: watching or consuming too much of this product could be harmful to your mental and financial health! In reviewing Puzzle Piece #5, we will explore the damage you could be inflicting on both your person and your portfolio if you are not careful.

What is financial journalism? If you're anything like me, you're bombarded by financial headlines and stories all day every day. I personally read 600–800 pages per month of economic and investment commentary. Before cable news networks launched and Al Gore invented the internet, financial journalism generally meant reading *The Wall Street Journal* and a few other financial periodicals such as *Money*, *Forbes*, *Businessweek*, *Fortune*, and *Barron's*.

Since the 1989 founding of CNBC, there has been an explosion of options from which you can obtain financial news and information. A quick internet search of financial media outlets today yields more than two dozen. A few of the more prominent ones are the following:

- CNBC
- *The Economist*

- Bloomberg
- Yahoo! Finance
- Business Insider
- CNN Business
- MarketWatch
- *Barron's*
- *The Wall Street Journal*
- The Motley Fool
- *Forbes*
- Reuters
- TheStreet.com
- Investopedia
- *Entrepreneur Magazine*
- *Business Today*
- *The Financial Express*[78]

While one may think that having access to so much financial news and information would be helpful, we find that often the opposite is true. Please remember that having access to information does not necessarily mean you have the wisdom to apply it. I believe that all computers should come with a warning label: "Wisdom sold separately."

When I started my career in 1987, most clients received quarterly investment account statements by mail. Mutual fund prices were quoted once per week in the newspaper. People did not have the ability to look at their accounts online daily. Therefore, they did not see or understand how the day-to-day ups and downs of the markets influenced their account values.

In 2008, *Cleveland Magazine* interviewed me and one of the client families I had helped achieve a successful transition from work life to retirement life. During the interview, they asked me, "What is the biggest change you have seen during the 20 years you've been a financial advisor?" I thought about it for a moment and shared that when I had started in the business, one of my biggest jobs had been delivering information to my clients about their financial options. Twenty years later, one of my biggest jobs had become helping clients sift through the mountain of economic data that was available to them to help them determine what was meaningful or applicable. This was largely due to the rise in financial journalism.

Have you noticed that every time you turn on the 24-hour cable news network (whether you are watching the ones that lean left or lean right), the airwaves are filled with unrest, disdain, and negativity? If you feel that way, not only are you not alone—you are also correct.

It seems that there are roughly 10 times more negative stories than positive stories being put out by the media. There are psychological and, of course, marketing reasons for this to happen, as ad revenue is what drives the content on cable news more than anything else. Please do not be deceived by the thought that the media's goal is to educate you. The media's *only* goal is to get you to watch more so that they can sell more ads and create more profits.

All of this affects your mindset and how you feel each day. That makes this a really important topic to understand. Studies show that even small doses of negative news increase anxiety and mood disturbance and that those unhealthy levels remain elevated for a prolonged period after viewing. This could be doing substantial damage to your psyche if you happen to be a homemaker or someone who works from home and you have cable news playing all day in the background.[79]

Let's explore some of the beliefs and behaviors that you can use to combat this negative news barrage.

Wisdom and Learning from History

> History repeats itself. That's one of the
> things that's wrong with history.
> — Clarence Darrow

It seems like the media is constantly telling us that we are in "unprecedented times." However, when we went through the Arab oil embargo in '73–'74, the stock market crash of 1987, the dot-com bubble, 9/11, and the Global Financial Crisis in '07–'08, the media told us the same thing.

Sir John Templeton famously said that the four most dangerous words that any investor can utter are "This time is different."[80] While he meant that valuations, earnings, interest rates, inflation, and GDP *always* matter, every crisis brings its own unique set of circumstances economically, politically—and sometimes medically and virally.

However, you can see from the next chart below that we have always solved problems that previously seemed insurmountable, leading us to new highs in the economy, wealth creation, and quality of life.

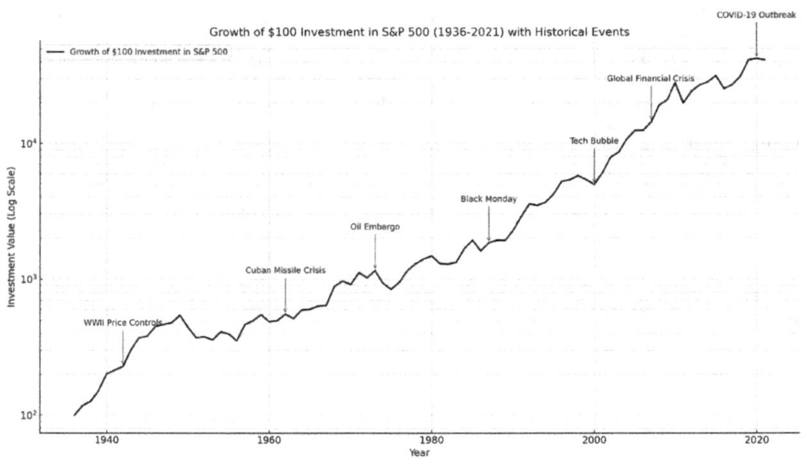

[81]

> I honestly believe it is better to know
> nothing than to know what ain't so.
> — John Billings

What do we know that is still true today that was true before the COVID-19 outbreak? Nick Murray has been a financial advisor for more than 50 years. I have read and followed his work for more than 20 years. He is an industry leader and a respected writer and speaker. I have often shared his thoughts and wisdom with my clients. The following truth is probably one of his most important. There are three emotional traits you need to be successful as a long-term investor and accumulator of wealth:

1. **Discipline:** When markets seem euphoric and valuations become unhinged from pricing, you need to stay disciplined with your diversification and asset allocation and not chase the latest hot dot or theme.
2. **Patience:** There are many times when it seems like the market grinds slowly up and down for a number of quarters and you feel like you are getting nowhere. We saw this play out during the 2015–2016 market cycle, when the markets seemed to go nowhere for two years. Subsequently, the market doubled in value in the five years from 2015 to 2019.
3. **Faith:** During times of dislocation, volatility, and downturn, you have to have faith that free markets, entrepreneurialism, innovation, and technology will bring us back, just like they always have. (See the previous chart.)[82]

During the early days of the pandemic, someone said to me that it was like we were living through the 1918 Spanish flu pandemic, the job loss of the Great Depression, and the 1965 Los Angeles Watts riots all at once.

Over those early months, we experienced the initial downturn in the stock, bond, and oil markets and the government-mandated shutdown of our economy. During that time, we tried to focus on controlling what we could control so that we did not make bad emotional decisions. We then moved into a longer-term period of uncertainty as we tried to restart the economy while maintaining social distancing and trying to solve the viral outbreak through treatment or future vaccines.

Cable news and social media tend to be negative because they know this will elicit an emotional response. In turn, this will keep us tuned in, watching or clicking, which will keep paying the bills by drawing advertising to the outlets.

However, be aware that there is a big difference between fear and danger. Fear is an emotion. It is not necessarily grounded in fact or risk. On the other hand, there are real risks that we face every day, often without giving them a second thought. Allow me to illustrate.

At age 10, I saw my first-ever PG-rated movie, *Jaws*. Ever since that movie came out, people in the United States have been more fearful of shark attacks.[83] According to the Florida Museum of Natural History, there have only been 10 fatal shark attacks in the last 10 years in the United States. However, this does not stop people from being fearful of sharks or thinking about them every time they go into the ocean.[84]

Contrast this with driving a car. Statistically, you are much more likely to be hurt in a car accident than to be bitten by a shark. On average, more than 38,000 people die every year in the United States in crashes on roadways.[85] According to the National Safety Council, each year, over five million people incur serious enough injuries in motor-vehicle-related incidents that they require medical attention.[86] Yet nobody I know has stopped driving because of the danger.

Cigarette smoking has been down in the United States over the last several decades. But, according to statistics from the CDC, it is still extremely dangerous. More than 480,000 people die each year in the United States from smoking-related deaths. This includes more than 41,000 deaths because of secondhand smoke. On average, smokers die 10 years earlier than nonsmokers.[87]

Let me share an anecdote that somebody told me many years ago to illustrate the difference between "scary" and "dangerous." A man is at the beach playing in the shallow waves when somebody yells, "*Shark!*" He jumps out of the water, gets into his car, drives to a fast-food restaurant for lunch, and lights up a cigarette on his way home. By responding to the emotion of fear, he has traded one scary activity for several more dangerous ones.

We now understand the difference between fear and risk. We also know that the media aims to incite emotions in their reporting to keep you tuned in. Now let's explore the real purpose and track record of financial journalism and its potential detrimental impact on your wealth.

What's the Purpose of Financial Journalism?

Being There is a 1979 political satire that tells the story of Chance, a middle-aged, uneducated gardener who unwittingly becomes a much sought-after political pundit. He eventually becomes an advisor to the president of the United States and those around him. In the movie, he is portrayed by Peter Sellers, who was nominated for the Academy Award for Best Actor and won the Golden Globe that year in the same category.

Chance has spent his entire life tending a garden for a wealthy old man in Washington, DC. He has never left the property, and other than his knowledge of gardening, everything else he knows comes from what he has seen on television.

When the owner of the estate dies, Chance is forced out into the real world for the first time. While aimlessly wandering the streets, he is hit by a limousine owned by an elderly businessman, Ben Rand. The car is occupied by Rand's much younger wife, Eve, who is played by Shirley

MacLaine. When she asks his name, he says, "Chance, the gardener." However, she believes she hears him say, "Chauncey Gardiner."

People mistake Chauncey's slow and measured speech and his stories about the garden as deep, thoughtful, and wise. The movie argues that if you look right, sound right, and have powerful friends, you can go far in society. Near the end of the movie, this uneducated and inexperienced person is seriously being proposed as a presidential candidate.

In what is yet another great example of art imitating life, we could point to many examples in the financial media in the years since the outbreak of the COVID-19 pandemic that would echo similarly.

We begin with one of the more egregious examples. Throughout much of 2022, many "expert" journalists in the financial media continually described Sam Bankman-Fried, a very young and high-profile crypto executive and business owner, as a genius. The August/September *Fortune* magazine hailed him as the next Warren Buffett. At that time, he was believed to have a net worth of more than $26 billion.[88] By November 11th of the same year, his crypto empire had crumbled, and his net worth was rumored to be less than $100,000.[89]

The movie *Being There* posited that an inexperienced and uneducated gardener was actually qualified to be at the highest levels of Washington's inner circles. Real life showed us that a con man running a Ponzi scheme could be hailed as both a billionaire and a genius. You can't make this $#@& up!

[90]

I have repeatedly cautioned people of the historical dangers when everybody, including the media, falls in love with and chases a single investment idea.

For those of us old enough to remember the tech mania of the late '90s, it culminated in multiple dot-com commercials during the Super Bowl in January 2000. The 2022 Super Bowl felt eerily familiar, as we saw multiple crypto endorsements from sports heroes and celebrities during the commercials. Knowing how the first episode ended foreshadowed what was likely to come.

There are numerous other examples of things that financial journalism has fallen in love with over the last few years that have turned out to be just as unrealistic and overhyped as the crypto craze. These include the meme stock phenomenon perpetrated by bloggers and day traders working from their moms' basements.

This also shows up in the top tech stocks. People could not get enough of these "grow forever" darlings from the market and the media. Most of these stocks eventually traded below the levels they did in February 2020, prior to the coronavirus outbreak.

We also had the infamous work-from-home stocks. Early in the pandemic, it was roundly decided that nobody would return to the office. Therefore, they could forever work from home, ride their smart bikes, watch their streaming services, and have all their meals and groceries delivered to their doors. The stocks of these home exercise, food delivery, and streaming service companies have also fallen dramatically from their initial stratospheric ascents.

All these media-loved and pushed investment themes have moved in the wrong direction for those who chased past performance, hoping that it would continue into the future. Mean reversion is a real phenomenon. Once again, attractive improbability turned out to be just that—improbable. The "attractive improbability" refers to the idea that people are often drawn to things that appear to be attractive and highly unlikely, rather than what is more easily attainable but less sexy. This phenomenon occurs when an investor realizes that the outsized returns an investment has recently experienced are unlikely to continue at the same pace in the future but is still enticed to allocate some of their resources to this idea on the outside chance that they may strike it rich.

I remember asking some clients who were endlessly caught up in the late '90s tech craze what they thought the purpose of the editors and reporters of these financial journals was. They naively stated that they thought the main purpose was to help educate them so that they could create themselves a brighter financial tomorrow. They could not be more wrong.

If journalists told you the simple truth—that long-term financial success comes from the compounded effect of good habits—you would never have to buy their publications again. If they told you that owning a diversified portfolio, adding to it regularly, and letting it compound over long periods of time would allow you to accumulate more wealth than you ever thought possible, you would simply have to buy their magazines *once*.

I am sharing this to inform you of the real purpose of all financial journalism. It is simply to get you to continue to watch, click on, share, post about, and comment on more and more of their largely inane and irrelevant content. Ultimately, financial journalists' real goal is to sell more advertising for the sake of the profit of their publishers. They have absolutely no incentive to help you succeed.

Like those listening to Chauncey Gardiner in *Being There*, many people breathlessly sit and wait for the next words of wisdom uttered by whatever financial news service they watch or read. I am here to remind you that you are better off—and that your family's wealth will likely compound far more quickly—if you simply follow the principles outlined above.

Financial Journalism Is Wrong—Again

Financial journalists love creating headlines that cause people to click or watch the latest epiphany they are sharing with the general public. Many people refer to this as "clickbait." Please remember that these journalists are not paid to be correct. Their goal is simply to get you to tune in or buy their publications.

From history, we know that these journalists have a track record of being wrong, especially at major turning points during economic and financial cycles. We know that in August 1979, *BusinessWeek* (the precursor to *Bloomberg Businessweek*) put out a cover story famously titled "The Death of Equities."[91] This article posits that the stock market has been slain by rising inflation (sound familiar?) and has been left for dead.

After this story was published, the stock market went on its longest bull market run ever from 1982 to 2000. During this 18-year run, the S&P 500 index went from below 200 to over 1,400, more than a sevenfold increase. So much for "The Death of Equities."

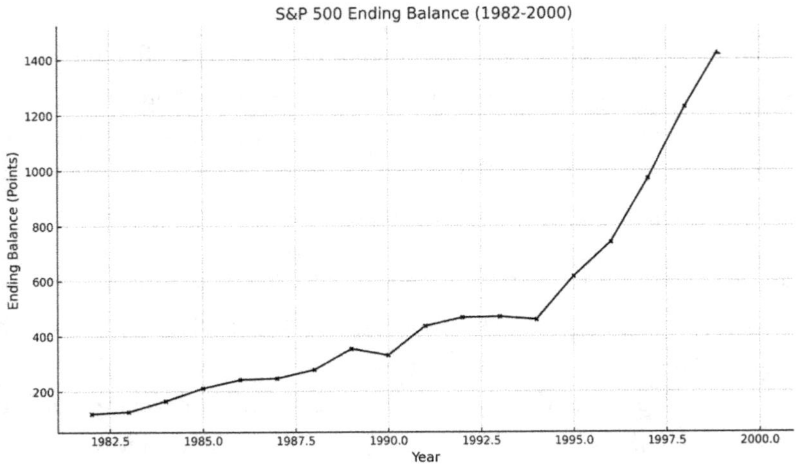

[92]

Fast-forward to April 2019, and once again, *Businessweek* asks whether inflation is dead.[93] As anyone who lived through 2022 and 2023 knows, inflation was definitely not dead. It rose from below 2%, where it had spent most of the previous dozen years or so since the '07–'08 Global Financial Crisis and subprime mortgage meltdown, to more than 9% in June '22.

I am not sharing these stories of journalistic failure just because they bring me joy—although I will admit that they do. They are to remind you that every time you hear the latest economic or political pundit stating with certainty what will happen—they don't really know. Therefore, you should turn off the TV or close your web browser and not emotionally react to the latest headline, no matter how confidently it may be stated.

For those of you who want a real thought challenge when seeing headlines such as these, you could ask yourself the question, "What would the smart thing be to do if they are wrong?" For example, if you thought the 1979 headline was wrong, you would naturally start buying equities while prices were low and therefore on sale. If they were wrong about the U.S. dollar, you might consider increasing exposure to foreign assets, whose value goes up when the dollar falls.

Strategic thinking and questioning confidently laid out prognostications are what CFP professionals are here to do on behalf of our clients. As we move forward, I would encourage you to ignore the most confidently stated headlines and instead enjoy life with your family and friends. If we all did this, we would be happier and have less stress in our lives, which in turn would allow us all to live life in a more joyful way.

As I have detailed above, financial journalism's track record of accurately predicting the future is abysmal. But what about Wall Street experts? Do the economists and market strategists that you see regularly pontificating on CNBC and other outlets have a better track record? Let's explore.

> It's tough to make predictions,
> especially about the future.
> — Attributed to many people, from Nobel prize-winning quantum physicist Niels Bohr to legendary baseball player and part-time philosopher Yogi Berra

Of course it would be much easier to make predictions about things that have already happened—although some people wouldn't believe what is really happening in the world today, even in hindsight.

Each December, economists and market strategists make predictions about where the markets will go in the upcoming year. It is an annual rite of passage on Wall Street. Looking at the track record of past predictions would make you wonder why anybody would put their reputation at risk for this process.

Let's go back to the beginning of 2022. The stock market, as measured by the S&P 500, was at an all-time high and was approaching 4,800. The economy was growing. There were still mountains of money flowing through the economy from COVID and post-COVID stimulus bills. Russia had not invaded Ukraine yet. However, the Federal Reserve Bank, after telling us for months that inflation was transitory, was threatening that they would have to begin raising rates to fight persistently rising prices.

Against this backdrop, Wall Street expected the S&P 500 to rise 9% to 5,100. It is interesting to note that no strategists predicted a negative year for the market in 2022. We can look back and see that the consensus was wrong. As the Fed raised interest rates much further and much faster than anyone expected, and as geopolitical threats injected uncertainty into the economy and caused energy prices to rise dramatically, the market fell 26% before ending the year just above 3,800, some 1,300 points lower than what the experts predicted.

As we entered 2023, the mood among the same Wall Street gurus was much more pessimistic, with most analysts expecting more muted returns for the market in the coming year....

Wall Street Year End 2023 Targets for S&P 500

Firm	SP& 500 Target	% Above '22 Close
Bank of America/Merrill Lynch	4000	3.90%
Barclays Bank	3675	-4.55%
BMO	4300	11.69%
Citi Group	3900	1.30%
Credit Suisse	4050	5.19%
Deutsche Bank	4500	16.88%
Goldman Sachs	4000	3.90%
JP Morgan	4200	9.09%
Morgan Stanley	3900	1.30%
RBS	4100	6.49%
Societe Generale	3800	-1.30%
UBS	3900	1.30%
Wells Fargo	4400	14.29%
as of 12/19/22 Median Targets	4000	3.90%
Closing Price Estimate		3850

Source: Evensky, Katz/Folder Newsletter Volume 17 #1 [94]

We can see that there were only a few market strategists who were brave enough to predict a double-digit return for the S&P 500. However, the average consensus was that the market would end the year around 4,000 with a gain of less than 5%. Let's see how our experts did when compared to where the index finished in 2023.

[95]

Even the most optimistic strategists underestimated the S&P 500's actual performance, which finished up more than 23% on the year.

It appears that the quote from Neils/Yogi was right. Predictions are tough to make—especially about the future. So, as you watch the news or read things online, and people confidently state where they think things will be 12 months from now, please look at the charts above and remember what a dubious track record of success predictions have before you put too much weight on them.

Another wise sage is Jeff Saut, the now-retired Raymond James chief investment strategist. You have likely seen him on CNBC, where he is a regular guest. When asked about his prediction for the market in the coming year, he generally quips, "I think stocks will be higher (or lower) by this time next year." And that, ladies and gentlemen, is *really* what people know about where the market will be in the future.

We will now consider a Bugs Bunny cartoon to explore the final point of this chapter. My goal is to help you understand that since 1950, we have lived through a multitude of economic and geopolitical events. Many of these have caused significant volatility and dislocation in the stock market. However, as you will see in the next section, these downturns were always temporary. The market always came back to reach new highs. Therefore, selling when things were down only served to lock in your losses and make certain that you missed the future upside gains.

Where's the Kaboom?

According to Wikipedia:

> *Hare-Way to the Stars* is a 1958 American animated science fiction comedy short film directed by Chuck Jones and written by Michael Maltese. The short was released by Warner Bros. Pictures on March 29, 1958 as part of the *Looney Tunes* series, and stars Bugs Bunny and Marvin the Martian....
>
> The cartoon starts when Bugs Bunny, feeling the effects of mixing radish juice with carrot juice the night before, unknowingly climbs out of his hole and into a rocket ship that is about to be launched into space. He realizes what has happened once he screws open the tip of the ship, and is immediately hit by the satellite Sputnik and lands on what appears to be a space station. While there, Bugs meets Marvin the Martian who is trying to blow up the Earth with his Illudium Q-36 Explosive Space Modulator (which resembles a simple stick of dynamite) because "Earth obstructs his view of Venus."
>
> Marvin lights the fuse, just before an alarmed Bugs quietly extinguishes it and steals the explosive, as Marvin quickly discovers what has happened—giving rise to one

> of his most famous lines ("Where's the kaboom?...There was supposed to be an Earth-shattering kaboom!!!").[96]

In much the same way, our financial media always seems to be looking for the next Earth-shattering kaboom! I have now been a CFP for over 30 years. As I mentioned earlier, I started in the business in August 1987, just a few weeks before the stock market crash in October of that year. One of my claims to fame is that I was in the business during the October 1987 stock market crash, and none of my clients lost any money. That is largely because I had not been in the business long enough to really have any clients yet!

Subsequently, I have lived and walked with clients through two Persian Gulf wars, the fall of Long-Term Capital Management, the dot-com bubble, 9/11, the subprime mortgage crisis, the failure of Lehman Brothers/AIG, multiple fiscal cliffs, the COVID-19 pandemic, government shutdowns, massive fiscal and monetary stimulus, and the highest inflation in 40 years, which led to the Fed raising interest rates at the fastest pace in 40 years.

Over that time, we have lived through four separate recessions, according to the National Bureau of Economic Research (NBER), an American private nonprofit research organization. The NBER defines a recession as "a significant decline in economic activity spread across the economy, lasting more than a few months, normally visible in real gross domestic product (GDP), real income, employment, industrial production, and wholesale-retail sales."[97]

As you can see below, since I entered the business in 1987, we have also experienced nine different bear markets, which are defined as stock market declines of 20% or more. You will note that four of those drops hit 20% on an intraday basis; however, when the market closed, it was just less than a 20% drop. As an advisor fielding phone calls from nervous clients, though, I can tell you firsthand that in each of those scenarios, clients responded as if we were in a bear market, regardless of the technical definition.

S&P 500 Bear Markets Since 1950

Peak Date	Trough Date	Peak Price	Trough Price	Percentage Loss	Duration (Days)
7/15/1957	10/22/1957	49.13	38.98	-20.700%	99
12/12/1961	6/26/1962	72.64	52.32	-28.000%	196
2/9/1966	10/7/1966	94.06	73.2	-22.200%	240
11/29/1968	5/26/1970	108.37	69.29	-36.100%	543
1/11/1973	10/3/1974	120.24	62.28	-48.200%	630
9/21/1976	3/6/1978	107.83	86.9	-19.400%	531
11/28/1980	8/12/1982	140.52	102.42	-27.100%	622
8/25/1987	12/4/1987	336.77	223.92	-33.500%	101
7/16/1990	10/11/1990	368.95	295.46	-19.900%	87
7/17/1998	8/31/1998	1186.75	957.28	-19.300%	45
3/24/2000	10/9/2002	1527.46	776.76	-49.100%	929
10/9/2007	3/9/2009	1565.15	676.53	-56.800%	517
4/29/2011	10/3/2011	1363.61	1099.23	-19.400%	157
9/20/2018	12/24/2018	2930.75	2351.1	-19.800%	95
2/19/2020	3/23/2020	3386.15	2237.4	-33.900%	33
1/3/2022	10/12/2022	4796.56	3577.03	-25.400%	282

Source: Yardeni Research 98

You can clearly see from the chart above that each time the market went through one of these significant downturns, *it was temporary!* The market always recovered to reach new highs. Sometimes it happened quickly, like it did after the federal government and the Federal Reserve Bank opened the floodgates of liquidity and stimulus following the COVID-19 outbreak. Sometimes, it took several years to move back to a new high, like we saw after the market was cut approximately in half during the downturns that started in calendar years 2000 and 2007. But here is the important point of this section: the market *always came back*.

If history clearly shows us this pattern, why do people get so nervous every time they experience one of these events? In a single word, media! To expand on that thought, the combination of 24-hour cable news media and social media platforms both screaming that the sky is falling creates an emotional response in most people. This emotional response is real, even if it is not rational or based on economic and stock market history. One of the most important things that I have learned in my decades of working as a CFP is that it is OK to feel the feeling. However, it is almost always detrimental to act on it.

Clients who were born in 1962 turned 62 in 2024. Therefore, to help put things in context, we can look at three important data points from 1962—the year these clients were born—and where those data points ended in 2023.

1. The S&P 500 closed out 1962 at 63. It ended this past year at 4,770.[99]
2. The cash dividend paid out during 1962 was $2.15. In 2023, it was $70.30.
3. The Consumer Price Index ended 1962 at 30. It closed out 2023 at 307.[100]

To put it in mathematical terms:

S&P 500	+76x
Dividend	+33x
CPI	+10x

In looking at this data, you can see that the price of the S&P 500 has increased 76-fold over that 62-year period. The cash dividend of the S&P 500 increased 33 times, while inflation only went up 10 times. This means that for our clients' entire lives, U.S. stocks "have been the simplest and most effortless way of building real (net of inflation) wealth" while generating a dividend income stream that grows significantly faster than the rate of inflation.[101]

Despite the media pounding a negative drumbeat consistently throughout my 30-plus years in the business, the sky has not fallen, and the end of the world has been delayed once again. So, I join Marvin the Martian in asking, "Where's the kaboom?" According to the media, there should have been multiple Earth-shattering kabooms that never came to pass. Please remember this the next time you hear the media screaming like Chicken Little from the rooftops. Once again, your best course of action would be to turn off the TV or the computer and go do something fun and meaningful with the people you love.

I wanted to take a moment to remind you of this. We share messages like this with our clients regularly as a form of financial vitamin C. We know that your body and your psyche do not store these reminders. Therefore, we must give you these regular doses to combat the negative news and noise of the world.

It is my sincere hope that you now have a better understanding of the purpose and the value of financial journalism. We have learned that both the journalists and so-called financial experts who populate our cable news and social media outlets have a dubious track record at best. Therefore, we should not spend a significant amount of time watching or worrying about what they are saying on a day-to-day basis.

What we should be doing is focusing on activities and habits that, when compounded over long periods of time, will allow us to reach our financial goals. This will give us the resources we need to do the things that make life meaningful for us and our families.

We can see that, despite the constant drumbeat of financial journalism telling us what we should be worried about and what actions we should take to protect ourselves from the latest impending financial doom, we are often best served by doing nothing. We should simply continue pursuing the tactics and strategies that have helped people successfully build wealth throughout history.

Managing your beliefs and behaviors constructively is the puzzle piece we will explore in detail in the next chapter. It should be obvious that we don't want to follow the crowd. If the crowd were largely right, it would be wealthy. We know this is not the case, so we should pursue alternative strategies. Let's move on to Puzzle Piece #6.

PUZZLE PIECE

#6

Managing Your Beliefs and Behaviors

Arnold Schwarzenegger once said, "It's mind over matter—if you have no mind, it doesn't matter."[102] The very same thought applies to the wealth management process.

In the last chapter, we discussed how damaging the constant bombardment of negative news from cable TV and social media can be. As we begin to explore our next puzzle piece, we will discuss how much harm can be inflicted on your financial health and wealth if you allow these negative thoughts and stories to affect your behaviors and habits, especially as they relate to your investment decisions.

We know that financial markets inevitably go through up and down cycles. While the ups are fun, the downs are definitely not, and therein lies the problem. When the market is going up, so are the values of your investment accounts. You feel good about the smart decision you made to allocate a portion of your hard-earned income to accumulate wealth that will eventually allow you to retire successfully.

It is interesting that when markets are near all-time highs, you hear people talk about their latest and greatest investments in social settings. Think back to peak periods in the stock market, such as the top of the dot-com bubble, the top of the '07–'08 real estate bubble, and even the government stimulus-induced post-COVID bubble, and you will often hear people at parties, restaurants, and especially online, brag about their latest financial feats and accomplishments.

However, these peaks are inevitably followed by eventual downturns or pullbacks in the market. It is important to remember that every downturn has proven to be temporary, as the stock market has historically come back to make new all-time highs. When these periods of volatility occur, people are much quieter about their investing prowess, or they are happy to blame somebody else—anybody but the person looking back at them in the mirror, who is ultimately the one responsible. They may choose to blame the person who wrote the newsletter they subscribed to, their financial advisor (gasp!), or the person they listened to on CNBC. But one thing we know for sure is that when their account values go down, it is always someone else's fault.

As we look toward creating financial and retirement success, we need to get a firm grasp on Puzzle Piece #6. This means we need to understand psychology and human behavior's role in accumulating wealth. To do this, we will look at how the volatility that we have experienced since 2018 has driven investor behavior and people's accumulation—or lack thereof—of retirement wealth.

We will explore what happens when you follow the crowd. I will introduce you to the concepts of herd mentality and FOMO, the fear of missing out. Understanding but not responding to these strong psychological urges is one of the keys to investing success. Remember, I am not telling you that you shouldn't feel joy when your accounts go up and pain or regret when the markets go down. *You are allowed to feel things.* However, history has shown that it is generally detrimental to act on these feelings, especially when you are trying to build wealth.

I will share some real-life examples of what happens when people get caught up in the excitement and energy surrounding the latest greatest financial trends or fads. We will review examples from both the dot-com bubble of the late '90s and the real estate bubble of the mid-2000s.

We will begin by exploring what the financial planning industry has realized about the importance of psychology and human behavior in the wealth management process.

What Role Does Psychology Play in Wealth Management?

In 2008, the United States was in the midst of the Great Recession, brought about by the subprime mortgage crisis and the downturn in the U.S. real estate markets. The U.S. economy, banking system, and financial markets were in such distress that we implemented government interventions and bailouts.

That same year, I was asked to present financial planning as a career choice at a local high school's career fair. I was one of 50 presenters who spent an evening talking with students about their college and career options.

It quickly became apparent that many of the students who came did so to receive extra credit from their social studies teacher. To get the extra credit, students had to get their questions answered by three different career presenters. Unfortunately, most of the students asked the same three rote questions repeatedly without intentionality or thought about their future career paths. It was a somewhat boring night for me, and I am sure that it was monotonous for the students.

My faith in the next generation was soon restored by a young lady who was in her junior year, though. She approached me and asked me a question that, to this day, remains the best I've ever heard from a student. She asked, "If I were to pursue a career in financial planning, what courses would be most helpful to me, other than the economics and finance classes I would be required to take?"

This question showed considerable intuition and insight. After thinking about it for a moment, I realized the answer was clear. Anything related to psychology or human behavior would be enormously helpful to someone entering the financial planning field.

Most people like to think that they make decisions based on logic and data. However, a significant body of research in the field of neuroscience shows that this is not possible with the way information flows through the human brain. When most people think about family, goals, and their experiences in life, they tend to make decisions that are emotionally and behaviorally based and then justified by logic—not the other way around.

This is why, in an effort to get to know our clients better, we often ask questions such as the following:

- What was your first memory of money?
- What was the best or worst financial decision you have ever made?
- What is one life lesson or value that you would like to pass on to your kids and grandchildren?
- How would you rate your financial status on a scale of 1 to 10? What is something that would allow you to rate it higher?

Questions such as these help us get to know how our clients view money and how to best use their financial resources to accomplish what is most important to them in life. These are all psychological and behavioral aspects that play a large part in helping us serve our clients with excellence.

Apparently, the CFP Board of Standards agrees with this sentiment, as they have now added the psychology of financial planning to their key study topics for both continuing education credits and the CFP exam.

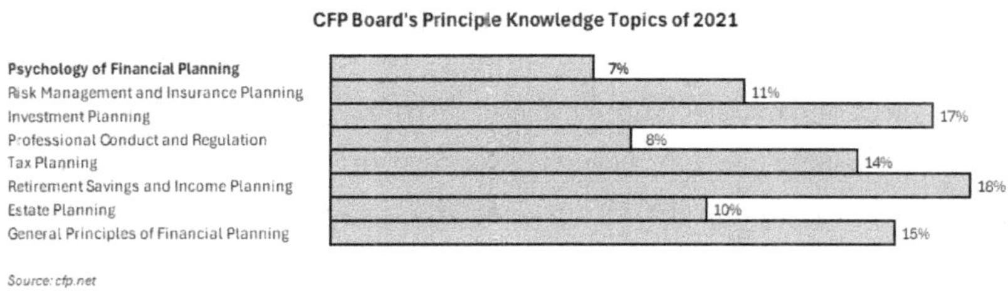

103

As you can see from the chart above, those hoping to become CFPs will now have to include this topic in their study. Representatives from the CFP Board decided to include behavioral finance as part of their curriculum because advisors have increasingly been interested in this topic. This is especially important to understand when you look at the emotional reactions people have to crises (such as 9/11, the '07–'08 Global Financial Crisis, or the coronavirus-induced economic shutdowns) and the financial market swings that tend to accompany them.

As a CFP, I believe this makes sense. Not only do I support this principle, but my company has incorporated it into our general financial consulting and counseling for many years. I am happy to see the CFP Board align their future curriculums and continuing education with this thought process. It is important as we continue to elevate our profession for the next generation of advisors.

The Last Six Years—How Has Behavior Affected Investment Results?

Investors who are trying to accumulate the resources necessary to make a successful transition from work life to retirements of significance, as well as those already retired who are trying to maintain their lifestyle, are justified in feeling frazzled and exhausted after living through the last few years.

Since 2018, we have lived through the outbreak of a global pandemic, unprecedented fiscal and monetary stimulus, two impeachments, a bitterly partisan election, massive supply chain disruptions, Russia's invasion of Ukraine, and the worst inflation we have seen in 40 years. All of this has been continually dissected and rehashed thanks to a 24-hour cable news cycle and social media spin cycle.

This has led to significant volatility in the global stock and bond markets. During this time, we have seen markets spike up and down with increasing speed and magnitude, as you can see in the chart below. In fact, you will note that in just over a six-year time frame, the stock market experienced four double-digit drops, with three of those being declines of more than 20%.

104

We know that investors love to own stocks when the market is moving up. It feels great to look at your account online or open your 401(k) statement and see that you have more wealth than ever before. Many times, this helps people to feel more confident about spending more. This can help drive the economy and lead to higher corporate earnings, which then continue to drive markets higher.

This is known as a positive feedback loop. However, when markets move up dramatically, so do valuation measures such as the P/E ratio. People tend to forget that their future returns are inversely correlated to the price at which they are buying today. The more expensive things are when you buy, the lower your future potential returns.

When the tide turns and markets take a substantial dip, emotions change quickly for the worse. During the last six years, the stock market, as measured by the S&P 500 index, has had three different drops of 20% or more. Each time the market fell, investor sentiment, as measured by the American Association of Individual Investors, fell right along with it. This sentiment index is taken from a weekly survey, and it typically shows that less than 30% of investors are bullish when markets go through major downturns, such as the depths of the '07–'08 Global Financial Crisis or the more recent COVID-19 market drop.

The negative sentiment that we experienced in 2023 seemed extreme, given that unemployment was at 3.6%[105] and consumers had less debt and more equity in their homes than they have had at any other point in the last three decades. What is really interesting is that low points in investor sentiment have historically led to great buying opportunities. Stansberry Research recently showed that when investor sentiment hits a 52-week low, investor returns over the two to three years that follow generally outperform the typical market averages.

Investor Sentiment Returns After Sentiment Hits 52 Week Low[106]

	6 Month	1 Year	2 Year	3 Year
After 52-Week Low	4.5%	7.4%	24.0%	31.2%
All Periods	3.9%	7.9%	16.4%	25.6%

Warren Buffett, legendary investor and founder of Berkshire Hathaway, has said many times over the years that investors should "Be fearful when others are greedy, and greedy when others are fearful."[107] I have often stated that Mr. Buffett is one of the most admired but least emulated investors of all time. People love what he says and admire his outstanding returns. However, few people do what he does. Data from the Investment Company Institute showed substantial outflows from both stock and bond funds in the fall of 2023.[108] This means that during the recent downturn, people were selling low once again.

What is the result of these actions over time? Well, a 2022 study by DALBAR, provided by J. P. Morgan Asset Management, of 20-year annualized returns through the calendar year 2021 shows that almost all asset classes outperformed the average investor. This statistical data shows asset class returns based on when investors bought or sold. Over that period, the average investor generated a total return of 3.6% per year. This was during a 20-year period when most asset classes, including stocks and bonds, did better than that.[109]

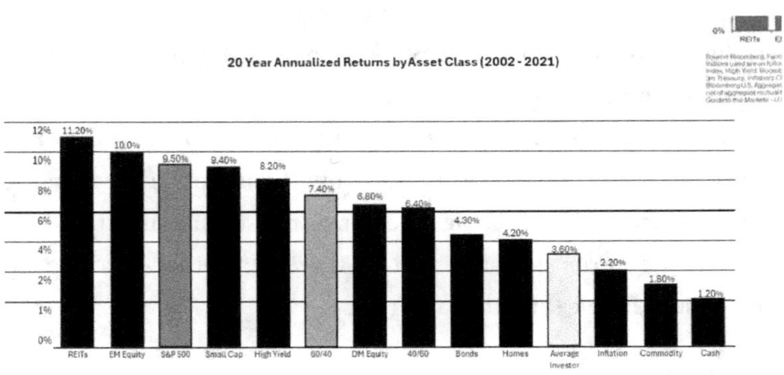

[110]

How can that be? In addition to not following Mr. Buffett's advice, most also spurned the advice of legendary investor Sir John Templeton, who, as you'll recall, told us that the four most dangerous words that any investor can say are "this time is different."[111] Allow me to share a real-life story to illustrate.

The Story of Cliff and Clair: The Lure of the Attractive Improbability

For our next client couple, we are going to draw inspiration from TV mom and dad Cliff and Clair Huxtable from *The Cosby Show*. Just as everybody loved the humor and wisdom the show's Cliff and Clair brought to everyday life and family situations, everyone on my team loves our real-life Cliff and Clair when they come to our office.

When I met Cliff and Clair in 1989, I was still young in the business, only 24 years old. Cliff was a successful mid-level engineer for a local utility company, and Clair had an inside sales support position at a pharmaceutical company. They were both in their early 30s and had two young children, both under the age of five.

At the time, they were trying to develop financial plans to provide for their children's college education and save for a future retirement. Over the next decade, we developed what I believe was a very strong and trusted advisor relationship. We talked often and met in person several times a year to make sure our investment portfolio was on course to reach their future financial goals.

Please remember that the 1990s were, by all measures, a very good time to invest in the stock market. In fact, the last five years of the decade saw the dot-com bubble continue to inflate. From an advisor's standpoint, times of significant volatility or downturn in the markets are always spent helping clients manage their emotions of fear and loss so they do not make the wrong decision at the wrong time and sell low.

However, the late '90s were a much more difficult time. Large-cap growth stocks, led by new technology companies and dot-com darlings that had not yet turned a profit, continued to rise dramatically. This led to conversations in 1998 or 1999 with clients who were disappointed that their portfolios had only gone up 18%–20%. Yes, that really happened. We would see clients comparing the returns of their well-designed portfolios to the latest hot stocks or mutual funds that had invested in a single idea or sector. Please remember that designing and implementing a well-diversified portfolio is not that difficult. What is difficult is staying disciplined with that diversification through the ups and downs of the market while the media screams, "You're missing out!"

In October 1999, I got a phone call from Cliff. He thanked me for everything I had done for them over the past 10 years. We had made great strides in helping Cliff and Clair accumulate the resources to meet their financial goals. However, Cliff felt that, going forward, it was no longer necessary to pay a professional an annual fee to help them. He felt that he could manage his own investments. He had been doing research and reading things online. He had made the decision to move all their investment assets to a mutual fund company that specialized in new-era tech and growth-oriented companies.

It seems that Cliff was taken in by attractive improbability. It is highly unlikely that a hot area of the market will continue to go up indefinitely. However, the allure of this is so great that many people have a hard time resisting. The logic goes like this: If they are right, they make a fortune. And if they are wrong, who can blame them? They were simply doing what everyone else was doing.

The dot-com bubble continued to inflate until March 2000. During those six months, Cliff was reassured that he had made the right move by transferring their nearly $500,000 of assets to his newfound investment strategy. Then the dot-com bubble started to deflate. Then 9/11 happened. Then the Enron/WorldCom fiasco unfolded. From March 2000 to October 2002, the stock market lost more than 45% of its value, and many tech and growth stocks that had done so well during the previous five years lost substantially more than this.

In late 2002, Clair called me. She told me that Cliff was going to call me the next day and asked if I would please take his call.

Cliff did indeed call the next day and told me that their $500,000 of investment assets had shrunk to approximately $240,000. He told me that Clair had told him in no uncertain terms that he needed to plead with me to take them back as clients, and if I agreed, he promised that from that day forward, he would follow my advice to the letter.

I had loved having Cliff and Clair as clients. I cared for their family and their children. I wanted to help them achieve their goals. That is what a CFP does. Against the advice of some of my peers, I agreed to reengage with them.

I am happy to report that more than 20 years later, we have had an extraordinarily successful relationship—professionally, financially, and personally. We were able to recoup and recover from the very difficult and financially harmful emotionally based decisions that had driven Cliff and Clair in 1999. We have worked hard to ensure that Cliff and Clair learned these lessons well and have not allowed their emotions to overrule sound judgment in their financial lives

Successful investors need a combination of faith, patience, and discipline to achieve their long-term goals and objectives. If you aspire to have results that differ from those of the masses, you need to act differently from the masses—which sometimes means *not* acting. As I've said before, if the masses were right, the masses would be rich. And trust me, that is not the case.

Your Mother Was Right!

When I was a kid, there were times when I wanted to do things because everybody else was doing them—things like participating in the latest fad or cool thing to do. This was my first introduction to herd mentality and FOMO.

No matter how much I tried to convince my mom that my life would be so much emptier if I didn't join my friends in the latest pursuit, my mom would inevitably say something like, "If all your friends were jumping off a bridge, would you do it too?"

My mom was trying to protect me and was trying to teach me to think for myself. Maybe she thought that if I followed the crowd, I might get hurt or disappointed. Well, those early instincts that my mom had would likely hold true as we look toward investor behavior.

As you can see in our first chart below, people tend to invest heavily in asset classes that have done well recently. This means they are buying high after prices go up. Note the significant positive fund flows around the peak of the dot-com bubble in the year 2000, as well as the multiple years of high contributions just before the '07–'08 Global Financial Crisis. You will also notice that in 2021, when markets were at all-time highs, we had our biggest year of deposits ever.

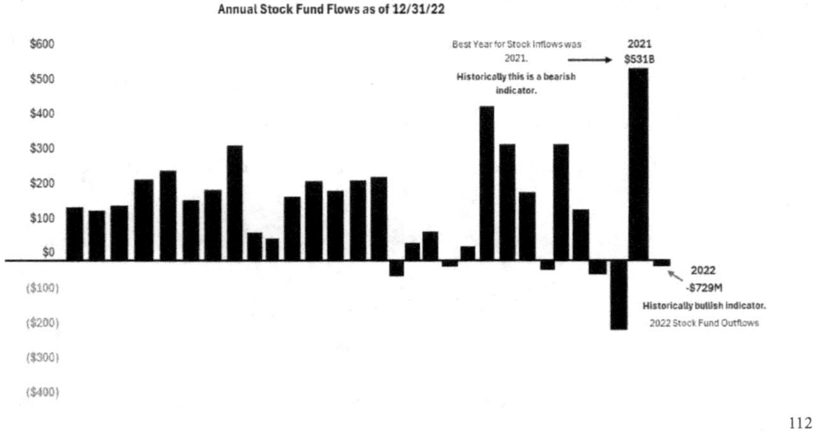

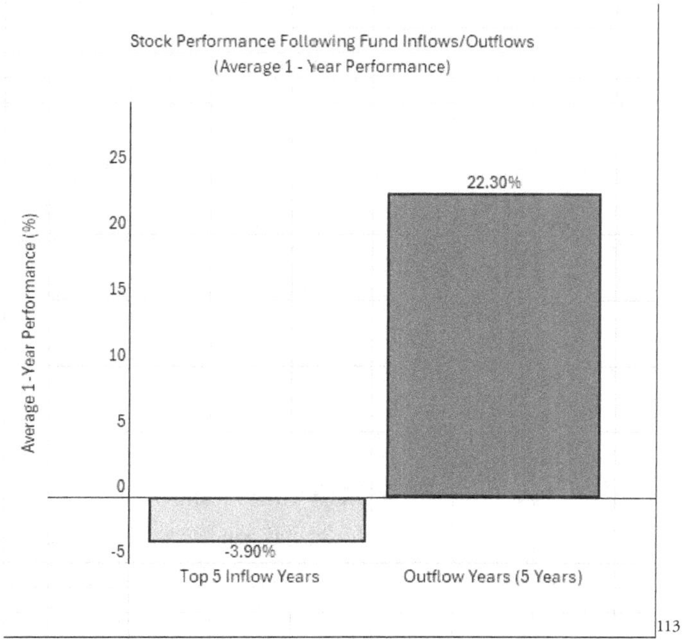

You may also observe that in years like 2008 and 2021, when markets were experiencing significant downturns and prices had dropped, people were pulling money out of the markets en masse—in other words, they were selling low. You will also see from the chart above that the market tends to do well in years following panic selling and price drops.

Our next chart gives you further insight into this. I love this chart because it literally coincides with when I started my career as a financial advisor in August 1987.

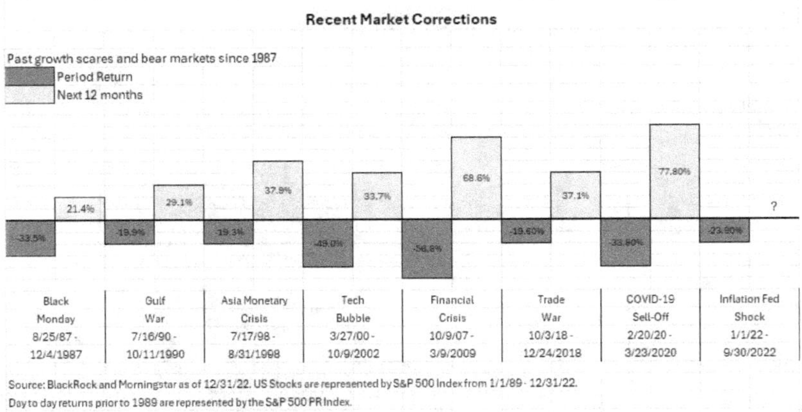

114

It is interesting to see how the markets turned and moved higher in the years following these significant financial events and market sell-offs. However, that also raises the questions, when is the bottom, and have we reached it yet? *That's the tricky part:* We won't know until several years down the road, when we are able to look back and clearly see where the bottom was. However, we do know that buying after prices have dropped—buying low—is a good idea, even if prices temporarily go lower before they move back up.

So, what has become cheap? As we look at our final chart, we can see that emerging market stocks have now experienced a negative five-year average rate of return. Many people are questioning the wisdom of investing in something that has performed so poorly. However, on a historical basis, investing in these markets when returns have been poor and prices are low has led to good returns in the three-to-five-year time periods that follow.

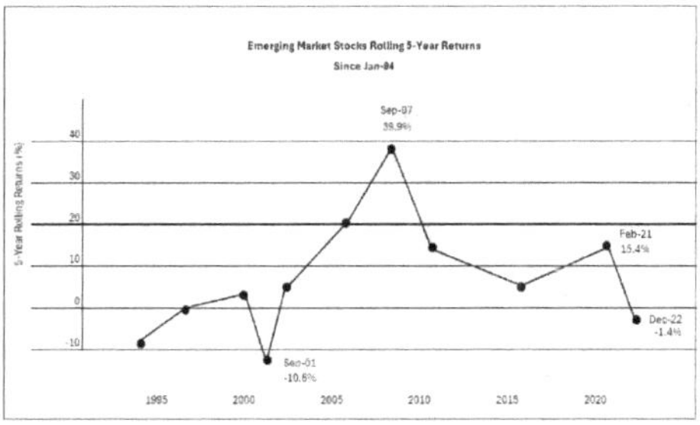

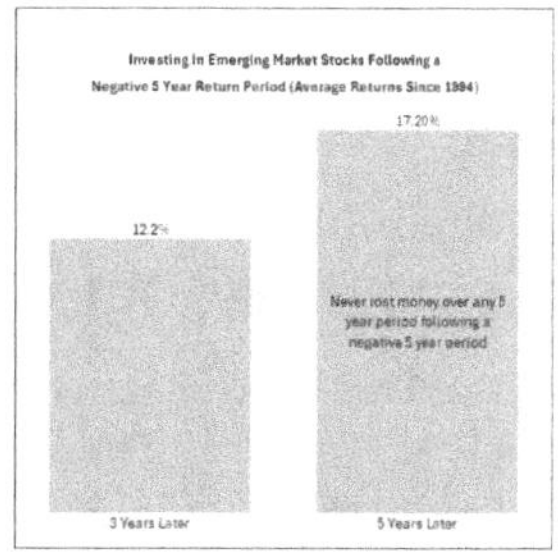

115

We know that when we experience major market downturns such as the dot-com bubble or the '07–'08 Global Financial Crisis, the asset class that previously led the market does not typically do as well in the next market upswing. So instead of looking backward and hoping that what did well previously will carry the banner forward once again, perhaps we should look to what did poorly recently and is therefore cheap, which might reemerge as a market leader.

It appears that we are transitioning from a period of low interest rates and low inflation to a cycle of higher inflation and higher interest rates. We should not expect the same type of stocks or investment asset classes to do well in the next cycle.

My mother was right. We should not follow the crowd. While herd mentality and FOMO are real, they *have not* been successful strategies for allocating investments.

The Story of Howard and Marion: A Case of Herd Mentality and FOMO

The twin psychological phenomenon of herd mentality and FOMO brings me to the story of Howard and Marion. Howard and Marion Cunningham from the TV show *Happy Days* were loving and engaged parents. The same can certainly be said for my clients Howard and Marion. I had known them for a number of years before they became clients in 1992. Howard worked in hospital administration, and Marion was a schoolteacher. Similar to Cliff and Clair, they were trying to achieve the dual goals of saving for a future retirement and paying for their children's future college education. They had two daughters and a son, and they were approximately 40 years old when they first became clients.

Like many of my clients here in the Midwest, Howard and Marion were fiscally conservative. They came from a strong faith base. They were not financial risk-takers. They liked paying cash for things. They wanted to allow the compounded cumulative effect of good habits to help them build the resources they needed to accomplish their financial goals over time.

So far, so good. That is, until they visited some friends who lived in Fort Lauderdale, Florida, in 2006. Their friends told them how much the value of their home had increased over the past seven years. They had purchased their condo in 1999 for $150,000, and now it was valued at more than $400,000. That seemed too good to be true, but the demand for Florida real estate was growing exponentially.

Unfortunately, a condo development was being built very near Howard and Marion's friends. While the developers were still building units in phase 1, they advertised that it was possible to buy condos in phase 3 and lock in the current prices with only a 10% down payment. Phase 3 condos were selling for $260,000, so that price could be locked in for just $26,000.

Here comes the lie and the attractive improbability once again.

The developer told Howard and Marion that, based on the price trajectory from the last few years, by the time their condo was built in phase 3, in approximately 15 months, it would be worth at least $300,000–$320,000. This meant that Howard and Marion would be able to sell the condo at that time and reap a $40,000–$60,000 gain on their $26,000 investment.

It seemed too good to be true, and it turned out that it was. At that time, Howard and Marion called me in Ohio to tell me about the opportunity. My normally very guarded and conservative clients wanted to know if it was OK for them to buy four of the units. You read that correctly: *four!*

They would need $104,000 from their investment portfolio to put down on this new opportunity. They would also be taking on mortgage debt of $936,000 on the four units until they could be sold. Remember, this was in 2006, when the real estate market was peaking. At that time, Howard and Marion expected that they would reap a large financial windfall and that all of this would take place over the next 18 months.

Most people expect that there will be periods of volatility and years with dramatic swings, both up and down, in the stock market. What made the '07–'08 Global Financial Crisis different was that it was precipitated by a downturn in residential real estate, something we had never seen before.

I told them that I thought this investment was a bad idea. Prices had already risen dramatically in Florida real estate, and we know that trees do not grow to the sky. Things do not keep going up forever.

We also know that there is an inverse relationship between the price at which you buy something and your future expected return. When you buy something expensive or that has already gone up in value dramatically, you cannot expect that asset to continue to appreciate at that pace indefinitely. Behavioral economics has discovered this problem with the human brain. It tends to look at things in a linear fashion and extrapolate current patterns indefinitely into the future.

I shared all this information with Howard and Marion. I had also recently seen a chart of Florida real estate prices juxtaposed against a chart of NASDAQ stocks from the late '90s. We know how quickly tech stocks went up during that time, but we also know how that story ended.

I am happy to report that I was successful in talking Howard and Marion out of purchasing *four* condos. However, I was not successful in talking them out of buying *one*. They put their $26,000 down in late 2006 and waited for their condo to be built, fully expecting that they would be able to sell it for $300,000 or more and reap a financial windfall.

However, by the time their condo was nearing completion, the real estate bubble had started to burst. By late 2007, the condo that they had paid $260,000 for only appraised at $230,000. This was stunning and disheartening to Howard and Marion.

Here comes mistake number two. Behavioral finance tells us that people tend to anchor their buy-and-sell decisions to the price point at which they purchased something, whether this makes rational sense or not. In the case of Howard and Marion, they had purchased the condo for $260,000 and could not bring themselves to think of selling it for less.

Therefore, since they could not sell the condo for what they had paid, they decided to rent it. They did so for the next 10 years. Their monthly cost for the mortgage, homeowners' association fee, utilities, and homeowners' insurance was approximately $1,700. Unfortunately, they were only able to rent the unit for $1,200 per month. This meant that they were upside down by $500 per month or $6,000 per year.

So, instead of selling the condo at a $30,000 loss and being done with it financially and psychologically, Howard and Marion slowly bled money from their financial resources for nearly a decade. The condo's value ultimately dropped below $150,000 in the aftermath of the deflating real estate bubble. There was no way that they could sell and absorb that type of loss.

This caused great emotional and financial strain for Howard and Marion, who, as you remember from my earlier description, were by nature very conservative. Eventually, real estate prices started to rebound, and in 2018, they got an offer to buy their condo for $225,000, which they accepted.

By this time, they were glad to walk away from the whole mess. They actually had to bring $8,000 to closing to make up the differential on the mortgage.

This meant that their "can't miss investment opportunity," from which they had expected to make $40,000–$60,000 of profit in just a year and a half, ended up costing them more than $70,000 along with 10 years of financial and emotional angst. The combination of the attractive improbability and the emotional decision-making tied to financial anchoring proved to be too much to overcome.

Luckily, the story has a happy ending. Howard and Marion have now been clients for more than 30 years. They were both hard workers and good savers. This allowed them to overcome the large and disappointing financial setback and still build the resources necessary to be able to transition from work life to a retirement of joy, family, and travel. However, that retirement could have likely started several years earlier had it not been for the real estate investment that seemed too good to be true—and ultimately was.

We have now spent two entire chapters trying to understand the potential negative impact of the 24-hour cable news and social media spin cycle. We explored the real purpose and track record of financial journalism. We reviewed how fear and danger can lead to emotional decision-making.

We also discussed the enormous role that managing your own behavior in the face of all this negative news and noise can have on your own financial outcomes. We introduced important behavioral finance concepts, such as attractive improbability, herd mentality, anchoring, and FOMO. Knowing and understanding that these emotional struggles will always exist is half the battle in winning and building wealth.

I took this much time to review and explain these concepts because they are *that important*. I trust that the real-life stories of clients and the lessons learned will serve as warning signs and reminders in your own financial life.

We will now move on to more economic and investment issues in the coming chapters. We will explore economic and investment topics such as the role of stocks and bonds in your retirement income portfolio. Let's begin by moving on to "Puzzle Piece #7: Understanding Economic Cycles and Investment History."

PUZZLE PIECE

#7

Understanding Economic Cycles and Investment History

"Investing your money in the market is like gambling!"

"I can't afford to put my money in the market and lose it!"

"There is no way for the little guy to win by putting their money in the stock market!"

These are all typical refrains from investors who need to allocate their resources to build the wealth necessary for a successful transition to retirement life. As we will see in this chapter, not only are the sentiments above misguided, but *they are also flat-out wrong.*

When I started in the business in 1987, I was given an analogy that a long-term investment in the stock market would resemble a person walking up a hill bouncing a yo-yo. The ups and downs of the yo-yo represented the inevitable bouts of volatility that would come with economic uncertainty, recessions, and geopolitical events. However, the upward slope of the hill represented the long-term and surprisingly consistent gains of the stock market over time. You can see how surprisingly accurate that depiction is in the next chart.

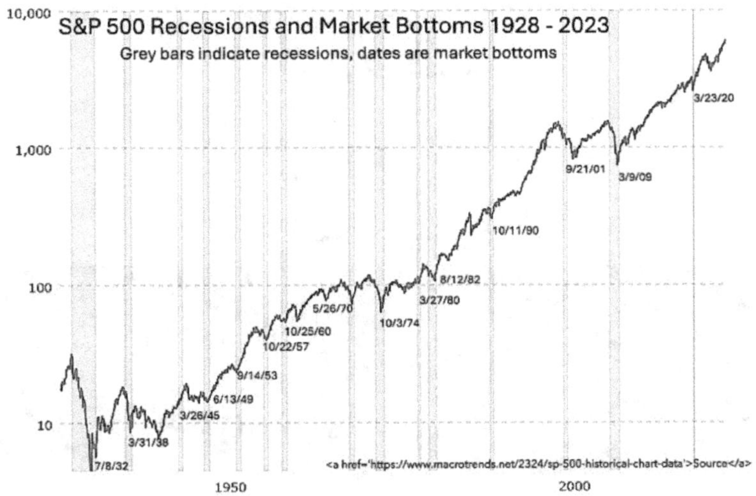

[116]

There are two really important things to note about this chart. The first is that you can't let the ups and downs of the yo-yo derail you from your long-term goals and objectives. If there is one thing we have learned over the last 25 years, it is that you cannot predict what global economic and geopolitical events will come along to create volatility in the markets.

All we have to do is look at the bursting of the dot-com bubble, 9/11, the subprime mortgage crisis, the failure of AIG and Lehman Brothers, the COVID-19 pandemic, and, more recently, inflation worse than we have seen in four decades. Each of these events was unknowable and unpredictable until it happened. Each one caused the stock market to drop more than 20%. However, each drop proved to be temporary.

This brings me to the second important thing we can learn from the chart above. That is the power of compounding over long periods of time. Many people think about their investments on a daily, monthly, quarterly, or annual basis. This is not irrational, as this coincides with when they look at their account values or receive their investment statements.

However, investing for retirement is a long-term venture. During your working years, you have several decades to deposit to your IRAs and

401(k) to accumulate wealth. Then, when you move into your retirement years and start taking withdrawals from your investments to fund your retirement lifestyle, *you also have decades.* This is where many investors start getting shortsighted. They forget that the average retirement lifespan can be 20 to 30 years or longer.

Therefore, it is extremely important to understand how the length of time your money is invested directly correlates to your investment success. Let's explore this concept in more detail.

Time Is on My Side

The song "Time Is On My Side" was written by Norman Meade and first recorded by a jazz trombonist named Kai Winding and his orchestra in 1963. Over the next two years, it was covered by soul singer Irma Thomas from New Orleans, a contemporary of both Aretha Franklin and Etta James, and more famously by the Rolling Stones in 1964.[117]

Just as Irma Thomas and the Rolling Stones sang, time is certainly on your side when it comes to the stock market. From a historical perspective, the longer your time frame for investing, the more favorable your odds become for a positive outcome.

The folks at American Funds looked at the S&P 500 index over the 96 years starting in 1927 and ending in 2023. Here is a summary of their findings.

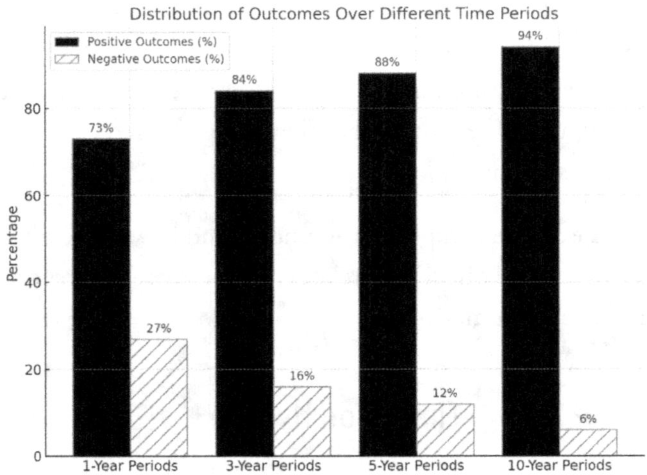

[118]

- For all one-year holding periods, the broad stock market, as measured by the index, was up 73% of the time and down 23% of the time.
- If you held the index for a three-year period of time, the odds of a positive return increased to 84%, with negative returns 16% of the time.
- Over rolling five-year periods of time, probability went to 88% up and 12% down.
- Finally, 10-year rolling periods produced positive returns 94% of the time.[119]

This is a reminder that during times of volatility, dislocation, and geopolitical uncertainty, it is important to remember that investing is a long-term venture. Many times, clients think they must get considerably more conservative as they move into their retirement years. However, as you'll recall, recent life expectancy statistics show that for a married couple, both age 65, there is a 50% probability that one of them will live to age 90.

This means that the average retiree should still consider their investment timeline to be 20 to 30 years. Based on these statistics, this should lead people to believe that investing in quality companies with growing earnings will allow them to build wealth throughout their lifetimes. This will likely benefit both them and their heirs down the road.

While building an age- and risk-appropriate asset allocation is relatively simple, asset allocations are sometimes not easily maintained during emotionally charged times. As we discussed previously, this is exacerbated by the news and noise of the media. However, my goal is to help our clients pursue activities that are contrary to those of the masses. Remember, if the masses were right, the masses would be rich, and by and large they are not. So, let's endeavor to pursue different behaviors.

As the most successful investor of our lifetimes, Warren Buffett, has said, "Our favorite holding period is forever."[120]

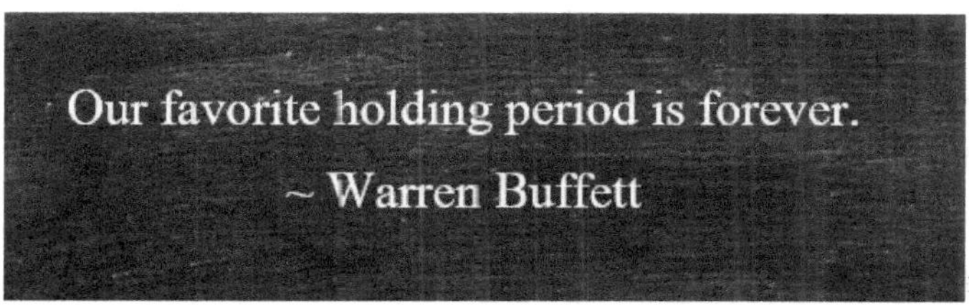

[121]

Next, we are going to explore two unique attributes of stocks that have kept them moving up that long-term hill you saw in the previous chart. Successful companies have historically seen both their earnings and their dividends grow over time. This is due to the fact that innovation and leadership in a free-market capitalist economy allows companies to create products and services that consumers want to buy. Therefore, if companies deliver products and services that the consumers want, they will buy them, and this will drive corporate earnings and dividends higher. It has long been known that stock prices follow earnings. We will explore this further next.

Higher and Higher!

According to Wikipedia, "(Your Love Keeps Lifting Me) Higher and Higher" is an R&B song written by Gary Jackson, Raynard Miner, and Carl Smith. It was recorded by Jackie Wilson for his album *Higher and Higher*....Released in August 1967, the song reached number one on the US *Billboard* R&B chart and, in November, peaked on the *Billboard* Hot 100 at No. 6."[122]

More than 100 cover versions of the song have been recorded since its release.[123] One of my favorite versions comes from the 2009 Rock and Roll Hall of Fame induction ceremony, where it was performed by Bruce Springsteen and the E Street Band along with Darlene Love, John Fogerty, Sam Moore, Billy Joel, and Tom Morello. You can find this amazing and fun performance on YouTube.

I am using this song as a metaphor to remind you that two other things also keep lifting us higher and higher. These are the earnings of America's best-run companies and the dividends they pay to their shareholders.

We know that in order to get the historically superior returns that the stock market has provided over time, you must be willing to hold on through the significant and unpredictable ups and downs of the market. You can see from our first chart that between 2018 and 2023, we experienced three significant periods of volatility, each leading to a drop of 20% or more in the stock market.

Nevertheless, due to a psychological phenomenon known as recency bias, most people do not remember why the market fell 20% from September 20th to December 24th, 2018. (By the way, the drop was caused by the Fed raising interest rates and creating fears of a recession.) This is because the unprecedented and painful events caused by the COVID-19 pandemic led to a 34% drop in February and March of 2020. The more recent event is top of mind.[124]

125

Staying invested while on this roller coaster ride requires a fair amount of discipline and the belief that a free-market capitalist economy will produce returns that will help you and your family build the resources necessary to accomplish your long-term financial goals.

To help bolster your understanding and belief, I will share another chart that takes us through the three bear market downturns of 40% or more that have occurred in the last 50 years. This chart also shows us how much the stock market, corporate earnings, dividends, and inflation have risen during that time.

[126]

	12/31/72	12/31/22
S&P 500	118	3,840
Earnings	$6.17	$219E
Dividend	3.19	66.92
CPI	43	297

A quick glance at the chart shows that over 50 years, from 1972 to 2022, inflation rose 7 times. However, the earnings of the 500 largest companies in the United States grew by more than 35 times during the same time, while the dividends they paid their shareholders grew by more than 21 times. This led the S&P 500 to rise more than 32 times over those 50 years, more than quadrupling the rise of inflation.

We strive to help our clients endure the volatile and uncertain sequence of returns by maintaining two to three years of reserves in cash, short-term bonds, and the ongoing dividend payments created by their portfolios. We have found that having enough liquidity to cover one's income needs several years in advance helps people endure the inevitable bouts of volatility that accompany their financial journeys.

We find that this visual reminder of the three bears helps give clients an extra dose of confidence and wisdom during the seemingly never-ending stream of negative financial news. As I have stated before, this type of financial encouragement is like vitamin C. You need a dose on a regular basis because your body does not store it.

My goal is to provide you with the antidote to negative financial journalism so that you and your family can accumulate the resources needed to live your best life. The next time you are feeling nervous or uncertain, please pull out the three bears chart and take another dose of financial vitamin C. You will then be reminded that corporate earnings and stock dividends have lifted us higher and higher, just as Jackie Wilson and Bruce Springsteen sang.

Let's turn our attention to math. I have loved math my entire life. When I was a young child in elementary school, one of my favorite activities was the timed math test we took to memorize our addition, subtraction, and multiplication tables. I was always the first one done, and I always scored 100% correct. I am not trying to brag; I can't figure out any foreign language—or, for that matter, anything mechanical—to save my life.

I am blessed that I get to work with numbers and help people with their financial lives. This is what makes me tick. They say that if you do what you love, you never work a day in your life. I truly understand this concept and get to live it every day.

I was lucky to have good math teachers throughout my high school years. Whether I was taking geometry, Algebra II, precalculus and calculus, probability and statistics, or trigonometry, I was blessed with great teachers who helped me learn not only the concepts but also the practical application of math in real life. We are now going to explore a concept that is extremely important to your investing and financial success: the mathematics of loss.

Spinning Wheel—What Goes Up

According to Wikipedia:

> "Spinning Wheel" is a song recorded in 1968 by Jazz fusion/Rock band Blood, Sweat & Tears; it was written by Canadian lead vocalist David Clayton-Thomas and included on their eponymous album, released in 1968.
>
> The song, released as a single in 1969, peaked at no. 2 on the *Billboard* Hot 100 chart in July that year, remaining in the runner-up position for three weeks.
>
> Clayton-Thomas was quoted as describing the song as being "written in an age when psychedelic imagery was all over lyrics…it was my way of saying, 'Don't get too caught up, because everything comes full circle.'"[127]

Interestingly, the song was also recorded by artists as diverse as Peggy Lee, Sammy Davis Jr., Shirley Bassey, James Brown, and even Barbara Eden of TV's *I Dream of Jeannie.*

The song is instantly recognizable from its opening line. If you were invested in the market between June 2021 and June 2023, you probably felt like that song represented the ups and downs of the stock market during that time pretty well. Despite all the negative headlines and economic events we lived through, the market was basically flat over those two years, as measured by the S&P 500 index. You can see in the following chart that there were a lot of ups and downs, but we ended up back where we started. What went up also went down—just as the song lyrics say.

128

There are a couple of things I want to remind you of in this type of environment. The first is about the mathematics of loss. If something was worth $100 and went down 20%, its value would drop to $80. If it then rose in value by 20%, it would be worth $96. This is because 20% of $80 is less than 20% of $100. Going up and down at the same rate time after time actually results in losing money, as you can see in the chart below.

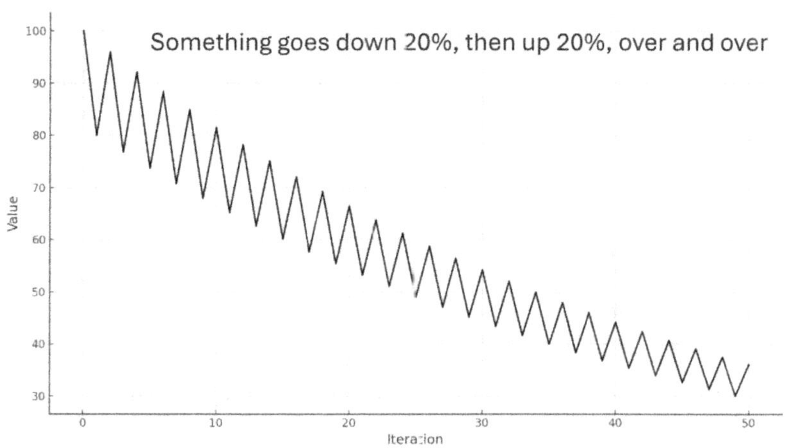

129

The first takeaway to remember is that *math matters*. It is important for your gains to outpace your losses over time. In fact, the mutual fund research company Morningstar uses a set of statistics that they call upside capture and downside capture to help advisors screen for investments that may provide a better probability of success as we construct our portfolios.

The second thing to remember is that the markets have worked in our favor throughout the various economic and business cycles we have lived through. As you can see in the next chart, the market's ups during times of economic growth far exceed the losses during recessions and times of economic dislocation. However, it has been my experience over several decades that the downs always feel worse to investors.

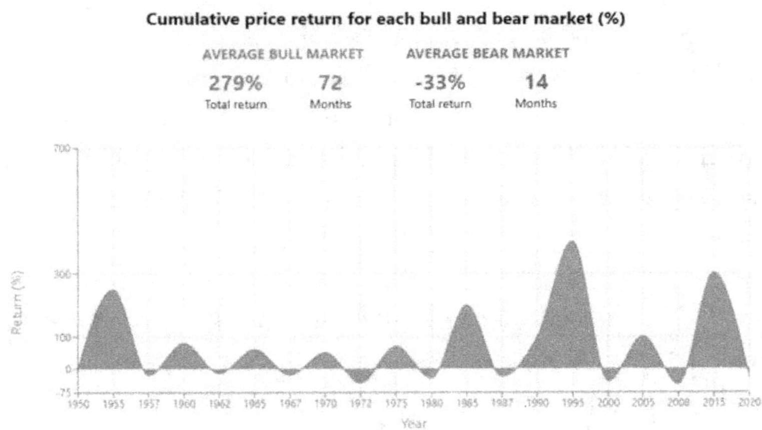

Sources: Capital Group, RIMES, Standard & Poor's. Returns shown on a logarithmic scale. Returns are in USD.

130

Historically, the gains have outpaced the losses, both in duration and magnitude, but you only benefit from those gains if you are invested throughout the entire cycle. This requires patience, discipline, and a belief that free-market capitalist economies produce superior returns.

My goal is to help you make good decisions during the inevitable ups and downs of the market cycles. It is extremely important to remember the math lesson above. To be successful in the long run, what goes up needs to exceed what goes down.

So far, we have explored the value of time, the significance of growing corporate earnings and dividends, and the role of mathematics in building the wealth you and your family will need to retire successfully.

Next, I am going to share one of my favorite stories about what happens when people get caught up in an investment idea that seems too good to be true. In the aftermath of the dot-com bubble and 9/11, as well as the Global Financial Crisis brought on by the failure of AIG and Lehman Brothers, many people forgot the story and the lessons that we should have learned from the failure of the hedge fund Long-Term Capital Management.

If nothing else, this tale should have served as foreshadowing for what eventually occurred just a decade later. Let's turn the clock back to the late '90s to explore what happened!

A Silver Jubilee

A Silver Jubilee marks a 25th anniversary. It could denote a wedding anniversary, the 25th year of a monarch's reign, or anything that has completed or is entering its 25-year mark. It is also known as the silver anniversary, as many people exchange presents made of silver to commemorate 25 years. In 2023, we marked the 25-year anniversary of the failure of Long-Term Capital Management, LTCM.

What was LTCM, and why are we commemorating the demise of a hedge fund 25 years after the fact? Let's explore.

LTCM was a large hedge fund led by Nobel Prize-winning economists and renowned Wall Street traders. LTCM was founded in 1994 by John Meriwether after his successful bond trading career at Salomon Brothers. Myron Scholes and Robert Merton were also on its team, and they received the 1997 Nobel Memorial Prize in Economic Sciences. David Mullins Jr., who had previously served as the vice chairman of the Federal Reserve under Alan Greenspan, was also an employee.[131]

LTCM literally had many of the smartest and most well-credentialed people in the world running their fund. This attracted a great amount of attention from Wall Street investors. LTCM was profitable for both its early investors and its founders, drawing over $1 billion of investor capital by promising that its arbitrage strategy would yield outsized returns while managing downside risk. You can see in our first chart below, which has been truncated on the right so as not to spoil the ending, that a dollar invested in the fund would have nearly quadrupled from March 1994 to March 1998.

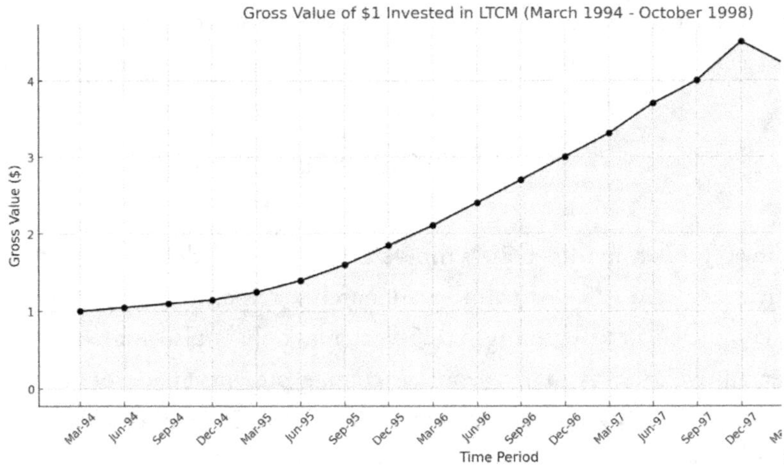

[132]

Just like anything else that seems too good to be true, the fund continued to attract investors and new deposits. The management team had created an investment formula that seemingly could not lose unless a three times standard deviation event occurred, sometimes known as a black swan (extremely rare) event. Not only did Wall Street banks such as Bear Stearns and Lehman Brothers invest heavily, but so did other financial institutions such as the insurance conglomerate AIG. Notice a pattern here? These institutions also borrowed money to invest, creating significant leverage in the financial system. All of this worked great...*until it didn't.*

LTCM used 25 times or more leverage in 1998. This means that a 4% loss on a trade could deplete the firm's capital, forcing it to either raise money or fail. LTCM was investing heavily in emerging markets bonds when Russia defaulted on its bonds in 1998. As a result of the unexpected default, there was a huge flight to quality U.S. Treasury bonds, leading to significant losses for LTCM and all its trading partners.[133]

This had the potential to create a chain reaction within the entire financial system. The NY Fed, then headed by future treasury secretary Timothy Geithner, organized a bailout of $3.63 billion, and a more significant crisis was averted for the time being. However, flash forward just 10 years, and we know that a very similar crisis, with many of the same players, came to pass.

This time, the object of investors' affection was subprime mortgages. It was thought that these could not lose value since residential real estate historically does not go down in value. Of course, this led to the '07–'08 Global Financial Crisis and even more significant bailouts by both the federal government and the Federal Reserve Bank. It seems that some people and institutions never learn, especially when huge potential profits are being dangled in front of them.

History shows us that people are drawn to attractive improbability. However, we believe that the road to long-term financial success can be reached by striving toward what we call less attractive probability. You do this through disciplined diversification, regular rebalancing, dollar cost averaging, and letting your financial plan be your guide—rather than being influenced by the latest hot stock or hot area of the market.

And how did this saga turn out for LTCM's investors? As Paul Harvey used to say, the full chart tells us "the rest of the story."

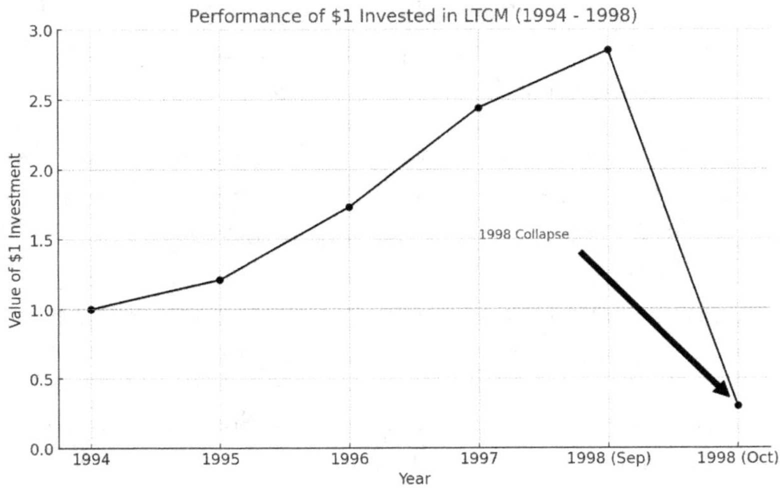

[134]

While LTCM's failure 25 years ago is certainly nothing to celebrate, it does provide a cautionary tale that we should pay close attention to, given the uncertainty in today's financial and economic markets.

To conclude this chapter, let's combine what we have learned with a couple of the lessons we explored in the previous two chapters about the impact of negative news and the importance of managing one's behaviors.

Economic and investment history is replete with examples of people pursuing unrealistic investment returns while disregarding risk and any semblance of reasonable due diligence.

As we will see, following the herd has not historically been a great way to build or maintain wealth. We will use a song from the Beatles to help set the stage for this important topic.

All Together Now

Many of you will remember "All Together Now," which was released by the Beatles on their album *Yellow Submarine*. The album was not only the soundtrack to an animated movie, but it was also the Beatle's 10th album, released in January 1969.[135]

While "All Together Now" may be a nice concept to sing about, it has not traditionally been a great idea for investing money. I have been a financial advisor for more than 30 years, and whenever I see a herd of people moving en masse toward a single investment idea or theme, it always seems to end badly.

In the late '90s, technology and dot-com stocks became all the rage. We were told, "This time is different," which you will recall Sir John Templeton told us are four of the most dangerous words you will ever hear about investing.[136] We were told that historically important investment metrics, such as earnings, profitability, and valuation, no longer mattered. In fact, if you saw commercials on television during that time, we were led to believe that it was so easy to make money that a baby or a tow truck driver could day trade as a side hustle.

[137]

138

Do You Remember?

In the mid-2000s, we experienced a similar phenomenon with residential real estate. It seemed that everybody was buying homes because they believed they always went up in value. I had more than one person tell me of their plans to invest in multiple properties because they could borrow money at cheap interest rates to leverage up their rate of return.

Who could blame people for wanting to get in on the action? Even Federal Reserve Bank chairman Ben Bernanke told CNBC that there was no problem with the real estate market in 2005. When pressed on this by anchor Maria Bartiromo, he said that he did not really buy the premise of her question because we had never seen real estate go down on a national basis before.[139]

This sounded too good to be true, and eventually, it was. Movies and books such as *Too Big to Fail* and *The Big Short* chronicle what happened when things didn't turn out as planned. It seems that eventually, things can go wrong when people decide to invest "All Together Now."

This is known as herd mentality. The *Merriam-Webster* dictionary defines *herd mentality* as "the tendency of the people in a group to think and behave in ways that conform with others in the group rather than as individuals."[140]

Watching this play out over the years, I realized that there are two emotional justifications that affect people's actions. First, they tell themselves, "Everyone else is getting rich by investing in tech stocks or housing, so I should be doing that too"—in other words, it's FOMO. Second, they tell themselves, "If I am wrong, nobody can blame me because I was just doing the same thing as everyone else."

Why am I mentioning this now? Because when everybody is talking about and investing in the same thing, it should make you nervous. Remember, if the masses were right, the masses would be rich, and by and large, they are not. Therefore, when everybody is talking about how much money they made from a single idea at cocktail parties and social gatherings, you typically want to pursue an alternative investment thesis.

Two incidents had me revisiting this. The first came when my wife and I were at a restaurant in Florida in mid-December 2021. Our very nice young waiter, who was in his mid-20s, asked me what I did for a living. When he found out, he told me that, in his opinion, investing in the stock market was old school and that he and his friends were making all their money by trading cryptocurrencies (can somebody say tow truck driver?). It seems that an overabundance of optimism and the promise of easy money was again attracting the masses.

The second was when actors or sports stars began endorsing and promoting the same investment idea in television ads. This began happening en masse in late 2021 as well. It doesn't matter whether the person had experience, knowledge, or past success with the investment they were touting; people were influenced by their celebrity status. There was a segment on CNBC discussing how those same crypto investments had declined in value since the commercials started.

When waiters and actors start giving me the same investment advice, I will see that as somebody giving me a divine sign to invest dollars elsewhere. I have seen this movie before. We also know from history that when financial capital moves in one direction, it typically leaves lower-priced opportunities in places no one is looking.

Thus, when this happens, my company continues to seek out and allocate our clients' hard-earned capital to these less appealing but more reasonably valued investments. We do not want to be distracted by attractive improbability. We would much rather do our homework and look for less attractive and less loved probabilities.

We have never found the herd mentality and following the crowd to be successful strategies. "All Together Now" may have been a fun two-minute pop song from one of the greatest rock bands of all time, but it is not a wealth accumulation strategy that we want to follow. Instead, a better approach may be to "Get Back" to the time-tested investment fundamentals (sorry, I couldn't resist).

Many brilliant people and historical leaders have cautioned us about forgetting the lessons of the past. The writer-philosopher George Santayana once wrote "Those who cannot remember the past are condemned to repeat it."[141] Winston Churchill is said to have said, "Those that fail to learn from history are doomed to repeat it." No matter the origin, the sentiments are real, and the wisdom should be heeded.

Unfortunately, both individual and institutional investors seem to have a very short memory when it comes to economic and investment history. This has often been to their detriment, as you can see in the stories above. My goal with Puzzle Piece #7 was to give you the history, stories, and wisdom that will allow you to avoid making the same mistakes in your own financial and investing life.

With this understanding and perspective in place, we can now start to look at the asset classes we will use to build your portfolio. As we move to Puzzle Piece #8, we will explore the role that bonds play in creating retirement income and managing investment risk.

PUZZLE PIECE

#8

The Role of Bonds in Your Retirement Income Portfolio

"Bonds are boring!"

This was the basic message I got during my early years of studying economics, investments, and finance. Whether it was what I was told in a macroeconomics class I took at the University of Akron or what I read in the pages of *The Wall Street Journal* each day during my lunch break while working as a bank teller at Huntington Bank, I learned that stocks were exciting and sexy. However, bonds were relegated to the newspaper's back pages and not talked about much in class.

Stocks represent *ownership* of a company. Each share of stock you purchase means that you own a small piece of that company. This gives you opportunities for profits and dividends, and you get to participate in the future growth of the organization. You even get voting rights as a shareholder. This gives you the ability to cast your vote on important proxy issues, such as who will represent your interest on the board of directors of the company.

On the other hand, bonds represent *loanership*. When you purchase a bond, you simply loan your money to the company or government entity.

They pay interest on your money each year. At the end of the bond's term, assuming the entity is still in existence and its finances are in good standing, you get your original principal amount back. Inevitably, that principal value will be worth less than the amount you originally invested simply due to inflation.

So why would an investor want to invest in bonds to begin with? Great question—I am glad you asked. From a historical standpoint, people put money into bonds to generate guaranteed income. Prior to the major stock market downturns in 2000 and 2007, interest rates on government and investment-grade corporate bonds had typically ranged from 4% to 8% over the previous 20 years.

This was an attractive rate of return. From an asset allocation standpoint, bonds also helped to mitigate some of the risk and volatility that people knew would occur within the stock portion of their portfolios. Since stock market and bond market returns were not highly correlated to each other, mixing them together in a portfolio often reduced risk. This can be seen through the efficient frontier next chart. As you will note, a portfolio containing roughly 60% stocks and 40% bonds had a higher return but roughly the same risk as a portfolio of all bonds during the nearly 50-year timeline of the chart.

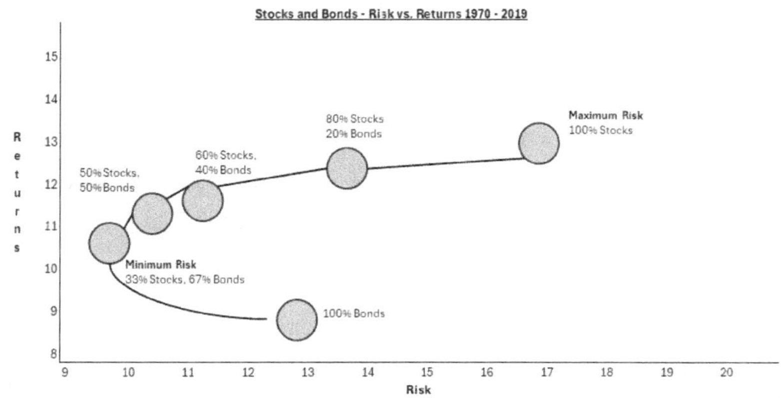

142

Bonds started becoming much more complicated and began to have the potential for greater returns with the invention of the junk bond market in the 1980s. This was primarily credited to financial engineering pioneers such as Ivan Boesky and Michael Milken, both of whom eventually did time in jail for insider trading and securities fraud. The invention of junk bonds fueled the leveraged buyout boom. This was portrayed in the 1987 movie *Wall Street* featuring Michael Douglas, who won the Academy Award for Best Actor. Douglas's character, Gordon Gekko, was said to be a composite of many *Wall Street* personalities, including Boesky and Milken.

Bonds grew in financial complexity in the 2000s as we moved toward the subprime mortgage crisis. Low-rated subprime mortgage bonds could be pooled together into what are known as collateralized loan obligations, or CLOs. In ways that I will never understand, a bunch of low-rated bonds could be thrown together into one investment vehicle, and the rating agencies would give this new entity, filled with junk, an investment grade rating and tell us that it was low risk. This all worked great…until it didn't.

Suddenly, investors realized that bonds weren't boring anymore. They also realized that they had better do their homework if they wanted to get their hard-earned principal back when the loan or bond matured.

Then came 2022. After the COVID-19 pandemic and economic lockdowns, the Federal Reserve Bank and the federal government unleashed a torrent of fiscal and monetary stimuli unlike anything we had seen before. This caused our money supply, as measured by M2, to experience 10 years' worth of growth in under two years. According to Investopedia, "M2 is a measure of the money supply that includes cash, checking deposits, and other deposits readily convertible to cash, such as CDs."[143]

This ultimately led to inflation rising faster than we had seen since the late 1970s and early 1980s. Unfortunately, as interest rates rise, bond prices drop. It became apparent to me that this would be a problem in late November 2021, when the Federal Reserve Bank finally retired the use of the word *transitory* when describing inflation. Let's explore how rapidly rising interest rates have historically created risk to bonds, even before the Fed began its fastest rate increase campaign in 40 years.

Could the Bond Market Give Us a Cherry Bomb?

When my friends and I were in second grade at Indian Trail Elementary School, we couldn't wait to get outside and play during recess. Many of us packed our lunches so that we would not have to wait in the cafeteria line. That way, we could get outside as quickly as possible and maximize our time on the playground.

The teeter-totter was one of the first pieces of equipment that we ran to. And one of the promises we made each other make whenever we got on the teeter-totter together was *no cherry bombs!*

For those who may not remember, a cherry bomb is when the person on one end of the teeter-totter waits until their "friend" is at the highest point and then jumps off. This causes the friend to fall back to Earth, jarring their entire body suddenly. Cherry bombs caused many hurt feelings and hurt backsides.

144

For those of you wondering why I am sharing this memory, the bond market in 2022 was poised to do the same thing to investment portfolios that our friends did to us on the playground. It is referred to as the "Teeter Totter Principle." In case you are not aware, there is an inverse relationship between interest rates and bond values. Bond prices go down when interest rates go up, as shown in the graphic below.

When Interest Rates Rise, Bond Prices Fall!

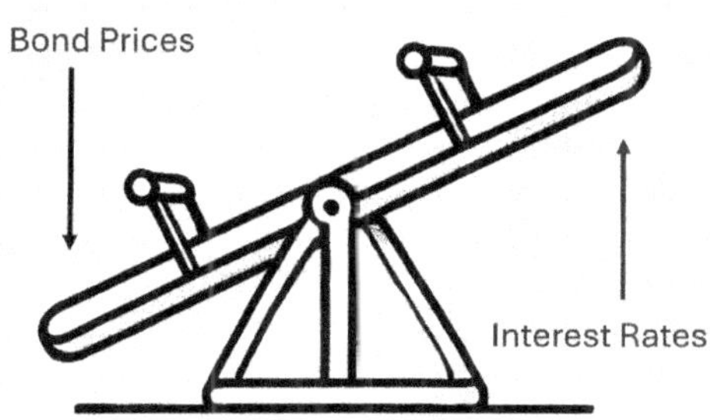

145

In 2021, the aggregate bond market index dropped by more than 1.5%.[146] What is interesting about this is that during that year, the Federal Reserve did not raise interest rates. The bond market allowed interest rates on the 10-year Treasury bonds to rise in anticipation of the Fed responding to combat ever-higher inflation.

Negative years in the bond market are relatively rare. They also do not have the same variability of returns that the stock market can have. A really bad year in the bond market can produce a negative return in the low single digits, while a bad year in the stock market can produce a negative return of 30% or more.

In summer 2021, the Fed told us they were not planning to raise interest rates at all in the 2022 calendar year. But at their meeting in January 2022, they told us that they planned to raise interest rates at least three times and possibly more.[147] This was a massive shift in policy which led to the potential for a second consecutive negative year for the bond market.

How rare is that? As you can see in the following chart, the last time the bond market had back-to-back negative years was in the late 1950s. This is important for retired and risk-averse investors, who typically have more bonds in their portfolios to dampen stock market risk and volatility.

Consecutive Years with Negative Bond Returns

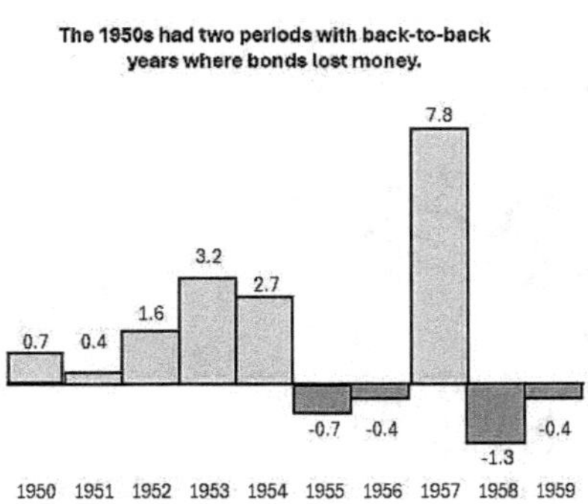

Bonds have not lost money in back-to-back years since the 1950s until now.

Year	Return	Following Yr
1994	-2.9	18.5
1931	-2.3	8.8
2013	-2	6
2021	-1.3	-13.02
1958	-1.3	-0.4
1999	-0.8	11.6
1969	-0.7	16.9
1955	-0.7	-0.4
1956	-0.4	7.8
1959	-0.4	11.8

[148]

It looked like the bond market and the Fed were getting ready to give investors a cherry bomb. Cherry bombs in your investment portfolio can hurt more and last longer than those on the playground. Luckily, there are several strategies that can be used to help minimize the damage to investor portfolios as rates go up and bond prices go down. These include shortening maturities on bond portfolios, looking to alternative asset classes, and investing in inflation-correlated assets.

By the end of 2022, we could look back to see how this perceived risk played out in real life. Results in the bond market were far worse than I had initially feared. Bond returns are driven by two primary factors: the interest rate being paid on the bonds and the direction of interest rate changes by the Federal Reserve Bank.

Let's put this in historical context. In 1994, the Fed raised interest rates six times. However, that year, the starting interest rate for most government bonds was about 7%. The 10% loss in principal value on the bonds was offset by a 7% income return on the bonds themselves, resulting in a net total return of -3%.[149]

The big problem in 2022 was that the starting point for government bond interest rates was under 2%.[150] This meant that there was little interest income to offset the principal loss from the Federal Reserve Bank aggressively raising interest rates. That combination caused losses in the bond market that were four times the largest amount we had seen in any calendar year over the last century.

As we began 2022, the Federal Reserve Bank had not yet started raising interest rates from their historically low levels. In fact, they were still buying $120 billion of government and mortgage bonds each month to further suppress long-term interest rates. They told us that once supply chain issues were fixed, inflation would be back down in the 4% range in short order.

Of course, none of this turned out to be true. Then, on January 5th, the minutes from the December Fed meeting were released. The message from the Fed's minutes immediately began to shake the global stock and bond markets. As mentioned before, the Fed decided to retire the word *transitory* a few weeks before this in November. They also stated that they would need to begin to increase interest rates to combat rapidly rising and persistent inflation.

At that time, I feared that bond prices would suffer if the Fed started to raise interest rates aggressively. This was like an early warning of the potential damage that could occur in what is typically the more conservative part of investor portfolios. Remember, historically, people allocate funds to bonds to help offset the market volatility and economic risks of the stock portion of their portfolios.

My concerns turned out to be massively understated, as the Fed embarked on its fastest interest rate increase campaign in decades. From a longer-term historical basis, this made 2022 one of the four worst years of bond market performance in the last 300 years. Similar losses were seen in 1721 (with the bursting of the South Sea Company bubble), 1865 (associated with the post–Civil War era), and 1920 (associated with the conclusion of World War I).

For most of the last 30 years, periods of economic downturn and falling stock markets were accompanied by the Federal Reserve Bank lowering interest rates to spur economic growth. Consider the dot-com bubble and 9/11, the '07–'08 Global Financial Crisis, and the COVID lockdowns of 2020. Of course, cutting interest rates also caused bond prices to rise, based on the teeter-totter principle we discussed before.

This is an important and complex topic. Many retirees have anywhere from 30% to 50% of their assets in bonds. I want to help you avoid mistakes based on the emotional response generated by looking solely at recent performance. As you can see from the next chart, 2022 was a brutal year for both stocks and bonds, and it is natural to feel pain and fear when you look at your account values during times like this.

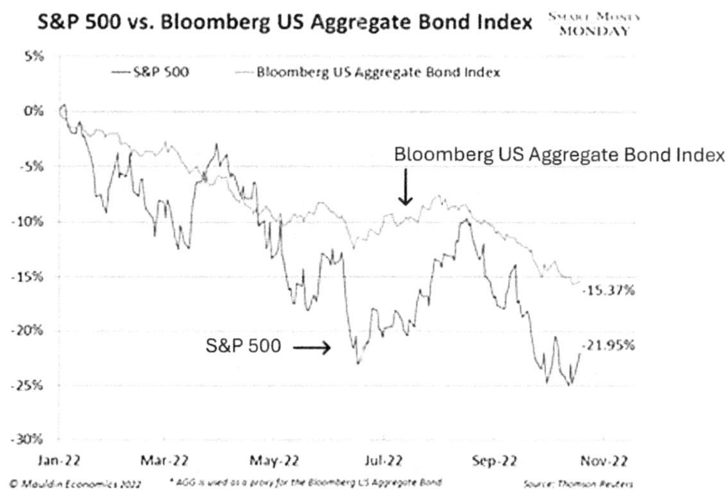

151

It has been nearly four decades since the Fed aggressively raised rates in the face of a slowing economy and a falling stock market. If you were invested in bonds in 2022, you may feel like you got dropped from the high end of the teeter-totter. The cherry bomb we feared from the bond market in February actually turned out to be far worse than we expected.

As bond investors turned the calendar to 2023, they wanted to know whether the worst was over. At the time, we didn't know the answer because the Federal Reserve Bank had told us they were not done raising interest rates yet. This meant that bond investors could be in for even further losses.

Successful investing is somewhat like driving a car. While the pain of recent losses is still top of mind, it is clearly in the rearview mirror. We all know how difficult it would be to drive a car if we only looked in the rearview mirror.

Two things will drive future returns in the bond market. The first is the current interest rates bonds are paying, which rose dramatically in step with the Fed's interest rate increase campaign. The second is potential increases in bond prices based on interest rates eventually coming back down to more historically neutral levels.

The ability to view the bond market's future returns in a more constructive way is akin to driving your car while looking through the windshield toward the future of what the investment and economic landscape may bring. The ability to separate past pain from future potential gain is key to generating positive returns from your portfolio.

Was the Bond Market Abby Normal?

According to Wikipedia, "*Young Frankenstein* is a 1974 American comedy horror film directed by Mel Brooks. The screenplay was co-written by Brooks and [the actor who played the title character] Gene Wilder....The film is a parody of the classic horror film genre, in particular the various film adaptations of Mary Shelley's 1818 novel *Frankenstein*."[152]

Young Frankenstein was shot in black-and-white, using numerous filming techniques from the classic 1930s movies that many of us grew up watching.

In one particularly famous scene from the movie, Dr. Frankenstein begins to question whether the brain he has transplanted into a recently deceased criminal was really the brain of "scientist and saint" Hans Delbrück. When questioning his assistant Igor, he finally learns the truth. Igor had dropped and ruined the brain he was supposed to get for his boss. Instead, he took a brain labeled abnormal. He eventually confesses:

> Dr. Frankenstein: Now, that brain that you gave me. Was it Hans Delbruck's?

> Igor: …No.
>
> Dr. Frankenstein: Ah! Very good. Would you mind telling me whose brain I *did* put in?
>
> Igor: Then you won't be angry?
>
> Dr. Frankenstein: I will *not* be angry.
>
> Igor: Abby someone.
>
> Dr. Frankenstein: …Abby someone. Abby who?
>
> Igor: Abby…Normal.
>
> Dr. Frankenstein: …Abby Normal?
>
> Igor: I'm almost sure that was the name.
>
> Dr. Frankenstein: Are you saying that I put an abnormal brain into a seven and a half foot long, fifty-four inch wide *gorilla?*[153]

2022 also turned out to be Abby Normal for the bond market. During that year, the Federal Reserve Bank embarked on its fastest interest rate increase campaign in decades. After initially dismissing rising inflation as temporary, the Fed finally took the threat of higher prices seriously and began raising interest rates in March 2022. They proceeded to raise rates seven times in 2022, totaling 4.25%. They told us that there was more to come in 2023. Remember, bond prices move inversely with interest rates. These rate increases produced losses in the bond market four times worse than any time over the previous 100 years.

The Worst Years for U.S. Bonds Since 1926

Year	Return	Next 12 Months
2022	-13.0	5.5
1994	-2.9	18.5
1931	-2.3	8.8
2013	-2.0	6.0
2021	-1.5	-13.0
1958	-1.3	-0.4
1999	-0.8	11.6
1969	-0.7	16.9
1955	-0.7	-0.4
1956	-0.4	7.8
Average	-2.6	6.2

A second chart puts this even further in perspective. You can see that the distribution of bond returns had historically fallen in a rather tight range—until 2022. Looking at the bottom left of the chart, you will see that 2022 was truly a negative outlier. In economic terms, this is known as left tail risk or a black swan event.

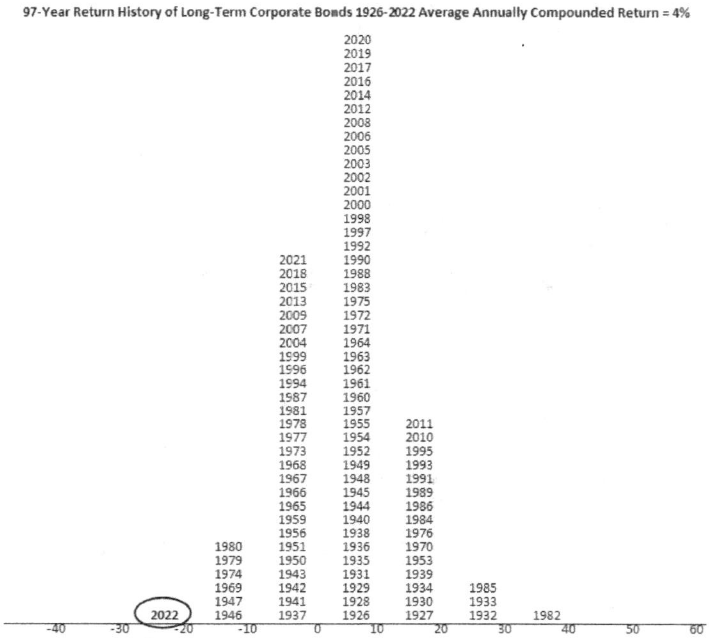

Source: Target Data Solutions [154]

However, many economists, market strategists, and bond fund portfolio managers became more excited about future bond returns than they had been in some time. This is because bonds were paying higher interest rates than we had seen in at least 15 years.[155] At that time, many market strategists and bond portfolio managers concluded that you could get reasonably high yields without having to go out to the far end of the credit risk spectrum (i.e., take too much risk).

We know that when the Fed feels that inflation has fallen sufficiently, it will eventually stop raising interest rates and begin cutting them to bring them back down toward what have historically been considered neutral levels. When this occurs, people who own bonds will not only earn historically above-average yields, but they will also reap appreciation on those same bonds as interest rates fall.

[156]

In 2022, the role of economic Dr. Frankenstein was played by Fed chair Jerome "Jay" Powell. Like the title character of the movie, Chairman Powell created an Abby Normal bond market. As painful as this was, past investment pain can lead to future gains for those who stay patient and disciplined.

The swiftness and severity of the bond market downturn in 2022 caught many investors and economists off guard. Next, we will examine what happens when this trend reverses course.

We know that, by raising rates, the Fed ushered in negative returns that the bond market had not experienced in over 100 years. In turn, simply hinting that the Fed may be done raising rates and will likely begin cutting rates soon could send the bond market significantly higher. Now that we have experienced more than two years of pain and disappointment in the bond market, let's explore what might come next.

How Far Can You Push a Beach Ball Underwater?

When we were kids, we often looked for relief from the summer heat by finding a pool or a pond to jump into and cool off. Most homes in my neighborhood did not have central air conditioning back then. Eventually, my parents put a window A/C unit in their bedroom, but we were rarely allowed in that room, and certainly not on days when we had Little League baseball games, for reasons our baseball coaches could never quite explain.

For most of us, getting into a pool meant that we had to put one together. Our pools had flimsy metal sides and vinyl liners that you clipped to the outside with pieces of plastic. Nobody I knew had a permanent above-ground pool, and the idea of putting an in-ground pool into a home in Northeast Ohio, where you could only use it a few months a year, seemed ludicrous at the time.

For those of you who have no idea what I am talking about, here is a picture of one of those relics.

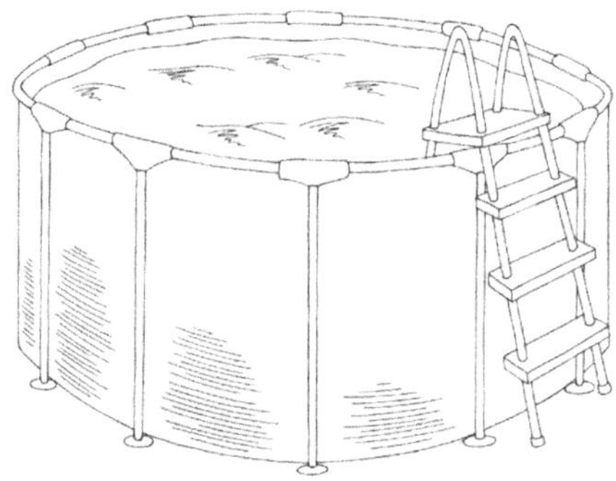

157

To amuse ourselves, we would sometimes see how far we could push beach balls under the water. As the air-filled balls were pushed further and further underwater, we knew they would go higher and higher when they were eventually released.

If you were an investor with a portion of your assets invested in bonds, the last couple of years may have felt like somebody was using this part of your portfolio as a beach ball that was getting shoved further and further underwater.

Historically, bonds have been used to reduce portfolio volatility, which is typically caused by gyrations in the stock market. As you can see from the graph below, the bond market only experienced four negative years in the five decades before 2022.

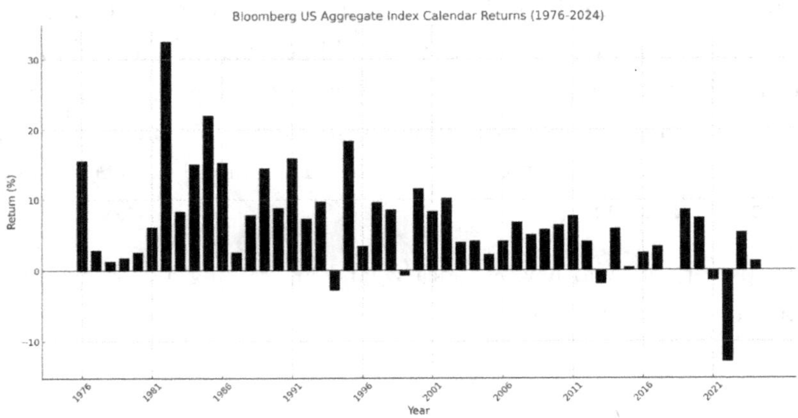

158

In February 2022, the Fed decided that inflation was no longer transitory and that they would have to begin raising interest rates to combat the massive amounts of fiscal and monetary stimulus that had been dished out since the onset of the COVID-19 pandemic.

As you can see in our next chart, as the Fed raised rates at its fastest pace in 40 years, the AGG, which is the bond market equivalent of the S&P 500, put in its worst two-year performance in over 100 years, falling from 114 to 92 (-19%). This was akin to pushing the bond beach ball further and further underwater.

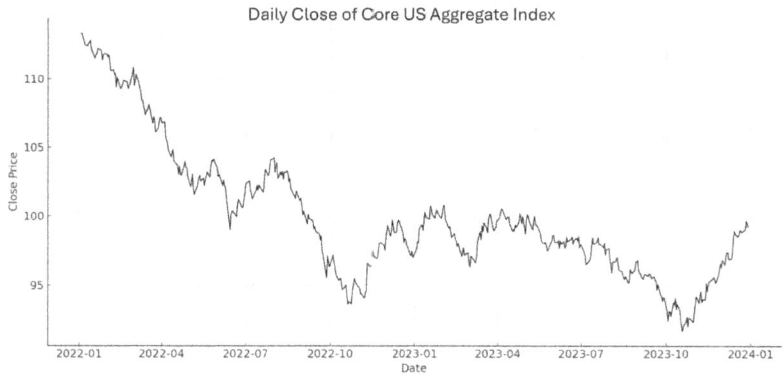

159

We knew that the Fed would eventually stop raising rates as inflation fell from a peak of 9.1% in June 2022 to 3.1% in early 2024. The narrative from the early November 2023 Federal Reserve Bank meeting and the unemployment and CPI reports released that month indicated that they might be done raising interest rates.

As a result, the bond market came shooting back up like a beach ball that had been held underwater. As you can see in our last chart, bonds experienced six consecutive negative months from May through October 2023, something that had not happened since this metric began being tracked in 1926.

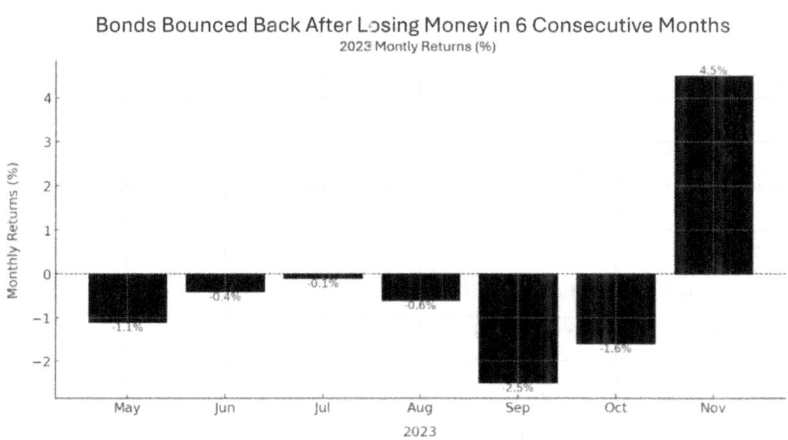

160

November turned out to be the bond market's 8th-best monthly return in the past 100 years. For those of you who have been concerned or frustrated that bonds have not been performing their historical role as a counterbalance to stock market volatility, the coming years may look very different from what we have experienced recently, as the Fed is now indicating that it will reverse course.

Recall that the teeter-totter works both ways. At the press conference following the December 2023 meeting, Fed chairman Jay Powell said that the Fed was not only done raising interest rates but would likely cut rates at least three times in 2024. As painful as the bond market downturn was, bond investors hoped the reverse would be true going forward.

Remember that I told you at the beginning of this chapter that bonds are boring? In researching and putting together the material for this chapter, I realized that I was as guilty of ignoring the bond market as my macroeconomics teacher and the writers of *The Wall Street Journal*. Prior to 2022, I had never written about the bond market. That is mostly due to the fact that there was not much to write about.

From a historical perspective, bonds have largely performed in line with expectations. They primarily serve three roles in client portfolios. First, they provide regular and consistent income, especially for retired clients who need that cash flow to help provide for their standard of living. Second, they serve as a diversification tool to help mitigate stock market risk due to their noncorrelated returns. And third, they provide for the protection of principal. During times when the stock market is down, which happens on a somewhat regular basis, as we shall see in the next chapter, bonds have historically held their value or gone up. This allows retirees, who need to withdraw from their portfolios, to have an asset class that they can sell while prices are still up.

Now that U.S. interest rates have moved out of the failed zero interest rate experiment of central banks after the Global Financial Crisis, we expect bonds to resume a more normal role in portfolios going forward. Therefore, we believe most retired clients should construct their portfolios to have enough bond exposure to help reduce risk and provide liquidity during the inevitable times of stock market volatility and dislocation.

As our friend and the title character of the 1986 movie *Ferris Bueller's Day Off* famously said, "Life moves pretty fast."[161] Historically, the bond market was a much slower and more boring place to invest your money. All of this changed in our post-Global Financial Crisis and post-COVID world. However, I still believe that having a disciplined diversification within the bond portion of your portfolio, along with periodic rebalancing to take advantage of market fluctuations, continues to make sense for most retirees.

As we move to Puzzle Piece #9, we will begin exploring stocks. This asset class has historically had much more volatility, both up and down. Equities have historically made up a large portion of people's investment portfolios. This is true both for younger people trying to accumulate the resources necessary to educate their children or retire comfortably and for retirees who want to see their portfolios and dividend income continue to grow through their retirement years.

PUZZLE PIECE

#9

The Role of Stocks in Building Your Retirement Wealth

"On which end of your investing lifetime do you want to take greater risks so that you have less risk on the other end?"

This is an important question as you try to build the wealth you will need for a successful retirement. We are going to explore it in more detail in this chapter.

In Puzzle Piece #7, we spent a significant amount of time trying to understand economic and investment history and why historical stock market returns should give you confidence that you can build wealth as a long-term investor. We then reviewed the role of bonds in your retirement income portfolio in Puzzle Piece #8.

We are now going to turn our attention to the stock market. We know that most famous investors and portfolio managers built both their reputations and fortunes by investing in stocks over multiple decades. You didn't get to know the names of Peter Lynch (of Fidelity Magellan fame), John Bogle (founder of Vanguard Funds), Sir John Templeton (founder of Templeton Funds and grandfather of foreign stock investing), or Warren Buffett (of

Berkshire Hathaway) because they invested successfully in Treasury bills. No, they built their wealth by investing in stocks for the long run.

There is a direct correlation between volatility and returns. If investors stick to low-risk assets, they will likely obtain low long-term returns. On the other hand, if investors are willing to allocate resources to an asset class that subjects its holders to more variability of returns, they will give themselves the opportunity to compound their assets at a much higher historical rate of return. We can see this in the chart below, which shows how a dollar invested in various assets would have grown from 1926 to 2022.

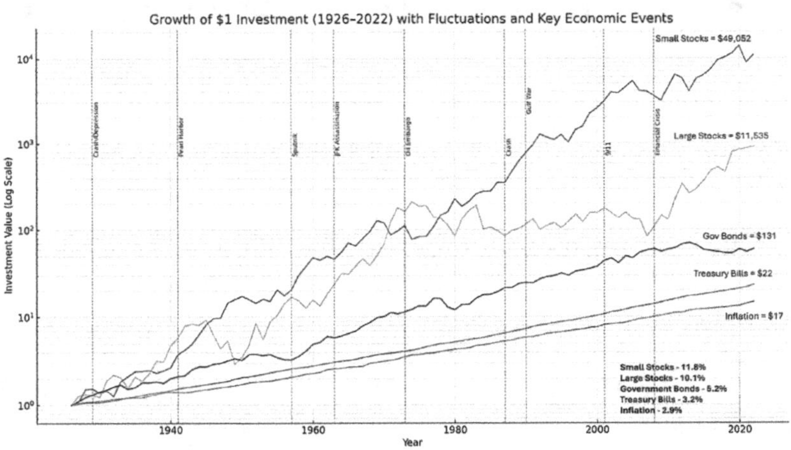

[162]

You will note that both large company and small company stocks had much greater volatility in their year-to-year results, but they both experienced double-digit returns over the long term. This meant that a dollar invested in either in 1926 grew and compounded to five-figure sums. At the same time, money invested in much lower-risk assets like government bonds and Treasury bills compounded at much lower rates. This led to accumulations that were not only much smaller but barely outpaced inflation.

Earlier, I asked this thought-provoking question: "On which end of your investing lifetime do you want to take greater risks so that you have less risk on the other end?" You could choose to invest all your funds in low-volatility options like CDs and Treasury bills, which would shield you from market risk and volatility. However, the modest returns from those investments might not be sufficient to build enough assets to fund a comfortable retirement or fulfill the aspirations you have for yourself and your loved ones. Most investors believe that they can eliminate risk from their portfolios. *That is not true.* You simply trade one risk for another. In this example, you trade market/volatility risk for longevity risk. At the end of the day, there are *no* risk-free options!

Alternatively, you can invest your resources in assets that have a much higher degree of volatility or variability of returns. This will produce much more uncertainty early on, and you will likely have some years with returns that will not feel comfortable as we go through inevitable geopolitical events, economic uncertainties, and recessions. Nevertheless, based on investment history, it is highly probable that you will accumulate the resources you need to retire successfully and live the life to which you and your family aspire.

Many people equate investing in the stock market with gambling. However, history does not show this to be an accurate analogy. You see, the longer you play a game of chance in a casino, the greater the odds are that the house will win and you will lose. The opposite is true when it comes to investing in the stock market. Historically, the longer you stay invested, the greater your odds are of being successful. This does not sound like gambling to me. Let's explore this idea in more detail.

"You Better You Bet"

In 1982, I was a sophomore in high school. One day at noon, it was announced that one of my favorite rock bands, the Who, was going to be coming to Cleveland—or more accurately, to the Richfield Coliseum—on what was supposed to be their farewell tour. Tickets were going to go on sale at Ticketmaster at 4 p.m. that day. To get a ticket, I would have to leave immediately from school at the end of the day to head to Chapel Hill Mall, get in line, and hope there were still tickets available. (Our children and grandchildren have no idea what I am referring to in this story.)

There was one major problem: I did not have enough money with me to buy a ticket. If I drove home to get the money after school, the tickets would certainly be gone by the time I got back to the mall. Fortunately, Ms. Griffith, my Algebra II teacher who had been a music hippie in the '60s and '70s, loaned me $20 (yes, you could see a concert from a major musical act back then for just $20) so I could buy a ticket to my very first rock concert.

The previous year, the Who had recorded their first album since the passing of drummer Keith Moon, entitled *Face Dances*. This album included what is still one of my favorite songs from the band, "You Better You Bet." According to Wikipedia, "it was the last single by the band that reached the top 20 on the *Billboard* Hot 100 [U.S. charts]," and it was their last top 10 single in the UK.[163]

Speaking of betting, approximately 68 million Americans were expected to bet on the 2024 Super Bowl, a 35% increase from the previous year. The collective wagers were expected to total as much as $23.1 billion (a 35% increase), according to the American Gaming Association.[164]

These year-to-year increases are largely being driven by the increasing availability of online betting sites. Several years ago, the Supreme Court overturned a 1992 federal law banning sports gambling.[165] This has led to legalized gambling in many states, with more states likely to join the virtual party.

It is interesting that during the first six months after the outbreak of the COVID-19 pandemic, both online betting platforms and online stock trading platforms saw their volumes increase dramatically. That change held steady until the economy reopened, people returned to work, and the government-funded stimulus checks and enhanced employment benefits began to be depleted.

We know that the markets have a way of separating people who are focused on short-term time frames and emotions from their hard-earned dollars. Betting and speculation are not investment strategies that have historically led to success when trying to build wealth.

It is extraordinarily important to differentiate betting from investing. We know that historically, markets go up more than they go down, although the downs are financially and emotionally difficult to endure. We also know that the longer your holding period, the higher the probability of success, as you can see in the next chart.

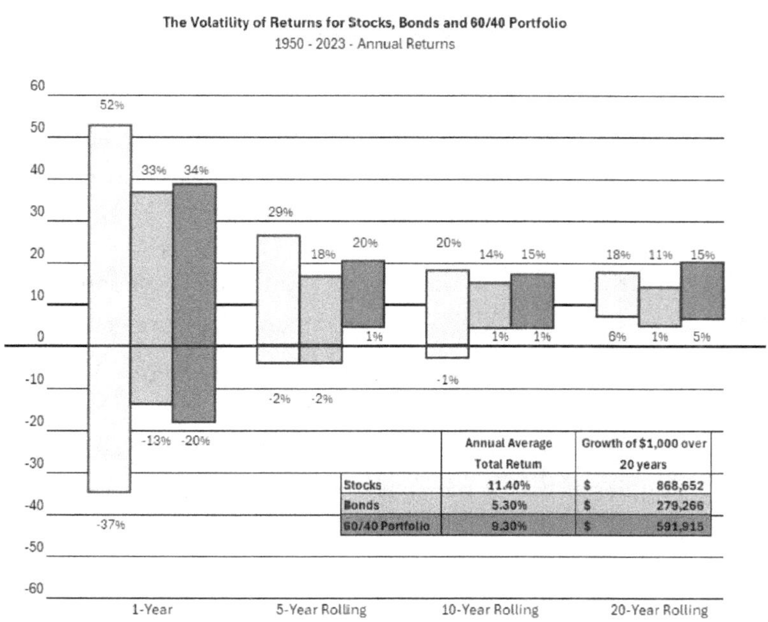

166

I want to thank Ms. Griffith, who bet I would pay her back (which I did the next day using my paper route and baseball umpiring money), for allowing me to see my first concert. "You Better You Bet" is a fun song that I still enjoy listening to every time it comes on radio or streaming platforms. I thought this would be a fun way to remind you that while many more people are betting on sports games, it is not a strategy I recommend for managing your family's hard-earned assets.

There is also a great amount of confusion about the stock market and the economy. *They are not one and the same.* While stocks do follow corporate profits and earnings over the long term, and these are somewhat correlated to the growth of the economy, the two do not move in tandem. As a matter of fact, the stock market often moves up or down long before the economy does. This often frustrates and confuses investors, especially in the short run. Let's dig a little deeper into this topic next.

Should We Watch the Stock Market or the Economy?

There are many times when the economy looks very different from the stock market. We only have to look at the last few years to see this in action.

In calendar year 2018, the United States experienced economic growth of 2.9%, as measured by GDP. This was one of the strongest years we have experienced since the '07–'08 Global Financial Crisis. This was also a 0.5% increase from the previous year.[167] Therefore, most people would expect that the stock market would have done similarly well. They would be wrong. A quick check of the facts shows that the S&P 500 dropped 4.4% that year.

By contrast, the United States' GDP grew by 2.29% in 2019.[168] This was relatively disappointing and also a 0.65% decline from the previous year.

However, the United States stock market responded by going up 31.5%. The disconnect between the two is confusing to many.

So, what exactly is going on? The stock market is a leading economic indicator. It is one of 10 such indicators in the Conference Board's Leading Economic Index for the U.S.[169] This means that the stock market generally moves down before a recession starts and typically moves higher before a recession ends.

This helps explain why the stock market bottomed in March 2020, in the midst of the COVID-19 shutdowns and a policy-induced recession. The stock market sniffed out that the massive stimulus from the federal government and the Federal Reserve Bank was going to eventually cause an upturn in the economy and consumer spending, therefore sending corporate profits higher. The stock market moved up well before the economy bottomed out.

What does this mean for future stock market returns? Our next chart shows that historically, when economic growth is strong, stock market returns are generally positive, albeit punctuated by more bouts of volatility. The key is to look for early warning signs that economic growth is starting to deteriorate, which may be early indicators of the next recession. We must also remember that no one can accurately predict geopolitical risks and economic shocks such as 9/11 or COVID-19.

Best 10 Years U.S. Real GDP Growth Since 1950

Year	Real GDP YoY	S&P 500 Return	Max Drawdown
1950	8.7%	31.5%	-14.0%
1951	8.1%	24.0%	-9.0%
1955	7.1%	12.0%	-9.0%
1959	6.9%	-8.7%	-26.8%
1962	6.1%	-10.0%	-22.2%
1964	5.8%	-14.7%	-23.4%
1965	6.5%	12.5%	9.9%
1966	6.6%	16.4%	-3.2%
1973	5.6%	6.2%	-12.6%
1984	7.3%	31.4%	-10.6%
Average:		10.0%	-12.1%

170

Understanding this historical context gives us a lens through which to view the future. It is important to remember that the stock market and the economy are not the same thing as we navigate the landscape throughout our investing lifetimes.

We also know that how people feel about the economy and their individual financial situations drives their spending habits and activities.

Next, we are going to try to better understand how consumer sentiment affects economic growth and stock market returns over time.

Are You Satisfied with the Economy?

American business author and former management professor at the University of New Orleans Michael LeBoeuf reminds us of something that most of us intuitively know: "A satisfied customer is the best business strategy of all."[171]

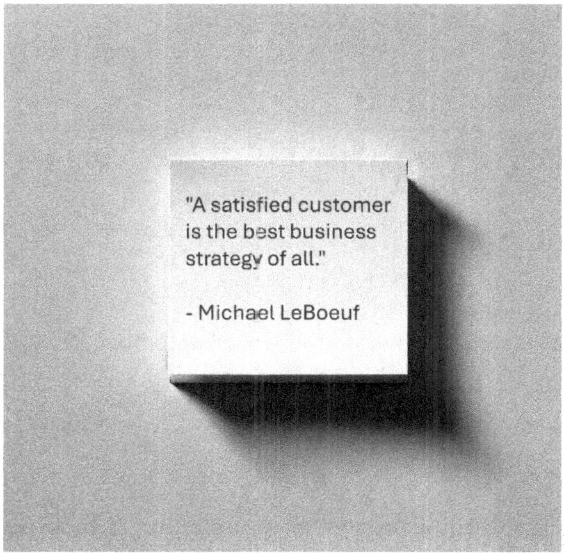

172

My goal as a small business owner is to create a customer service culture that produces not just happy clients but raving fans, people who are not only loyal to our business but become brand ambassadors, referring their friends and loved ones to the CFPs of Impel Wealth Management. They want to see their friends and loved ones helped in the same way they have been. In my opinion, this is the ultimate measure of client satisfaction.

When we explore satisfaction and sentiment from an investment standpoint, we intuitively know that uncertainty and volatility create both anxiety and dissatisfaction. We can observe this plainly in the sentiment poll from the American Association of Individual Investors that you can see in the next chart. A reading from the spring of 2022 showed a bullish, or optimistic, sentiment of only 15.8%.

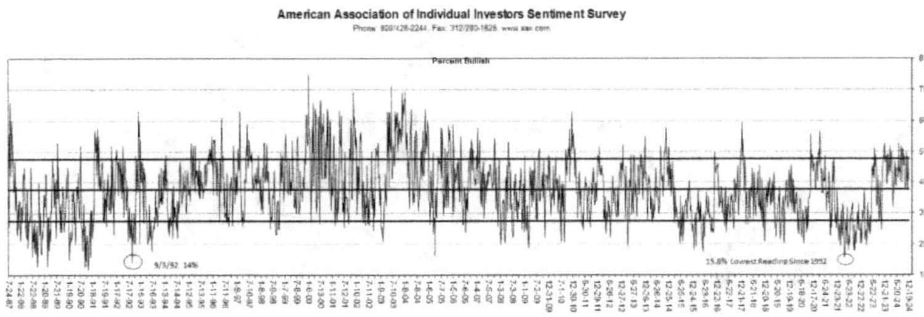

[173]

Surprisingly, this was the lowest level since September 1992! Think about everything that has happened in the last 30 years. This would include the dot-com bubble, 9/11, the Global Financial Crisis, and the COVID-19 outbreak, to name just a few.

It seems that the combination of rising inflation (which pushed prices for food, fuel, and most things we buy significantly higher) and rapidly rising interest rates, geopolitical uncertainty (including Russia's invasion of Ukraine), and the upcoming midterm elections created a great deal of anxiety among Americans.

An additional poll conducted by Morningstar and Gallup published March 31, 2022, also showed a very low level of satisfaction here at home. The percentage of Americans who were satisfied with the way things are going in the United States was at a historically low level similar to when we lived through the previous crises outlined above.

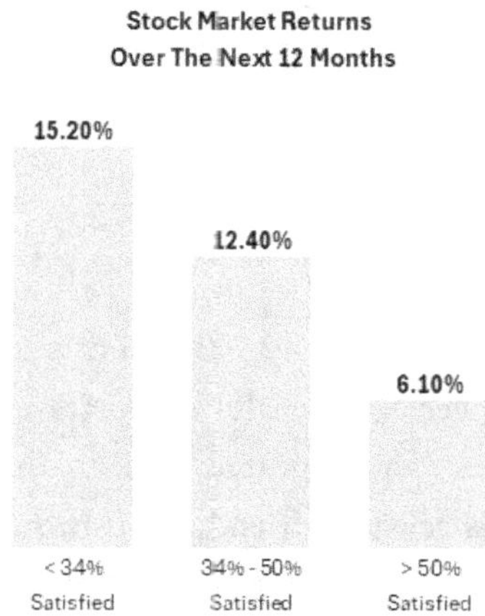

Source: Poll by Morningstar and Gallup, published 3/31/2022 [174]

What may be very surprising for most people to learn is that optimism and satisfaction surveys are often *contrarian indicators*. The highest level of satisfaction came in February 1999 when the economy was humming along, we were creating budget surpluses, and the stock market was going gangbusters. However, returns in the stock market over the next 10 years were very disappointing, as we lived through two stock market drops that both exceeded 45%.

As you will note in the chart, when the number of people satisfied is below 34%, which was clearly the case in early 2022, stock market returns over the 12 months that follow, as measured by the S&P 500 index, tend to be in excess of 15%. Please remember that there are no guarantees, and past performance does not predict future returns.

Sometimes, pessimism and dissatisfaction lead people to sell at the wrong times in an effort to reduce risk. This has often led to people missing out on the rebounds that occur, thereby compounding the error by reducing the growth of their financial resources.

We also know that our economy is dynamic and evolves over time. This means that innovation and entrepreneurialism in a capitalistic society create new companies and new opportunities for profit and growth. We will explore this dynamic further in our next section.

Back to the Future

Back to the Future was released in July 1985. In this comedic science fiction classic, California teenager Marty McFly, portrayed by Michael J. Fox (of Alex P. Keaton fame), is transported back to the 1950s when a time travel experiment by his scientist friend, Doc Brown, goes awry. Marty eventually runs into teenage versions of his parents. He spends most of the movie trying to figure out how to get back to his own time and save Doc Brown from a nefarious fate without disrupting the lives of his parents.

Looking at the past and imagining the future can benefit us, too—it can teach us lessons about how economies and markets evolve over time.

In 1980, Ronald Reagan won his first presidential election, inflation and interest rates were double digits, U.S. hostages were being held in Iran, and I was finishing my freshman year of high school. As we look back at how our world and the stock market have changed in the 44 years between 1980 and 2024, the chart below helps tell the story of our economy and how what we value has evolved.

Ten Most Valuable US Stocks

1980	2000	2024
Exxon Mobile	General Motors	Microsoft
General Motors	Wal-Mart Stores	Apple
Mobil	Exxon Mobil	Nvidia
Ford Motor	Ford Motor	Alphabet
Texaco	General Electric	Amazon
ChevronTexaco	IBM	Meta Platforms
Gulf Oil	Citigroup	Eli Lilly
IBM	AT&T	Broadcom
General Electric	Altria Group	Tesla
Amoco	Boeing	Visa

Source: 1980 and 2000 Data from Money.com and 2024 Data from Statistia.com 175

If you look back to 1980, you will note that seven of the 10 largest and most valuable companies in the U.S. stock market at the time were related to the oil industry. By the calendar year 2000, only five companies from 20 years earlier were still on the list, and only one of those was related to the oil industry. Flash-forward to today, and no company from 2000 remains on the list. Today's top 10 list is heavily weighted towards tech and AI-driven companies, one of which nobody had heard of just a few years ago.

What will this list look like in 10, 20, or 40 years? It will probably be much different than you or I would think or guess. The world, technology, and innovation are evolving much more quickly than anyone would have expected, and the pace of that change will only increase in the coming years.

If you had told someone in 1980 that the major oil companies that were the most valuable publicly traded companies at that time would all disappear from the list shortly, they likely would not have believed you. What changes will be coming, how might life evolve, and how will those changes benefit you and your family in the years to come?

As the economy and markets evolve and experience their inevitable ups and downs, investors will also experience different emotional cycles. There will be times when markets have moved up, your account statements look great, and you feel confident about buying more of what has recently performed well. The potential problem is that you will likely be buying when prices are also high.

On the contrary, when the markets go through their downturns, it will not feel nearly as good to log in and look at your account. However, it is usually a good idea to buy more of what you were previously willing to purchase while prices are lower. It is interesting that consumers like to buy things when they are on sale, but somehow, that does not always translate the same way when they are allocating new monies to their investment portfolios.

Buying when prices are low and investments are on sale is difficult. As discussed, it requires faith, patience, and discipline. Let's discuss how to be successful in this endeavor next.

Everybody Loves a Sale!

When I was a young child, I learned that buying things on sale was important. You see, I was the oldest of three children. Our family of five was supported by my dad's income as a navy-trained electrician. While we were not technically poor, I remember that being able to go to the back-to-school sales at Kmart or Sears and get a pair of jeans or a couple of T-shirts for the start of a new school year was a big deal.

My next experience with sales came when I turned 11 years old. I wanted to buy a 10-speed bike, so I began working as an after-school newspaper delivery boy for the *Akron Beacon Journal*. Whenever there was a major sale, it produced a significant number of sales flyers, which, in turn, made the newspapers I carried much heavier. Judging by the typical weight of the Sunday newspaper, it seemed like there were sales going on all the time.

176

The importance of sales was what I learned next. This lesson came during my first two years of college, which I paid for in large part by loading and unloading trucks for O'Neil's (which has since merged with Macy's department stores).

Any and every occasion was viewed as a reason to have a sale: after Thanksgiving, pre-Christmas, after Christmas, Presidents' Day, Easter, Memorial Day, etc., etc., etc. O'Neil's even figured out that if there was no reason to have a sale, they could have one anyway and call it the One-Day Sale. They typically had several One-Day Sales each month. Why the focus on sales? That's a great question; let's explore it together. Americans value being able to buy things at a discount. Few things make people happier than feeling like they got a deal on something they needed (or wanted).

This seems to extend to all areas of life except for the purchase of financial assets. I have now worked as a financial advisor for more than 35 years. Unfortunately, financial assets go on sale on a somewhat regular basis when their prices drop. This allows people to buy more of things they previously wanted at a lower price. Instead, people tend to panic, which generally does not help if their goal is accumulating wealth.

In fact, people who are looking to accumulate the financial resources they will need to retire comfortably or educate their children and grandchildren often tend to invest more when prices are high. I could give you multiple examples, but I will limit today's discussion to just a couple of obvious ones that I have seen over the last three decades.

In the late '90s, anything related to the internet or dot-com theme saw its price rise significantly. It did not matter whether the company had a great business model or even if they had growing sales, profits, or both. This speculation seemed to hit a peak around the time of the Super Bowl in 2000—though many of the companies featured in those ads ceased to exist in the next few years.

We watched a similar phenomenon take place just a few years later as the real estate bubble enticed people to continue to buy real estate, even after prices had risen dramatically. It seemed too good to be true, which should always be a warning sign, but on a historical basis, real estate prices had never gone down nationally. You'll recall that even then, Federal Reserve chairman Ben Bernanke had said this in a CNBC interview with anchor Maria Bartiromo.[177] *All of this worked great until it didn't.*

It has been said that the New York Stock Exchange is the only place on Earth where, when they have a huge sale, everyone runs screaming out of the store.

Warren Buffett, who, as I stated before, is one of the most successful but least emulated investors of all time, has often used stories when explaining how he likes to buy stocks on sale. The following analogy has been attributed to him: "If you owned a bakery, and the price of flour went on sale for 20% off, you would back up the truck and buy all you could while prices were down." This is a logical behavior that people would use to accrue almost anything else they wanted to buy. Buffett has used many similar analogies to emphasize the importance of purchasing quality investments when their prices are low, comparing it to buying essential supplies at a discount.

Investors often think of the S&P 500 as just an index, when in reality, it is a composite of 500 of the largest, most profitable, and most innovative companies headquartered in the United States. The leaders of these companies are charged with generating sales and profits, regardless of the economic backdrop and without regard to who is in the White House or on Capitol Hill.

It is quite likely that stocks will go on sale again at some point this year, as they do in most years. You can see from the next chart that since 1980, the stock market has averaged a 14% intrayear downturn on an annual basis.

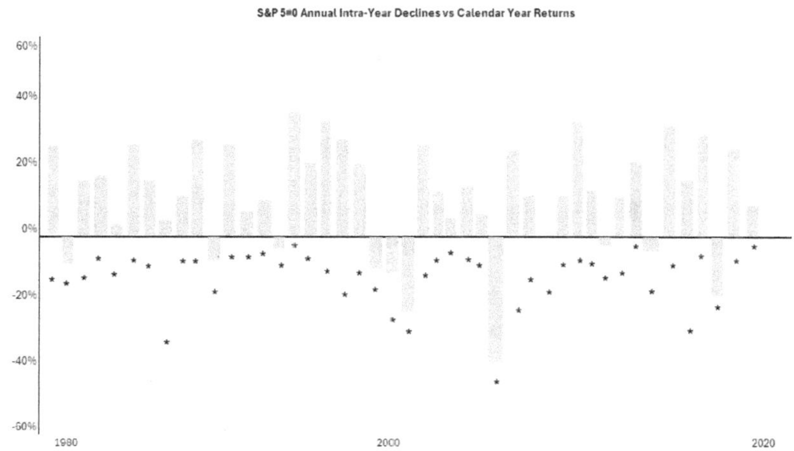

[178]

Each time this happens, the financial media begins to scream that the end of the financial world is coming—again. And each time, a few of our clients listen to these market commentators and prognosticators and call us, panicked. They know who they are. Looking at more than 200 years of stock market returns, as well as more economic and geopolitical crises than you can count on your fingers and toes, we can confidently say that each time the market went through a downturn, it was temporary. Each time, the market subsequently moved to a new all-time high, and the world's end was postponed yet again.

So, the next time this happens, let's treat it like somebody put an ad in the Sunday newspaper announcing that stocks have gone on sale. Let's rush to buy instead of panicking or selling just because so-called experts on social media and the 24-hour cable news outlets are telling us to. Please remember that if we do what most people do, we will get the results that most people get. Since most people are not wealthy, we do not want to follow their habits or actions.

In exploring Puzzle Piece #9, we have reviewed that, despite negative news, consumer sentiment, recessions, and geopolitical events, stocks have been the best-performing asset class over the last century. The impact of higher compounded returns over long periods of time has allowed many investors to accumulate the resources needed to educate their children and grandchildren, donate to the causes that are important to them, and, most importantly, transition from work life to retirements of significance.

It is also important to understand that this compounded growth has allowed investors' resources to grow far more quickly than costs have risen. As we will explore in our next chapter, the negative impact of inflation can cause significant damage to your long-term financial goals.

Until recently, many people have not thought much about inflation over the last couple of decades, as it has been relatively benign. However, the recent flare-up in prices has brought this risk that many people had not thought about since the late '70s and early '80s to the forefront once again. Please join me as we explore the risk of rising prices to your retirement in more detail next.

PUZZLE PIECE

#10

The Risk of Rising Prices During Your Retirement Years

Inflation is like a river that erodes your hard-earned financial assets! Sometimes this happens slowly, as we saw in the years following the '07–'08 Global Financial Crisis, when inflation rarely reached 2% annually. Other times, it seems to come quickly for your checkbook, like we experienced during the late 1970s and again more recently during the post-COVID price flare-up. Regardless of how quickly or slowly inflation rises, it is like a river slowly wearing away its rock bed over many years.

The most well-known example of erosion in the world is the Grand Canyon. Scientists and archaeologists estimate that the Colorado River took more than 70 million years to slowly create its path through many miles and layers of rock, shaping the canyon into what nearly 5 million park visitors see each year.[179] More importantly, even though it is invisible to those visiting and viewing the canyon now, the process of erosion slowly continues.

Inflation, like erosion, slowly eats away at the value of each dollar, leaving it to buy fewer goods and services than it would have just a few years ago. We aren't always aware of this over a few weeks or months. However, over longer periods of time, consumers inevitably feel the substantial impact of those rising prices. The chart below provides a helpful visual representation of how the value of your hard-earned dollars has been slowly eroded by inflation over time.

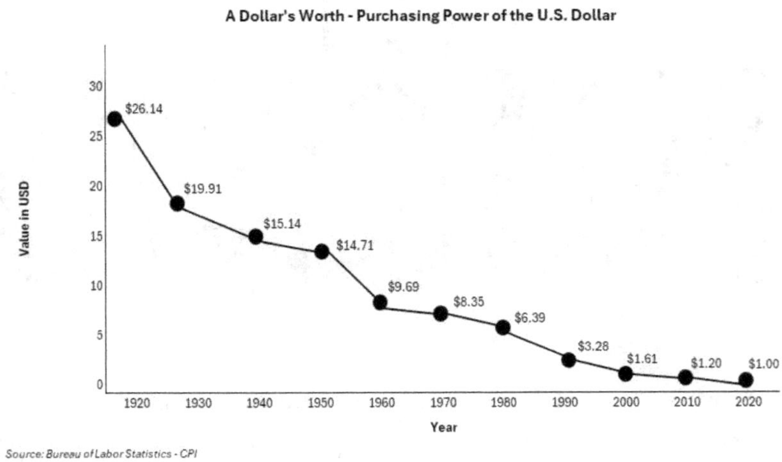

[180]

As you can see from the chart, it took $26.14 in 2020 to purchase what $1.00 would have when President Woodrow Wilson signed the Federal Reserve Act into law on December 23, 1913.

Unfortunately, many people who are trying to save and build the resources necessary to retire comfortably spend their time fretting over day-to-day market volatility when the real enemy is the impact of inflation over long periods. Let's visit France before World War II to illustrate what happens when we spend time fighting the wrong battle in a different war.

During World War I, France had lacked adequate protection against German invasion. The Maginot Line was built in the 1930s by France to prevent another German invasion. The line was named after the French minister of war André Maginot. As you can see in the map, it is "a line of concrete fortifications, obstacles, and weapon installations" meant to deter invasion along the French/German border.[181]

182

Military experts around the world believed that the Maginot Line was a work of genius that would successfully protect France from invasion. The line was "impervious to most forms of attack."[183] The French were confident that they had protected themselves, leading them to a false sense of security and complacency.

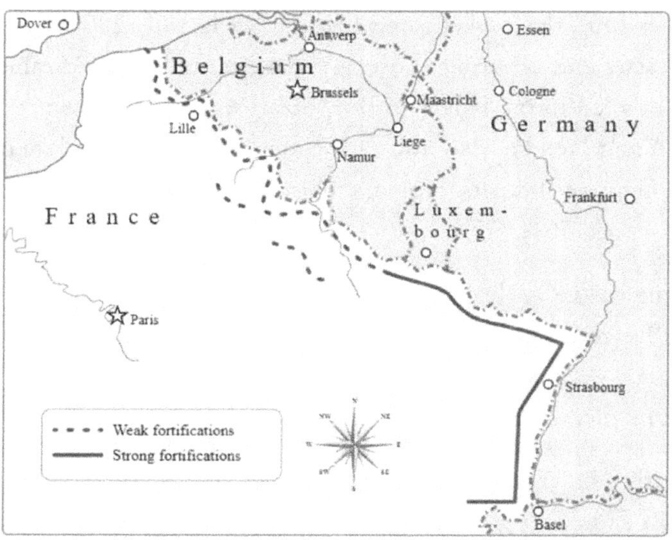

184

However, when Adolf Hitler decided it was time for Germany to invade France in the spring of 1940, they simply went around the Maginot Line and invaded through Belgium, outflanking the line of protection. At the end of the day, the French had created a tool that would have protected them during the last world war, but not the current one.

When I began my career as a financial advisor in 1987, many investors were worried about protecting their investment capital from the inevitable bouts of volatility that accompany investing in the stock market. At the time, many of these individuals had memories of the Great Depression or had been raised by parents who had lived through it and drilled into their heads that they should never trust banks or financial markets.

Fast-forward to today, and many people have been scarred by the multiple significant market downturns we have experienced since the turn of the century. We began with a 49% pullback in the S&P 500 in the 2½ years from the peak of the dot-com bubble in March 2000 to the trough in October 2002 in the wake of the Enron/WorldCom scandal.[185] Let's not forget that we lived through the 9/11 attacks in between those bookends.

In October 2007, the market barely broke above its early 2000 highs when the real estate and subprime mortgage markets started to crumble. This subsequently led to the failure of Bear Stearns, the government takeover of FNMA and Freddie Mac, and the September 15, 2008, failure of both AIG and Lehman Brothers. From October 2007 to March 2009, the stock market dropped 56%.[186]

Then came the COVID-19 government-mandated economic shutdowns and massive recession. Our country had not experienced a significant health pandemic since the Spanish flu outbreak in 1920. This resulted in the stock market dropping 34% in just six weeks.

Stock market downturns, like those outlined above, are extraordinarily difficult to endure. It is never fun to see the value of your accounts drop by a third or more while you are trying to accumulate the resources necessary to retire successfully. However, as I shared with you previously, each of these bouts of volatility *was temporary.* The market subsequently moved to new all-time highs after each one of these events, no matter how emotionally difficult they were at the time.

In the meantime, inflation slowly but surely continues to erode our purchasing power every year. It is important to remember that, at the historical inflation rate of 3%, the cost of living will double every 24 years. This does not consider that many items that retirees spend money on, such as travel and health-care expenses, tend to see prices increase faster than the general inflation rate.

All this leads me to the following conclusion: many investors are allocating their financial resources to protect against short-term financial volatility, while the real danger is inflation, which will eat away their purchasing power over their retirement lifetimes.

Please remember that the Maginot Line, which would have prevented invasion across the French-German border during World War I, did not protect against the German invasion in World War II, and the results were disastrous. There is a significant financial and economic analogy that we should all be paying attention to.

In order to avoid making a similar mistake in our financial lives, we need to understand what inflation looks like, what causes it, how we measure it, and what significant negative impact it could have on our retirement goals.

What Does Inflation Look Like?

In the mid-90s, most people still had vivid memories of what a period of rising and persistent inflation looked like. Those who lived through the late '70s and early '80s can remember the impact of double-digit inflation, double-digit interest rates, and the accompanying recessions on our families and financial lives. This includes home mortgages at 16%,

CDs at 14%, and the Federal Reserve's prime overnight lending rate hiked to 19% in an effort to squelch rising prices.

Financial advisor and author Nick Murray often used postage stamps as a straightforward illustration of rising prices.[187] He would simply show the price of a postage stamp from some previous date, such as 1975, and then show the cost of the same stamp 20 years later. The rise in price of the stamps mirrored the inflation that we had *all* experienced over that time. This metaphor resonated with both advisors and financial institutions. Many of them created marketing pieces around this idea. Here is one that I have had in my briefcase for nearly 30 years, created in 1995.

188

This is a simple yet vivid illustration of the impact of rising prices on everyday costs and goods. Remember, many retirees live on relatively fixed incomes. As prices rise, people spend more of their limited resources on the same milk, eggs, gasoline, and stamps. This leaves less cash flow to pursue the other interests, hobbies, travel, and lifestyle goals that make life meaningful.

A survey conducted by CNBC and Momentive finds that many American consumers are cutting back on their spending due to the impact of rising inflation.[189] As much as 60% of the U.S. population lives paycheck to paycheck and has less than $1,000 in savings.[190] This means that many people have to make difficult decisions about where to spend their finite resources. Lower-income households are most at risk and have to make unwelcome decisions and trade-offs about which necessary expenses to cut back on.

However, the survey also finds that Americans with incomes of at least $100,000 are also cutting back their spending. This is extremely important economically, as higher-income constituents make up nearly three-quarters of consumer spending.[191] Remember that consumer spending makes up about 70% of the GDP.[192] This will be an important indicator to watch when the next recession comes along.

What Caused Inflation to Come Roaring Back?

Inflation is when you pay fifteen dollars
for the ten-dollar haircut you used to get
for five dollars when you had hair.
— Attributed to Sam Ewing

As we entered 2021, most people had not heard much about inflation over the previous two decades. For most of that time, the Federal Reserve Bank had been trying to get inflation back up toward its 2% per year target goal. It was largely unsuccessful in this quest, as inflation averaged approximately 1.5% annually in the aftermath of the Great Recession of 2008–2009.[193]

However, the rollout of the COVID-19 vaccine slowly allowed the service sector of the economy to reopen. The U.S. government and the Fed had also dumped unprecedented amounts of fiscal and monetary stimulus onto the recovering economy. On top of this, the Fed had pledged to keep interest rates low until at least 2023.

The above combination caused many people to worry about a resurgence of inflation. Let's take a moment to remind you what this could look like, as inflation scares are a distant memory to many people. The era of high single-digit or low double-digit inflation of the late 1970s and early 1980s is 40 years into our memory banks.

When I was in elementary school, I occasionally got to watch the game show *The Price Is Right* during summer vacation or on days off from school. They sometimes played a game on the show called Lucky Seven, where the contestant had to guess the price of a car. The first number of the car price when I was in elementary school was always four, as vehicles cost about $4,000 at that time.

[194]

By 2021, the valuation analysts at Kelley Blue Book reported that the average cost of a new vehicle in the United States was $40,857.[195] This was up 5.45% over the previous year and 10 times what vehicles had cost in the 1970s, back when I was watching *The Price Is Right.* The subsequent surge in inflation drove the average new vehicle price to nearly $50,000 by 2024.

Part of this spike in inflation measurements is due to what is known as the base effect. Inflation is measured year over year. This means that the spring and summer months of 2021 were measured against the meager inflation from the same period in 2020, which was lower due to the coronavirus shutdowns, quarantines, and social distancing requirements. This is partly what caused the most significant increase in inflation that we have seen in many years.

There was a lot of debate about whether this would be an ongoing price surge or just a temporary issue. The Fed and several economists initially told us that inflation would be transitory and, within a year or so, would come back down to the reasonable levels that we have become comfortable with. This would be primarily due to the one-time effects of the stimulus, aging demographic trends, and continued technological advancements. Other economists believed that we were ushering in a new era of higher inflation due to all the excess money being printed by the government.

The crucial question is which set of economists and their outlook was correct. Since inflation can cause significant harm to people's cash flow during their retirement years, please remember that even at 3% inflation, prices will double every 24 years. This means that somebody retiring at age 60 would need twice as much money to maintain the same standard of living in their early 80s as they did when they first retired. If inflation were to creep higher than that, the impact could be devastating. Inflation also puts a disproportionate burden on lower-wage individuals, who have a more challenging time paying higher prices for basic living needs.

How Do We Measure Inflation?

196

The following chart shows some conflicting information about the CPI, how it is measured, and how it compares to its underlying price components.

As you will see in our next chart, from 2000 to 2021, the CPI rose 62.5%, approximately 2.25% per year. Core CPI, which excludes the volatile categories of food and energy, has gone up slightly less, at 56.9%. From these numbers alone, it seemed that consumer inflation was relatively tame and had been under control for most of the last two decades. The chart also shows eight different components measured within the CPI.

What is interesting about this chart is what is measured and what is not.

Notably, energy, which went up 119.8% during this time, is not included. Neither are college tuition and fees, which rose a staggering 172% over the period. However, medical care is included and has increased substantially more than other CPI components, rising 106.6%. If you were to judge by CPI alone, inflation would appear to be relatively low and under control, assuming that you were not paying any money for energy, health care, or education. These are things that most people cannot live without.

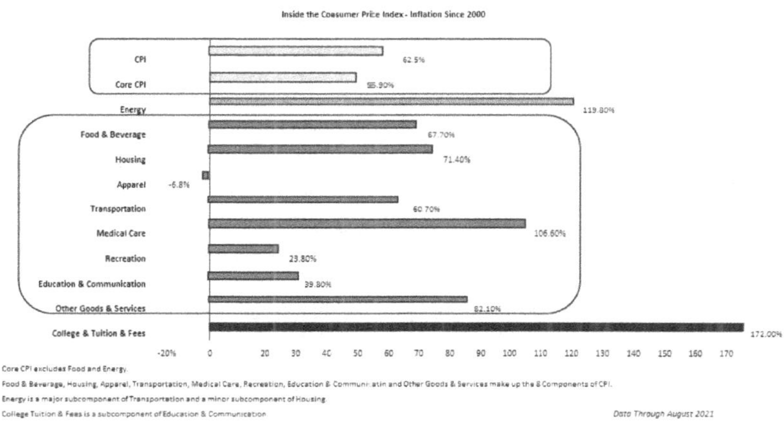

[197]

Let me now shine a light on a second issue with the way we measure inflation. As you can see from the following chart provided by Bloomberg and RSM, the biggest weighting in CPI is something known as owners' equivalent rent, OER, which makes up more than 23% of the index. Most people have never heard of OER.

The Bureau of Labor Statistics gets this number from doing a monthly phone survey. Respondents are asked if they rent or own their homes. Renters are asked how much they pay each month. Homeowners are asked what they would charge somebody to live in their home if it were empty and unfurnished. This makes this number completely subjective.[198]

Have you ever considered what you would charge to let somebody rent your home? And how likely is it that you have thought about whether you would raise or lower rent regularly? While most homeowners don't think much about these things, OER, which the Bureau of Labor Statistics reports monthly, comprises nearly a quarter of this inflation measurement.

It is hard to believe that in today's world of high-frequency data, where we can instantly tell how many people drove on the turnpike yesterday or how many people ate out at a restaurant last night in Cleveland, Ohio, the federal government still uses such an arcane and dated system to help determine such an economically significant number.

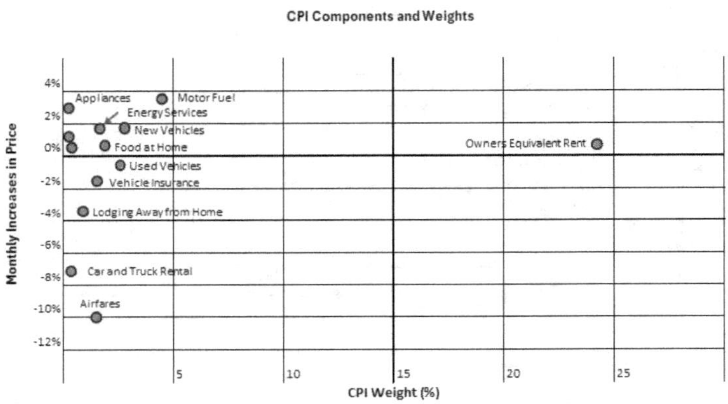

Source: BLS

199

Please review our next chart to see how much this number is disconnected from what is happening in the real world. It shows that in the first half of 2021, rents rose by more than 5% on a year-over-year basis. However, over the same time frame, the OER only went up 2.6%, nearly 3% less. This tells us that the largest component of CPI was underreported by almost 3% during that time. We now know that this measurement of inflation lags real-time data both on the way up and on the way down.

This means that the inflation measurements that economists and politicians watch closely and constantly discuss are substantially outdated. This leaves the Federal Reserve Bank, which is in charge of trying to maintain low and stable inflation, to rely on backward-looking data. This is akin to trying to drive a car down the highway while only looking in the rearview mirror. As I discussed earlier, this is not a wise idea.

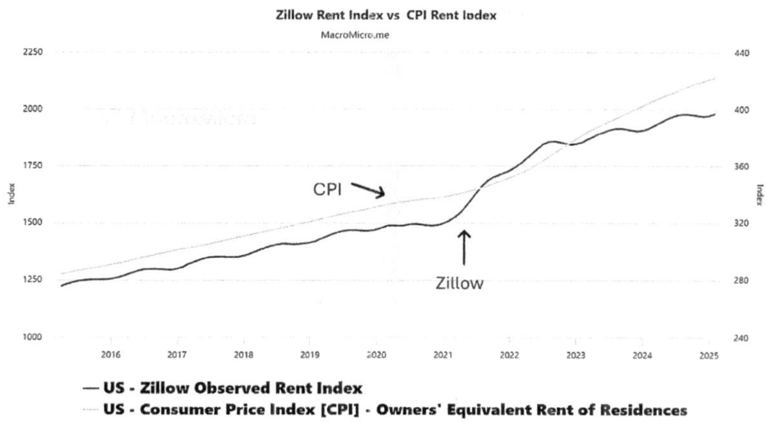

[200]

I am not saying that the government's reporting of these numbers is unethical or nefarious. I simply want you to know that there are substantial issues and distortions in the reported data in a very large and complex economy. My goal is for you to be informed as you read and hear about these issues in the media and online.

Did Inflation Go Metric?

Those of you who are old enough may remember that 1975 was a challenging and interesting time to be alive. We had recently closed the door on the Vietnam War and Watergate. We were anxiously looking forward to the U.S. Bicentennial celebration the following year. The stock market was starting to rebound from its biggest two-year drop since the Great Depression. We had recently come through the Arab oil embargo and the long gas lines that accompanied it. Inflation was starting to rage, and the misery index—which combines unemployment and inflation—was rising sharply.

To add to this stress, Congress passed the Metric Conversion Act of 1975, which declared the metric system "the preferred system of weights and measures for United States trade and commerce."[201] This was around the same time that many other countries were switching over to the metric system. At the time, I was 10 years old and in fourth grade. I loved all things related to math and was very comfortable with the imperial system, where things are measured in feet, inches, pounds, ounces, and so on. But suddenly, my teacher was talking about things such as kilometers, millimeters, liters, and grams. Unfortunately, instead of learning the absolutes of the new system, we were generally taught to compare things—kilometers to miles, yards to meters, and liters to quarts.

Use of the metric system never entirely caught on in the United States, and we are still one of only three countries in the world (along with Myanmar and Liberia—how's that for the company?) that have not fully adopted the metric system.[202]

In a similar fashion to trying to change to the metric system, and unbeknownst to most people, the U.S. Bureau of Labor Statistics has made several adjustments over the last 40 years to how it calculates inflation via the CPI. These have significantly affected the inflation rate reported each month, especially compared to what Americans feel and experience at the grocery store and gas pump.

As you can see from the following chart, inflation would have been significantly higher in 2021 if we had used the same methodology to calculate it in 1990 or 1980. Very few people know that these changes were made or how they affect the Bureau of Labor Statistics' monthly reporting. This change to the inflation calculation was similar to your child's teacher changed the grading scale on their report card without telling them what was needed to get an A.

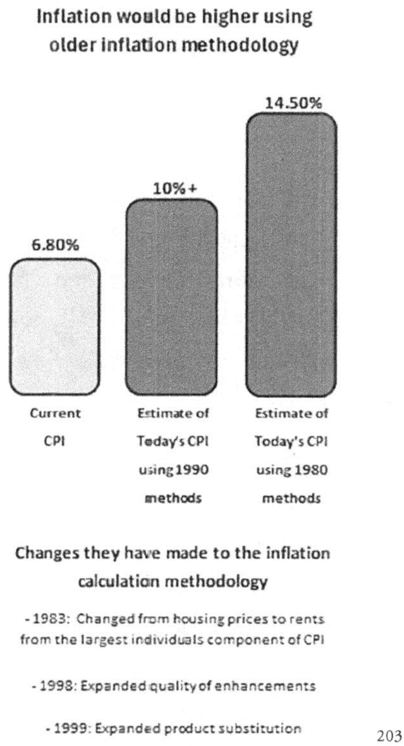

I will draw your attention to two major changes that were made and how they affect the numbers reported. First, in 1983, the Bureau of Labor Statistics changed how they measured the housing component of CPI, which makes up nearly 23% of the index, from the actual change in housing prices to OER, which we discussed previously.

This means that one of the most important pieces of data that is released every month is based on random phone calls to individuals, who do not have a firm idea or financial anchor for how much their home would really rent for. This astounds me every time I see this number discussed.

Then, in 1999, the formula was changed again to allow for expanded product substitution, the theory that, if a consumer were going to buy a product (say, steak) at the grocery store and the price was too high, they would likely purchase a cheaper product (say, ground beef) instead. By substituting ground beef for steak, the consumer spends less money, and inflation remains lower than the actual price increase at the cash register (do they still call them cash registers?).

As you can see in the chart, inflation was reported at 6.8% in December 2021. However, using the methodology used in 1980, the last time we experienced double-digit inflation, we would have had an inflation rate of 14.9%. That number coincides more realistically with what many people were experiencing when managing their cash flow and expenses in the post-COVID world.

In anecdotal conversations I had with two business owners during this time, they both shared extreme frustration with higher material and labor costs, which had risen dramatically since the pandemic. One told me that the price of copper wiring he had to purchase for his business had increased 300% in the past year. He also had to give his employees raises of $5 per hour or risk losing them to competitors. A restaurant owner I was talking with at the time said that he was going to have to raise menu prices for the third time that year. He feared that people would stop coming to his restaurant. He was also dealing with significant employee turnover due to wage pressures.

Looking at these government statistics makes me feel like I am back in my classroom in 1975. I understand things in terms of inches, pounds, and gallons, while my teachers are telling me that things are really measured in centimeters, kilograms, and liters. If you feel like the changes to the inflation calculations are akin to your own teacher from 1975 trying to teach you the metric system, you are not alone. There are changes taking place that no one told you about, and these affect your life every day.

Finally, we will examine what these inflation metrics mean to today's average consumer and retiree and discuss their significant impact on those at the lower end of the wage spectrum.

The Opposite of Robin Hood

Almost all of us have some picture in our heads of who Robin Hood is or what he represents. For our retired clients, this may come from seeing the swashbuckling Errol Flynn play the title character in the 1938 movie. Some people remember Kevin Costner's portrayal in 1991's *Robin Hood: Prince of Thieves*. I even remember Daffy Duck trying to convince Porky Pig that he was the hero in a 1958 Warner Bros. cartoon.

Whether you are a fan of Robin Hood or not, it seems like he has been working in reverse. While Robin Hood is known for stealing from the rich to give to the poor, right now inflation is taking the most from the poor, who have limited resources. And the results are annoying more people than just Princess Fiona, who famously clocked Robin Hood during his dance routine in the first *Shrek* movie from 2001. Many people have rightly been frustrated by the growing income, wealth, and education inequality in our world today. We have seen these disparities grow over the last 20 years during both times of economic growth and economic downturn. These patterns have continued during both Democratic and Republican presidencies, regardless of who controls Congress.

According to data from the Federal Reserve Bank, from 2008 to 2020, incomes for those in the bottom 20% of wage earners grew by 33.6%. During the same time, incomes for the top 5% rose by 53.1%.[204] From a wealth standpoint, the top 1% of all households saw their wealth increase by nearly $4 trillion during the COVID year of 2020. This means that of all the wealth created in 2020, 35% went to the top 1% of wealthy households, while the bottom half captured approximately 4% of the newly created wealth.

This has now been exacerbated by rising inflation, driven mainly by higher food and fuel costs. This disproportionately hurts those at the lower end of the income and wealth spectrum because these costs comprise a higher percentage of their expenses. This is even more pronounced in poorer countries, where inflation has caused the price of food to rise so high that it has plunged millions of people into famine. It appears that inflation is harming everyone.

What was the Fed's response to this rising inflation? It raised interest rates aggressively. This slowed the growth of the real estate market. The bond market dropped in value by double digits, and the stock market declined by more than 20%. These actions combined to significantly harm the wealth of those at the top of the ladder.

It seems that right now, the Fed and the financial markets are acting as the anti-Robin Hood. They are taking from the rich, but it is not helping the poor at all. It would be great if people from both sides of the aisle and those in charge of our economy would focus on creating policies that would help. Everyone feels the pain, albeit to different degrees and in various ways.

It would be great if we could see a focus on longer-term structural policies that would address these problems over time. Investing in education, job training, housing, and infrastructure would likely affect people's income and wealth far more than raising interest or tax rates.

Unfortunately, there are no easy answers. More than 20 years of excess have led to only hard answers. Thinking back to *Shrek,* Princess Fiona's attempt to remove an arrow that had struck Shrek's behind caused him significant discomfort, and he told her that what she was doing was the opposite of help. It seems that many governmental and economic policies are doing the same thing to us—giving us all a giant pain in the behind.

Contrast this with my professional study group. I have been blessed to regularly meet with a group of some of the top financial advisors in the country. These are people who could be considered my competition. Yet, instead of taking a scarcity mentality and trying to protect our own pieces of a finite pie, we have an abundance mentality. We genuinely believe that by sharing our best ideas and best practices with each other, we can make the pie bigger for everyone.

I wish leaders at a higher level of government and the economy would take notice and do something similar. Instead of trying to divvy up a finite economic pie, we should be trying to make the pie bigger so that everyone can benefit. *What we need is a Robin Hood that allows everyone to participate in a growing economy.* The goal should be to create prosperity that everyone shares in. I hope that, eventually, we can move toward these types of solutions for the good of everyone in our society.

Periods of high inflation can be particularly challenging for retirees living on a fixed income. Just as the Colorado River slowly ate away at the bedrock to create the Grand Canyon, it sometimes feels like ongoing price increases are eating away at the financial resources we worked so hard to accumulate. While you want to float downstream toward your ideal retirement life, the impact of inflation may make it feel like you are paddling against the current.

I hope this chapter's exploration of this vital topic has given you a better understanding of one of the forces you will have to contend with to create the retirement life you envision. We will now move on to our next puzzle piece, which may surprise you: the challenge of aging demographics and low birth rates. It appears that these two forces are combining to create another hurdle for those hoping to create a retirement of significance. Let's explore this together.

PUZZLE PIECE

#11

The Challenge of Aging Demographics and Low Birth Rates

"Demographics are destiny." This phrase was coined by Richard Scammon and Ben Wattenberg in the book *The Real Majority*.[205] We know that evolving age dynamics can have a profound impact on growth, social norms, and political views. They can influence how people save, spend, and invest, with consequences for everything from marriage to retirement to migration. We are watching this play out in real time both in the United States and in other countries around the globe.

Here at home, we are dealing with both sides of the coin. Aging demographics indicate that more people are entering their retirement years than we have ever seen before. These citizens have paid into entitlement programs for their entire working lives and are counting on the benefits promised to them by Social Security and Medicare. However, due to the lower population sizes of younger generations, fewer young people are working and thus contributing payroll taxes to support these programs. This means that at some point down the road, something has to give.

We also know that people in the millennial and Gen Z generations are waiting much longer to get married and start families. They are also not having enough babies to keep our population growing. Population growth is one of the two key components needed to expand GDP. In this chapter, we will explore how the combination of an aging population and low birth rates is creating the perfect demographic storm that our citizens will have to weather over the coming decades.

David Rosenberg, the chief economist of Rosenberg Research, has shown that birth rates in the United States have fallen dramatically over the last 40 years. We also now have a much older population. Fifteen years ago, just over 10% of the United States population was above age 65. Within the decade that followed, we see this growing toward 20% in the near future. You may wonder why this is important. Consumer spending life cycles show that as people age, their spending tends to slowly decline. This suggests less potential economic growth in the future.

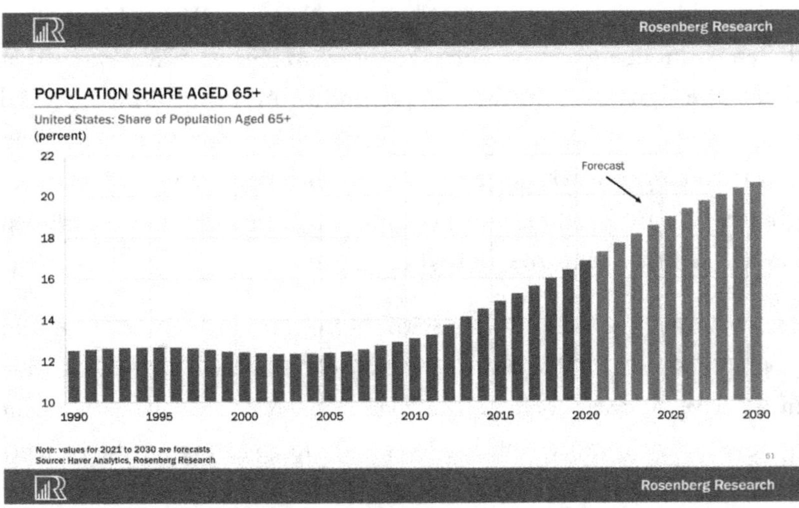

206

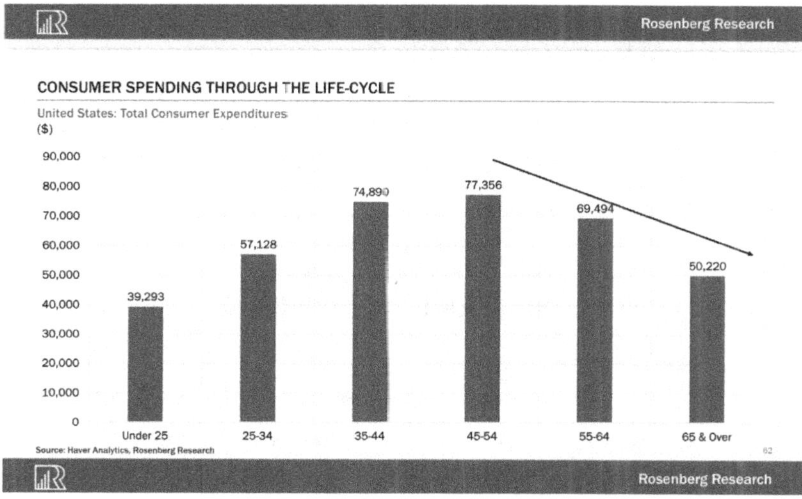

[207]

As CFPs, we build retirement plan projections for our clients based on very conservative assumptions that they will continue to spend at the same rate throughout their retirement, but the above chart shows what I have anecdotally observed over the last 35 years. As people age, they tend to spend less.

Numerous studies, as well as what I have observed in working with dozens of client families through the years, indicate that people spend at their peak levels during their first 10 years of retirement.[208] This makes sense. People are excited about this new phase of life. They are also younger and healthier than they will be in the future (unfortunately, aging happens to all of us). This means that, during this time, they travel more, play more golf, eat out more, and spend more money on entertainment such as sporting events, theater shows, or concerts.

These same studies show that in years 11 through 20 of retirement, people tend to spend approximately $0.87 for every dollar that they spent during their first 10 years. They also show that those who live to years 21 through 30 of retirement tend to spend approximately $0.70 on the dollar when compared to those early days postretirement.[209] These numbers are consistent with the trends in our previous chart.

Let's examine these demographic trends more comprehensively and explore what they will mean for the economy and for those of you hoping to enjoy your retirement years soon.

Let's Talk About "My Generation"

From my perspective, two important events occurred in October 1965. First, on October 5th, I was born. Later that same month, The Who released their classic song "My Generation." They later performed the song on the *Smothers Brothers* TV show and nearly blew up the set.

Written by Pete Townshend, "My Generation" is a song of youthful rebellion. The song's message indicates that the writer hopes to die before they get old. Anecdotally, unlike so many other tragic rock 'n' roll figures such as Jimi Hendrix, Jim Morrison, and The Who's own Keith Moon, Pete, who is nearing age 80, did not die before he got old. As a matter of fact, I recently got an email stating that he and Roger Daltrey, the other remaining original member of The Who, are going out on a farewell tour—again.

What does this have to do with economics? A lot, actually. Economic activity is largely driven by the spending patterns of people of different age groups and different demographic groups. In the next chart, you will notice that the older members of the baby boomer generation are now approaching their mid-70s and starting to pass away in greater numbers.

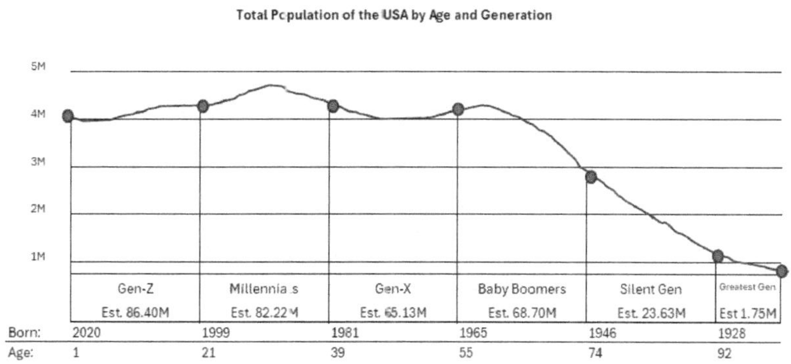

[210]

As we have discussed many times, this group has had an outsized impact on economic activity in the United States for decades. Originally numbering 76 million people, as of 2020, there were approximately 68.7 million of them remaining.

While Gen X, which was born from 1965 to 1981, is a smaller cohort, the millennials and Gen Z generations coming up behind are significantly larger. The mantle of spending money and accumulating wealth is now being passed on to the next generations.

As we look way out into the future, where do we see these trends going on a global basis? The next chart shows the recent population and the projected calendar year 2100 population for a number of countries. You can see that the United States population is projected to stay relatively stable over this time frame.

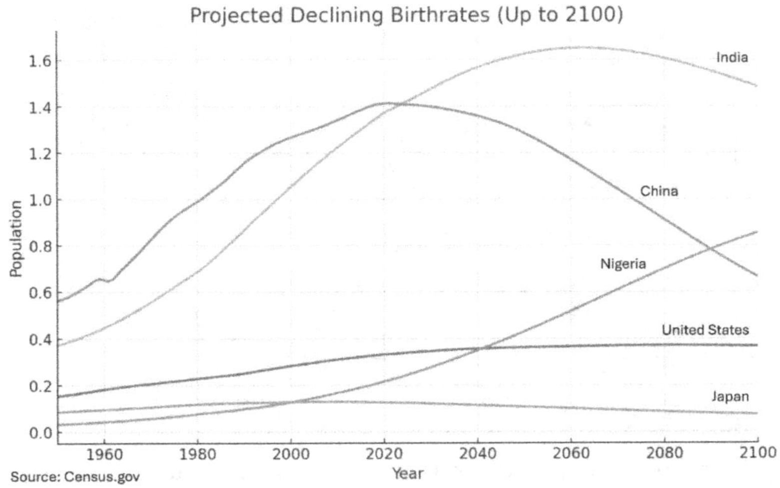

[211]

What immediately jumps off the page is the substantial population shrinkage that is projected to take place in China. This is primarily due to decades of the one-child policy, which is leading China to become both an aging and declining population force rapidly (we will explore this in more detail in the next section). You can see a similar but less severe population shrinkage in India.

Since China entered the World Trade Organization in December 2001, China's economy has grown to become the second largest globally.[212] Its ability to create low-cost goods, primarily due to low-wage labor, drove many of the lower inflation trends we experienced between the '08 financial crisis and the 2020 COVID-19 pandemic. As GDP growth is equal to population growth plus productivity growth, it will be difficult for China to continue to be a driver of global growth going forward.

That torch may be passed to other countries and economies in the future. As you can see in the chart above, Nigeria's population is projected to nearly triple over that same timeline. As stated above, population growth is a major factor in GDP growth, so it will be interesting to see what impact these population trends will have on future wealth creation.

While 80 years in the future seems like a long time away, looking at past events gives us a better lens through which to view this. It has been over 90 years since we were in the depths of the Great Depression. It was also more than 80 years ago that Pearl Harbor was bombed, propelling us into World War II.

Amid the day-to-day news, noise, social media posts, and tweets, keeping an eye on these longer-term trends should be interesting and should inform our long-term asset allocation decisions. Whether we are talking about my generation, your generation, or future generations, this should give you a different way to see the big picture.

Let's continue exploring how these aging demographic trends might affect economic spending patterns and the allocation of our finite resources, such as commercial real estate.

From Shopping Malls to Nursing Homes

In 1967, I was two years old. Those of you who live in Northeast Ohio will remember that this was the year that Chapel Hill Mall opened on the border of Cuyahoga Falls and North Akron. A few years later, in 1975, Rolling Acres Mall opened at the border of Akron and Barberton. As the parents of the baby boomers migrated toward the suburbs, and as transportation became more affordable for those families, these new shopping malls allowed families to have unique and varied shopping experiences, all within the confines of one geographic location.

213

For me and other members of the Stow High School class of '84, shopping malls were a very important meeting place. In addition to the food court, they also housed many of the movie theaters where we gathered to see everything from *Jaws* to *Star Wars* to *Back to the Future.*

As we moved toward the late '90s, new opportunities to shop became available with widespread access to the internet. The shiny retail behemoths, which had only been created 30 to 40 years earlier, eventually began to shut down after the Global Financial Crisis in the late 2000s. The last store at Rolling Acres Mall shut down in 2008, and Chapel Hill Mall finally gave up the ghost in 2021 after struggling for many years from a decline in both traffic and the quality of its stores. After 2016, visiting was a scary experience, and it no longer resembled the mall from my childhood.

Then something else started popping up en masse in place of the former malls. As our population continued to age, we started seeing nursing homes and assisted living facilities dot the landscape. My wife and I live on the border of Stow and Hudson, Ohio, and there are easily more than half a dozen of these facilities within a two-mile radius of our home. Many of these did not exist before 2010.

This has happened while the population of the United States has continued to grow. When Chapel Hill Mall opened in 1967, the U.S. population was just under 200 million people.[214] Today, the U.S. population is just over 341 million people.[215] Given the fact that birth rates in the United States have continued to decline, it is amazing that our population has grown by more than 140 million people over the last five decades. Even more amazing is the fact that between now and the end of the century, the U.S. population is expected to continue growing, albeit at a much slower pace.[216]

The population of many countries is projected to decline over the next 75 years. This is true even in places with large populations, such as China. You will likely remember that in 1980, the Chinese government implemented a one-child policy. Due to the fear of overpopulation, the Chinese government kept this policy in place until 2016. As a result, China has an uneven population distribution that is very top-heavy toward its rapidly aging segments. Their younger population is not growing quickly enough to support its elders.

The risk is that the Chinese economy may be heading toward a fertility-led depression. Since the onset of the COVID-19 pandemic, China's consumers have experienced a significant negative wealth effect, as they have seen drops in the value of their homes and stock portfolios. This has led to a drop in sentiment and confidence and a reduction in consumer spending.

As a result, young Chinese families are having fewer babies than at any point in the last 50 years, even though the one-child policy no longer exists. In 2022, there were only 950,000 births in China, the lowest ever recorded. This represents 50% fewer babies than just 10 years ago. You will note in our next chart that the fertility rate, which shows the number of births per woman, has been below 2.0 since 1991. In 2021 it dropped to an all-time low of 1.16. There are not enough children being born to replace the aging population.

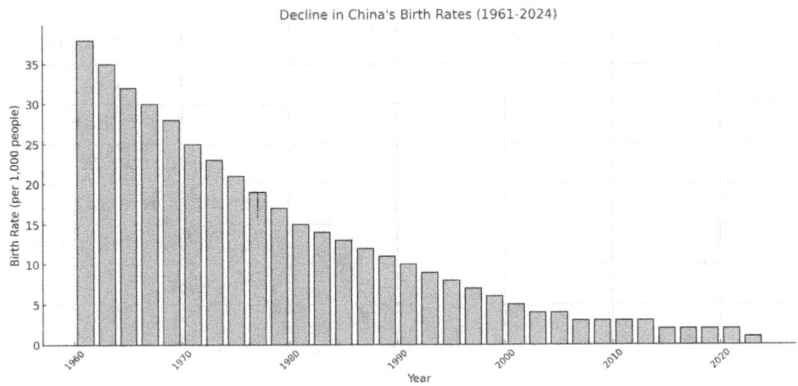

[217]

In both 2022 and 2023, China saw its population decline as it recorded more deaths than births. This is the first time China has seen a decline in population since 1961.[218] We know that GDP growth is equal to population growth and productivity. For many years, people have been concerned that China's economy was going to overtake that of the United States. We heard similar prognostications about Japan in the late '70s and early '80s. It is hard to imagine China's economy continuing to grow at a rapid pace while its population is declining.

China's population decline led Ed Yardeni, one of my favorite economists and market strategists, to author an article entitled "China: The World's Largest Nursing Home," which was published in November 2023.[219] I do not know how many shopping malls, such as Chapel Hill or Rolling Acres, were built in China during the 1960s or 1970s. However, based on demographic trends, more nursing homes and assisted living facilities may soon be popping up in China than in the United States.

We know that the large number of people moving toward retirement means that the United States government is going to have to spend a bigger percentage of the tax dollars it collects on mandatory entitlement programs, including Social Security and Medicare. Let's review how these mandatory spending dollars are affecting the allocation of the government's finite resources and what is left for discretionary spending to provide for the rest of our citizens.

A Different Government Mandate?

Since the onset of the COVID-19 pandemic, there has certainly been a lot of talk and debate about government mandates. We have dealt with vaccine mandates, mask mandates, remote school and work mandates, and more.

However, in this section, I would like to address a different type of government mandate: mandatory government spending. The government spends a significant and growing portion of the tax dollars it takes in on mandated entitlement programs, including Social Security, Medicare, and Medicaid.

The next chart shows the significant impact of this mandatory spending, especially as baby boomers age and the interest paid on our ever-growing national debt continues to balloon.

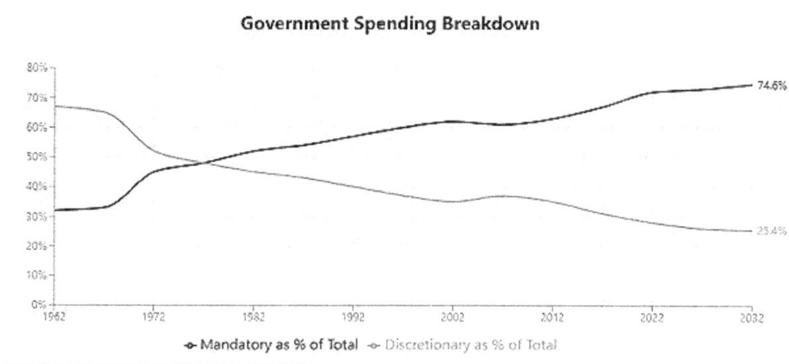

220

You can see that in the early 1960s, mandatory spending accounted for approximately one-third of the money the government paid out. This left two-thirds of tax receipts to invest in things that would generate future growth or infrastructure for the benefit of our country's residents.

In what is a disturbing trend that shows no sign of reversing, that fractional amount has completely flip-flopped. We are now spending approximately two-thirds of our tax dollars on entitlement programs and interest on the debt. These dollars are projected to grow from approximately two-thirds to three-quarters of our government spending in just the next 10 years.

It is important to note that much of our government debt has been financed by interest rates held artificially low for the dozen years following the onset of the Global Financial Crisis. But, now that the Federal Reserve Bank has begun an aggressive campaign of raising interest rates to fight rising and persistent inflation, the cost of interest on the federal debt will potentially skyrocket in the coming years.

This gap will continue to grow in the future as our population continues to age and as the baby boomer generation retires. Unfortunately, this demographic trend of a large number of older workers retired or retiring soon, along with smaller younger generations, is also hitting much of Europe and Japan.

I have always taken the position that I am short on government but long on humanity, innovation, and technology. These have brought great benefits to our society and our economy over time. We will have to pay close attention to these trends over the coming years. There are no easy answers, and as Fed chairman Jay Powell recently said in a speech from Jackson Hole, Wyoming, there will likely be shared pain for people across the country as we address these difficult issues.[221]

It is important for us to be aware of and understand trends and demographics as we move through the next decade. Trends and demographics are like a steamship or aircraft carrier—they move very slowly over time. While previously promised entitlement programs may not be a government mandate, it is spending that the government has committed to, and this will affect all of us in the future.

So, what options do we have to fill the gap created by the compounded effects of an aging population demanding more government resources and a younger population not producing enough babies to keep the population and tax revenues growing to meet the government's obligations?

One option is to rely on productivity gains from new technologies such as robotics and generative AI. While we think this will be part of the solution, we will likely also continue to rely on immigration. The United States has always been known as a country of immigrants.

Unless you are of Native American descent, your ancestors came here from somewhere else. My ancestry is primarily northern European, particularly English and German. My wife's family is from southern Europe and the Caribbean, with a few other pieces and parts sprinkled in for good measure. This is typical of our U.S. melting pot. Let's explore what the potential impact of more legal immigration could be on our economic growth.

Do We Want Growing Pains or Labor Pains?

I have avoided writing about the relationship between immigration and the labor market for several years due to the topic's politically charged nature. I will do my best to keep this discussion at an economic and mathematical level and not get into the public policy side of things.

Growing Pains was an ABC sitcom that aired from 1985 to 1992. The show ran for seven seasons and had 166 episodes. The series centered on the Seaver family, who lived on Long Island in New York.

The show ended up focusing much of its time and attention on the family's ornery son, Mike, played by Kirk Cameron. Mike was a lovable goofball who did not take life or school too seriously. While *Family Ties'* Alex P. Keaton was worried about the stock market and what was going on with politics, Mike and his friends Eddie and Boner showed a much simpler and goofier side of teenage life. Personally, I identified much more closely with Alex, but Mike seemed to have a lot more fun.

Currently, in the United States, we are living with a different type of growing pains, one that comes from demographics and is not easily fixed by any political policy. I opened our chapter with the old adage "Demographics are destiny." This is due to the fact that you must have population growth to have GDP or economic growth. As a matter of fact, the formula for GDP growth is as follows: Workforce growth (which is driven by population growth) × productivity growth = economic growth.

In short, if you don't have enough babies being born to keep your workforce growing, it is hard to have enough productivity growth to keep your economy moving forward. This is one of the reasons the AI revolution is potentially so important—it could increase our productivity dramatically while our population or workforce is growing much more slowly.

While artificial intelligence productivity gains may help this situation, if our birth rate does not pick up, one logical solution is to have more people of working age come into the country. As mentioned previously, the United States has historically been built on (legal) immigration.

One of the great concerns that U.S. citizens have is that lower-paid migrant workers could take the jobs of people born in the United States. Our next chart validates this, showing that from 2019 to 2023, foreign-born workers gained approximately 2.5 million jobs, while people born in the United States have cumulatively lost 1.3 million jobs over the same time frame.

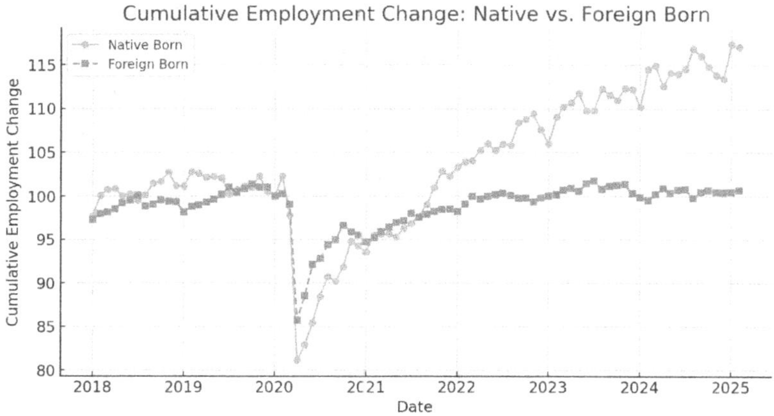

[222]

There are massive issues around border protection and legal versus illegal immigration. We will leave these to the politicians to solve for now. However, I wanted to frame the mathematical and economic numbers so that you have a better understanding of the overall issue.

Unless we adequately address the worker shortfall through higher birth rates, technology-driven productivity gains, better immigration policies, or some combination of the three, we will continue to face the struggle between labor pains and growing pains. Unfortunately, watching politicians grapple with this will not be nearly as fun as watching Mike and his friends on an episode of *Growing Pains.*

Finally, I would like to turn to a different issue that is affecting families in this time of aging demographics. That issue is the impact that caring for aging or ill parents or spouses is having on families.

After leaving Boston and the familiarity of his friends, Frasier Crane (of *Cheers* fame) moves to his hometown of Seattle to host a radio show. Frasier's aging father, Martin, moves in with him. Luckily, Frasier has the help of Martin's live-in caregiver, Daphne, to assist with his aging father's care.

Similarly, I was introduced to the topic of caring for an aging parent in the late 1980s when my client Frasier decided to take in his own father, who was suffering from Alzheimer's. Frasier was an only child, loved his dad, and felt obligated to care for him, even though he was still working. After Frasier moved his dad into his rather small two-bedroom condo, his dad went downhill rapidly for approximately six months. Then he plateaued for more than a year. He subsequently got pneumonia and passed away a few months later. The nearly two-year ordeal drained Frasier physically, emotionally, and financially. Unfortunately, I have seen this play out many times in different families over the last 35 years.

Let's review the potential impact caretaking can have on you and your family. These situations can cause significant strain and can also affect the quality of life you aspire to during your retirement years.

Our Back Pages

According to Wikipedia, "'My Back Pages' is a song written by Bob Dylan and included on his 1964 album *Another Side of Bob Dylan*....[The song] has been covered by artists as diverse as Keith Jarrett, the Byrds, the Ramones, the Nice, Steve Earle, Eric Johnson, and the Hollies. The Byrds' version, initially released on their 1967 album *Younger Than Yesterday*, was also issued as a single in 1967 and proved to be the band's last Top 40 hit in the U.S.[223]

Many believe that the lyrics show that Dylan had become disillusioned with the 1960s protest movement and that he intended to abandon that style of songwriting. The song is known for its repeated lament, in reverse chronological order, that the writer was a lot older then but is younger now.

Per Wikipedia, "At the 30th Anniversary Tribute Concert to Dylan at Madison Square Garden in 1992, 'My Back Pages' was performed in the Byrds' arrangement, with Roger McGuinn, Tom Petty, Neil Young, Eric

Clapton, Dylan himself, and George Harrison, all singing one verse in that order. This performance, which featured vocals from all six musicians, along with guitar solos by Clapton and Young...was released on *The 30th Anniversary Concert Celebration* album in 1993."[224] It can also be found on YouTube.

As incredible as the performance was and no matter how catchy the refrain is (I ended up singing and whistling it around the house all day when I wrote this, much to my wife's dismay), the rest of us tend to age in the more predictable order below.

As a matter of fact, United States demographic trends show that in 2024, our country hit a demographic milestone. According to statistics from the U.S. Census Bureau's population projections, during that year, the baby boomer population had 4.4 million people, or approximately 12,000 people per day, reach age 65.[225] This large number of people entering into both Medicare and Social Security is creating unique challenges for our rapidly aging society.

One such challenge is that many people are regularly serving as unpaid caregivers for their parents, grandparents, or spouses. As you can see next, just under 15% of our adult population, or approximately 37.1 million Americans, spends at least one hour a day as unpaid care providers. Simple math tells us that this is the financial equivalent of several million workers missing from the U.S. labor force.

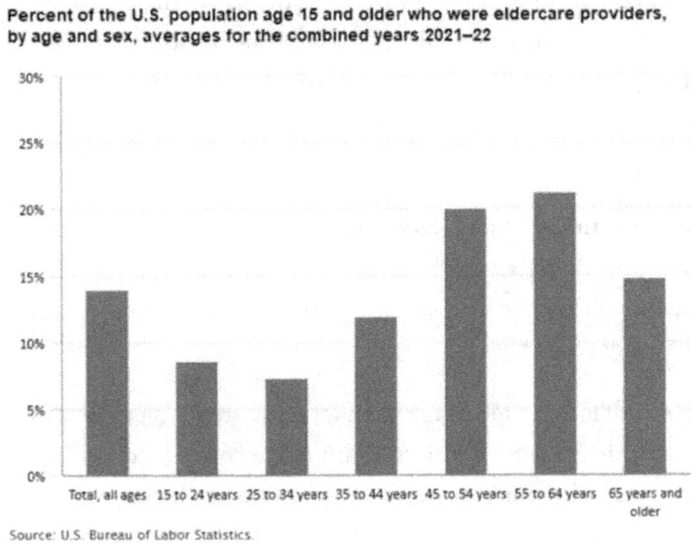

Source: BLS 226

This can create stress on both the individual caregiver and their family. Even if they feel called to provide care for their loved ones, it can be physically and emotionally draining. It also means that they are not present with the rest of their family for important moments or events.

From an economic standpoint, this is actually reducing GDP growth. The hours spent working as a volunteer do not show up in any government statistics. This also means that paid caregivers are not providing the service, slowing our national economic growth and reducing our national earned income.

Over the last 35 years, I have watched as clients deal with these situations while caring for sick or aging parents, grandparents, or spouses. The decision to become an unpaid caregiver can be driven by multiple factors. The first is the desire to care for the family members you love and keep them at home as long as possible. This is a beautiful and caring gesture. However, caregiver burnout is a real thing, and I have watched many clients who had the best of intentions to care for their spouse or other relative end up getting exhausted, injured, or both, trying to care for their loved one.

Some people make this decision because of the cost of long-term care in an assisted living facility or memory care unit. As you can see from the following chart, which includes data through 2021, the cost of these facilities has risen steadily and significantly over time.

Source: https://www.genworth.com/aging-and-you/finances/cost-of-care/cost-of-care-trends-and-insights

I know from recent conversations with clients that the cost of these facilities in the Northeast Ohio area is currently running anywhere from $5,000 to $7,500 per month depending on the level of care needed. It is important to remember that ancillary services such as medication management can be over and above this amount. This can add up to $60,000–$90,000 per year, which can deplete a family's hard-earned savings very quickly and leave the healthy or surviving family member with depleted resources and in a dangerous financial position in the future.

You can see that many factors contribute to choosing to be an unpaid caregiver. These can include positive emotional inputs such as devotion, love, and a desire to serve. The decision can also be driven by guilt or fear of financial loss. It is important to understand the emotional and financial drivers in the decision-making process so that you can make the best choice for your loved one and the rest of your family.

As we all continue to move toward our own back pages, we see the opposite of what Bob Dylan wrote: we were so much younger then, but we're older than that now. We are all moving down the road of aging, life, and health, and it is important to recognize what this means from a family and financial standpoint. I thought this was an important reminder to share for those of you who find yourself facing these challenges or in the midst of them.

I hope that this chapter gave you a lot to think about. Understanding the challenges that both aging demographics and low birth rates pose to the U.S. economy and to future retirees is an extremely important piece of the puzzle. This is a complex topic with many moving and intertwined parts. Unfortunately, politics and government policy will definitely influence these areas as we move forward.

We are now going to move to a much more fun discussion as we move to "Puzzle Piece #12: Permission to Spend—Enjoying Retirement Life." As we put the last pieces of our puzzle in place, it should give us the confidence to use the income and asset resources we have accumulated to do the things that bring us joy in our retirement years. Let's turn the page and enjoy the journey.

PUZZLE PIECE

#12

Permission to Spend—Enjoying Retirement Life

It's time to have some fun! This is the chapter you have been waiting for. We are going to explore the topics of spending money and enjoying life.

Over the preceding 11 puzzle pieces, we have discussed serious and complex financial, economic, and investment issues. Hopefully, you will agree that we were able to do this in a unique and fun way.

Now let's set the stage for our next topic. I want to bring back something I mentioned in Puzzle Piece #2. In the history of mankind, we have only ever figured out three things that you can do with money: *save it, spend it,* or *give it away.* Throughout the book, I've guided you on how to accumulate the resources you need to enjoy a retirement of significance—in other words, how to *save* enough during your working years so you can enjoy your best retirement life. This chapter is about empowering you with the freedom to choose how you use your money.

Another key point we discussed in Puzzle Piece #2 was the importance of creating a vision for what you will retire to, not just what you will retire from. Now, 10 chapters later, you've reached that point. You have put in the hard work, been diligent and intentional with your saving and investment plans, and accumulated the resources necessary to enjoy this next phase of life, pursuing the activities you love with the people you care about. This is your inspiration and your motivation for the future.

Now I am going to share some stories and principles about giving yourself permission to spend what you have built in order to enjoy this next phase of life. By the way, if you have saved enough, there are only two things left that you can do with your money: *spend it* or *give it away*. I will explore both options in this chapter.

While spending money sounds like fun, it is more difficult for many people than you might imagine. You see, habits become ingrained in people over long periods of time. If you spent three or four decades living a disciplined financial life so that you could create the wealth you will need to enjoy a great retirement, you have likely hardwired certain behaviors into your belief system.

Unfortunately, I have many clients who have been very successful in the accumulation phase of life. Yet they have a hard time flipping the switch and changing their behavior patterns so that they can enjoy the fruits of their efforts. This may sound strange to you, but I can assure you it is a real phenomenon.

The thought process goes something like this: "I have accumulated these resources because I did these behaviors over many years. The compounded effects of these habits allowed me to build more wealth than I ever thought I would have. However, if I change my behaviors and start spending instead of saving, the resources I worked so hard to accumulate might start to disappear."

Things That Make You Go Hmmm...

According to Wikipedia, "'Things That Make You Go Hmmm...' is a song by American dance group C+C Music Factory. It was released in June

1991 as the third single from their debut album, *Gonna Make You Sweat* (1990)....The song was inspired by a running gag on *The Arsenio Hall Show*, where Arsenio, while allegedly on a long drive, pondered certain thoughts and referred to them as "things that make you go hmmm...'"[228]

[229]

Given the state of today's world, all kinds of things could make you go hmmm. This becomes obvious when we look at our political divides, our society's economic and wealth disparities, and the passion with which people fight with others they barely know—or don't know at all—on social media platforms.

Today, like Arsenio Hall, I will explore one of the great questions I ponder: Why is it so hard to get many of our clients comfortable with spending money they have worked so hard to save?

Of course, this does not apply to everyone. Many of my clients spend at reasonable levels and achieve their cash flow and standard of living goals based on their assets and income resources. I also have a few who spend aggressively. I regularly have to discuss pumping the brakes with those clients and maintaining a sustainable withdrawal rate throughout their life expectancy. (If you're one of those clients and you're reading this, you know who you are.)

However, more than a third of my clients have resources beyond their needs, but they still struggle with spending these excess resources for their own enjoyment today, helping their kids or grandkids with current life needs, or having the peace of mind to be generous to others through charitable giving. (Once again, if you're one of those clients and you're reading this, you know who you are.)

Why is this? Great question. I firmly believe that much of it is rooted in habits formed during the accumulation phase of life. As I have mentioned previously, there are several habits that clients who are successful savers and accumulators tend to share:

- No matter what they make, they spend less than that, saving and investing the difference.
- They pay down debt quickly.
- They don't make impulse purchase decisions based on credit for things they don't really need.
- They don't make irrational investment decisions based on the latest tips they got at the golf course or the beauty shop or through some online blog.

Unsurprisingly, over long periods of time, these good habits can lead to the successful accumulation of wealth. Unfortunately, these same habits can cause people not to feel comfortable flipping the switch when they retire and spending the funds they worked so hard to accumulate for the things they want in this next phase of life.

Referring back to the BlackRock study from Puzzle Piece #2 reveals several important themes and lessons. One of the most important is that many retirees prefer not to touch their principal. They would rather feel financially secure than try to live it up during early retirement, when they are healthier and have more energy.[230]

This confirms my earlier thought process that saving and accumulation habits die hard. Many retirees fear that they may experience a financial or medical shock that could cause them to deplete their funds. There is also a general concern that they could outlive their money if they don't keep saving.

Another interesting finding was that retirees with defined benefit pension plans, much like many of our parents had, have more consistent income and, therefore, are less likely to spend down their assets. The study found that only 25% of retirees with pensions are likely to touch their savings. Meanwhile, 55% of people without pensions dipped into their retirement savings assets.[231]

The study also found that men and women approach their finances in retirement differently. Women tend to be more risk-averse and have higher levels of financial worry than men. These concerns are not without basis, as women often outlive their husbands and have longer life expectancies. This causes them to worry more about depleting their assets.[232]

Finally, think about everything we have lived through over the last 25 years from a financial and economic standpoint. The dot-com bubble, 9/11, the failure of AIG and Lehman Brothers, and COVID have caused many recent retirees to have less optimism and report higher levels of anxiety than people who retired many years ago.

We work hard to develop financial plans that give people the confidence to save and accumulate what they need to make a successful transition from work life to retirement life. We then want them to have the confidence to spend these hard-earned resources on the things that bring them joy and fulfillment during their retirement years.

There have been many times when I have observed a client's estate after they passed and wondered why they had so much money at the end. Why didn't they enjoy life more along the way? After more than 35 years as a financial planner, I find this is still undoubtedly one of the "things that make me go hmmm."

Sometimes, clients don't spend their money simply because they are afraid to. Sometimes, it is because they wait too long to start enjoying things and then life, family, or health interfere when they are finally ready to spend. There is only a certain window when you can use the gifts of time, health, and resources. If something happens to any one of those three, life changes.

Sophia: Save It for Later

The English Beat came out of Birmingham, England, in 1978. They were a New Wave band that fused pop, soul, punk, and reggae. Their first single was a cover of Smokey Robinson and the Miracles' "Tears of a Clown." The band was very popular in England and Australia. They also had a big following in the United States, largely thanks to the early days of MTV. According to Wikipedia, "The Beat toured the world with well-known artists including David Bowie, The Clash, The Police, The Pretenders, R.E.M., The Specials and Talking Heads."[233]

"Save It for Later" is my favorite English Beat song. It was released in 1982 on the band's album *Special Beat Service*. It is a very fun and catchy tune that you should look up on YouTube or your favorite streaming service if you're not familiar with it. The song has also been covered by Pete Townshend of The Who and Eddie Vedder of Pearl Jam. While the song's lyrics have nothing to do with our first topic, the song title leads us perfectly to my client Sophia, who did not have the same sense of humor as her *Golden Girls* namesake but certainly fits the character's age demographic.

Sophia was referred to me by her daughter in 1994. Sophia's daughter was a schoolteacher who was concerned that her mom was not using her income or asset resources in a way that allowed her to enjoy her retirement years. Sophia was a 78-year-old widow who primarily lived on her Social Security benefits and a very small pension that totaled approximately $1,500 per month or $18,000 per year.

In addition to her income sources, Sophia had approximately $400,000 in four checking accounts distributed among four separate banks. To make things worse, two of the checking accounts were non-interest-bearing. It is important to remember that at that time, the FDIC insurance limit was $100,000 per person. It is even more important to know that Sophia had been a teenager when the Great Depression hit. The painful memories from those years affected her financial habits and beliefs for the rest of her life.

Cumulatively, Sophia was earning approximately 1.25% interest on the $400,000 she had in the various banks. To help put this in context, in 1994, 10-year Treasury bonds were paying north of 6% interest. Shorter-term liquid investments, such as Treasury bills and short-term corporate bonds, were paying more than 4% interest at the time.

I shared this with Sophia and suggested that we move approximately $300,000 of her money to these liquid, low-volatility instruments. She could leave the rest in the bank for liquidity and to have the peace of mind of FDIC insurance. I showed her that earning 4% interest on this money would allow her to get $12,000 per year, or an additional $1,000 per month, of interest income. This, along with her pension and Social Security, would allow her to enjoy a higher quality of life.

We talked about what she might use the extra money for. She talked about getting new carpet for her condo, taking an Alaskan cruise, or replacing her aging automobile. And then she said something that has stuck with me for the next 30 years. She looked at me and said, "But Jesse, you don't understand. I can't spend that money on those things...because *I might need it later when I'm old.*"

I tried to assure her that she would still have all her principal available. I also reminded her as gently as I could that she was already 78 years old. If she didn't start enjoying some of the money now, she might never get the chance. Unfortunately, Sophia passed away at age 84 and never spent a dime of the money she had worked so hard to accumulate.

This had a profound effect on me as a young CFP. I made it my mission to use the financial planning process to help people like Sophia gain enough confidence to enjoy their wealth and their retirement years. Sophia was an extreme example, but throughout my career, I have had many clients who struggled to switch from saving to spending. I continue to coach and encourage clients to embrace a new thought process and new spending habits in this next phase of life.

Financial success during retirement is all about having enough cash flow to do the things that make life enjoyable. Some clients embrace this thought process more aggressively than they probably should. They want to enjoy life while they are young and healthy enough to do so. I caution them that there is a very real risk that comes with spending at such an aggressive rate. It is *never* fun to run out of money before you run out of life.

Sometimes, clients just want to blindly follow a certain preordained spending pattern they have in their heads, regardless of whether it is grounded in a sound financial strategy. During our regular semiannual check-ins, these clients generally want to discuss things at a high level and are not interested in the details of how things work or what the risks of their spending patterns may be.

Mona: Living on the Edge

According to Wikipedia, "'Livin' on the Edge" is a song by American hard rock band Aerosmith....It was released in March 1993 by Geffen Records as the first single from the band's commercially successful eleventh album, *Get a Grip* (1993). The single reached number 18 on the US *Billboard* Hot 100 chart."[234] The band's autobiography, *Walk This Way*, indicates that the song was inspired by the 1992 Los Angeles riots.[235] "Livin' on the Edge" is a perfect analogy for Mona, who, like her TV namesake Mona Robinson from *Who's the Boss*, wanted to live life large and really didn't care about the consequences of how much money she spent. She was the antithesis of Sophia, illustrated in the previous section.

I was lucky enough to be referred to Mona, a wonderful and fun 62-year-old lady, in late 2009. She had been employed by a local manufacturing company for nearly 30 years and wanted to know whether she had enough financial resources to retire. Her boss had been a client of mine for many years at that point. Remember, the markets had bottomed in March of that year after the subprime mortgage crisis and the failure of AIG and Lehman Brothers.

Up until that point, Mona had lived a relatively conservative and debt-free lifestyle. She had a modest home in Northeast Ohio, which was paid for. She was going to be receiving Social Security benefits of $1,600 per month and a small pension of $900 per month. The pension had been frozen many years before when her employer switched to a 401(k) plan, as many, if not most, employers had.

Mona had approximately $600,000 in her employer's 401(k) plan, and she wanted to roll it over to an IRA. She asked whether I could help her invest that money so that she could supplement her income each month. These combined income resources would allow her to live comfortably in her retirement years.

As many of you may recall, the 2010s were a pretty good decade for the economy and for investing in the financial markets. Although there were periods of volatility, we were living through a rebound period following the Global Financial Crisis. During this time, the stock market rose steadily, as you can see next.

236

From 2010 through 2019, Mona dutifully withdrew $3,500 every month—$42,000 per year—from her initial $600,000 investment. I cautioned her that this equated to a very aggressive 7% initial withdrawal rate. Mona took withdrawals of $420,000 over the ensuing decade. Over the same timeline, her account grew to more than $790,000 as the market compounded at a double-digit rate. Things turned out OK for Mona. However, I regularly remind clients that *a rising stock market can cover a multitude of withdrawal sins.*

In early 2020, before COVID, I met with Mona, and we reviewed her cash flow needs, tax situation, and investment account. I reviewed her portfolio construction and the historical risk and return statistics for her IRA. I was happy that I had been able to help Mona do the things that gave her retirement years meaning and joy. I was pleased that my professional capabilities, along with a rising market, had allowed her to achieve these life goals.

It was at that moment that Mona firmly reminded me of what mattered from the client's side of the table. She looked at me and very plainly said, "Jesse, do you know what's really important to me?" She then explained that as long as she received the $6,000 per month from her Social Security and pension checks, along with the monthly withdrawal from her investment account, she could do what she wanted in life.

She said that she knew that what I was talking about was important. However, most of what I had been saying was just noise to her. She just wanted to make sure she had the income she needed to live her best life each month. Mona was confident that I was well-versed in economic and investment history, and she knew that I loved sharing what was happening in the current world. However, she said that as much as I enjoyed talking about how the watch worked, *she just wanted to know what time it was.*

We are now going to turn our attention to the more fun and constructive things you can do with the financial resources you have accumulated throughout your working life. This includes giving yourself permission to spend money on things you really enjoy. We are also going to spend time talking about how you can use your financial surplus to bless others. This can include family and loved ones, as well as charitable and nonprofit organizations that align with your value system and passions.

We're in the Money: What to Do Next

According to Wikipedia, "'We're in the Money' is a song from the 1933 Warner Bros. film *Gold Diggers of 1933*, sung in the opening sequence by Ginger Rogers and chorus....The song's lyrics reflect a positive financial turnaround and a fantasized end to the Great Depression."[237] The song was also featured in the musical *42nd Street*, which "follows the rehearsal process of a Broadway show staged during the height of the Great Depression."[238]

The first thing I want to focus on is how you can use your financial resources to do the things that will make life and your retirement years fun, meaningful, and memorable. To help illustrate this, I am going to share with you the stories of two different clients who were definitely "in the money."

Phil and Vivian: Learning to Fly (First Class)

The first couple I would like to introduce you to is Phil and Vivian. They are very similar to TV couple Phil and Vivian Banks from the 1990s sitcom *The Fresh Prince of Bel-Air*, also known as Uncle Phil and Aunt Viv to Will Smith's streetwise character in the show. Phil and Vivian definitely had more than what it took to get along.

Phil was a very successful chemical engineer for a large publicly traded oil and gas company. He continually moved up the corporate ladder throughout his 40-year career. He retired at age 63 when the combination of his brother's passing and the realities of what was going on in the world during the COVID-19 pandemic led him to the realization that life was too short and that he and Vivian needed to start enjoying what they had worked so hard to create.

This proved to be easier said than done. Phil and Vivian were debt-free. They both had Social Security benefits, and Phil had a pension of $1,800 per month that he would begin receiving when he retired. They had diligently saved and invested, accumulating more than $2.2 million of investment assets.

You may remember from "Puzzle Piece #3: Determining How Much You Need to Retire (What's Your Number?)" that studies have shown that you can generally withdraw 4% per year from your investment assets, adjusted annually for inflation, over a 30-year retirement timeline. Based on the assets Phil and Vivian had accumulated, this would equate to $88,000 of annual investment income over and above their pension and Social Security incomes.

Phil and Vivian had two children who were both in their mid-30s when they retired. Luckily, both their children and their spouses were doing extremely well in their careers. They did not need their parents' money, and I was very happy that they both encouraged their mom and dad to use the money they had saved to enjoy their retirement years.

Phil and Vivian started off slowly. They were cautious about traveling and enjoying life in a post-COVID world. However, I continued to try to instill confidence in them that it was OK to spend their money and enjoy life. They started off taking some driving trips to see friends and loved ones throughout the southeastern United States. This then expanded to spending two months at a time out of the Northeast Ohio winter weather in Florida and Hilton Head.

As they got more comfortable with the idea that they could spend money and enjoy life without depleting their resources, they embarked on larger trips to the national parks out west. Recently, they took a two-week Alaskan land and sea vacation. I am very happy to report that they are planning a three-week trip to Australia and New Zealand next year. I actually got them to buy first-class tickets for the very long round-trip flights so that they can be comfortable and well-rested when they get there.

Phil and Vivian said they finally realized that if they didn't spend their money on first-class tickets, eventually, somebody else would!

239

The Griswolds and The Cleavers: Family Vacations (and Memories)

Poor Clark Griswold! He just wanted to create special moments and memories for his wife, Ellen, and his children, Audrey and Rusty.

According to Wikipedia, "*National Lampoon's Vacation*, sometimes referred to as simply *Vacation*, is a 1983 American black comedy road [trip] film directed by Harold Ramis starring Chevy Chase [and] Beverly D'Angelo.…It tells the fictitious story of the Griswold family on a cross-country trip to an amusement park and various locations as accidents occur along the way.…The film was a box-office hit, earning more than $60 million in the U.S. alone with an estimated budget of $15 million.… As a result of its success, five sequels have been produced."[240] As the family went from vacations out west to Wally World, Europe, Las Vegas, and even a staycation celebrating Christmas, a rotating cast of actors played the two Griswold children, as the cast members kept growing up.

[241]

Clark may have had an idealized and unrealistic vision for what would make for a successful family vacation. However, I believe he had the right idea. I have long been a big proponent of creating unique experiences and meaningful memories. This comes from an exercise I do with clients. I will ask them if they remember what they got for their 10th birthday or what special gift they got for Christmas when they were seven years old. Nobody remembers. That's because, just as cars depreciate the moment they are driven off the dealer's lot, the value of the "stuff" we buy goes down over time.

However, the value of shared experiences almost always stays with people throughout their lives. These memories also have a unique characteristic: they inevitably go up in value over time! When I ask the same clients whether they remember piling into the car for a family vacation or recall a parent coaching one of their sports teams, the answer is typically an enthusiastic *yes!* This is usually followed by an interesting or funny story about what happened along the way.

By the way, I practice what I preach in this regard. I told Rachel long ago that I did not need her to buy me another polo shirt or sweater for my birthday, an anniversary, or Christmas. I would much rather find something that we can do together that will create a new experience or memory that we can share for years to come.

I want to introduce you to my clients Ward and June Cleaver, whom I am modeling on the famous parents of the TV show *Leave It to Beaver*. They are amazing parents and grandparents and have embraced the value of experiences over possessions and created some incredible experiences and memories with their beautiful family. Ward and June have been my clients since 2002, when a coworker of Ward's, who had been a long-time client of mine, referred them to me. Ward and June were looking to build a relationship with a financial advisor who could help them determine whether they were on track to retire successfully in the next few years.

Ward was a financial analyst for a trucking company in Northeast Ohio, and June was a middle school guidance counselor in the Akron area. Once we determined through the financial planning process that they had accumulated enough resources to be able to retire comfortably, they decided to use some of the surplus they had built to start taking unique family vacations with as many of their kids and grandkids as they could. They knew the window for doing this would not be open forever, and they wanted to take advantage of it. They did so in a big way!

I could share many stories from their family adventures. However, one story in particular seems to best represent their unique family. Ward and June have two daughters who live in Northeast Ohio and a son who lives out of state. The children are all married, and they and their spouses are all very successful in their careers. Ward and June also have seven grandchildren. In my more than 20 years of working with Ward and June, I have always been amazed at how well the entire family gets along. It is a testament to what great parents and grandparents Ward and June have been.

Three years before Ward and June's 50th wedding anniversary, which was coming up in 2017, Ward and June approached me about planning a two-week family celebration in Hawaii. They had done their homework. They thought that they could cover the cost of flights, lodging, most meals, and several fun activities on two different islands for approximately $53,000. They wanted to know if this was something we could plan for within their budget. While I had certainly had other clients do meaningful things for their families, this was on a scale that I had not yet seen. I told them I was up for the challenge, and in early 2015, we began planning and saving for the trip.

While the family was in Hawaii, their granddaughter told Ward and June that she had arranged to get her senior pictures taken on the beach. She asked her grandparents to take her down to meet the photographer there. When they arrived, the entire family, along with a minister, was waiting for them so that they could renew their wedding vows for their 50th anniversary. Yes, it's that kind of amazing family.

In our office's library, which also serves as a client waiting room, the shelves are filled with family pictures from meaningful moments in clients' lives that we have helped them plan and save for. A family picture from Ward and June's Hawaii adventure sits proudly on those shelves. I love sharing their story with people coming to our office for the first time.

I could regale you with story after story from Ward and June's family, as well as from many of my other clients' families. The point is that Clark Griswold, no matter how misguided and accident-prone he was, was correct in his quest to create shared experiences and great family memories. It is my hope that you are inspired to use some of the wealth you build to create these types of memories for you and your loved ones. I truly believe they will only go up in value as the years go by.

We are going to finish this chapter by exploring other things you can give yourself permission to spend your money on. These involve sharing the excess resources you have accumulated with others—both the family members you want to be generous with and those you wish to help through smart charitable giving.

It's a Wonderful Life

According to Wikipedia, "[The 1946 film] *It's a Wonderful Life* is now considered to be one of the greatest films of all time and among the best Christmas films. It has been recognized by the American Film Institute as one of the 100 best American films ever made. It was No. 11 on the American Film Institute's 1998 greatest movie list…and No. 1 on its list of the most inspirational American films of all time.…On review aggregator Rotten Tomatoes, the film holds an approval rating of 94% based on 97 reviews, with an average rating of 9.0/10."[242]

Wikipedia also says, "The film stars James Stewart as George Bailey, a man who has given up his personal dreams in order to help others in his community and whose thoughts of suicide on Christmas Eve bring about the intervention of his guardian angel, Clarence Odbody. Clarence shows George all the lives he touched and what the world would be like if he had not existed."[243] You see, George's generosity and willingness to stand up for and help others less fortunate than him had had effects that had rippled throughout his community far beyond what he had realized. Commenting on the film, director Steven Spielberg once said, "*It's a Wonderful Life* shows that every human being on this Earth matters—and that's a very powerful message."[244]

It's a Wonderful Life is by far my wife Rachel's favorite Christmas movie. This means that at least once each holiday season, we spend an evening making dinner at home and watching the black-and-white classic.

Now that we have spent some time exploring meaningful ways to spend money on yourself and your family, let's explore how giving your excess money away can have a George Bailey-like impact on the lives of others.

Remember, as I said before, if you don't give your excess money away while you are living, you will give it away when you die because you can't take it with you! Therefore, since the financial planning process allows us to determine how much a client will need to do all the things that make life meaningful for them, it also allows us to see how much extra there will be to be generous with.

I often encourage clients not to wait until they are gone to let their will or trust distribute these excess funds to their loved ones and to future generations. I believe there is mutual benefit in starting the process earlier in life. With life expectancies stretching into the mid-80s and beyond, many times, when a client passes, they have adult children in or nearing retirement. By this time, those adult children have often built their own financial resources and independence. However, there were times earlier in those children's lives when they could have really used some help or a financial boost from their parents.

As we discussed in Puzzle Piece #10, rising prices and inflation have made it more difficult for future generations to do things we were able to do more easily. This includes buying homes, saving for future education needs, paying for day care, music lessons, and athletic teams, or even taking family vacations.

I have found that clients who know they have sufficient resources to accomplish their own goals and understand they have excess funds find it easier to be generous. This also means that they get to see the benefit of their generosity with their kids and grandkids. I don't believe wanting to witness these experiences is a narcissistic endeavor. I believe there can be real joy in seeing your family enjoy a vacation or once-in-a-lifetime experience together. I have had many grandparents relate the joy of seeing their grandchild walk across the stage when their name is called to get their diploma.

I could write an entire chapter on smart ways to make charitable gifts to help others. You may remember that in Puzzle Piece #2, I shared the story of Mike and Carol, who are now closing in on nearly $1 million of lifetime charitable gifts. Like George Bailey, they probably will never know how much of an impact they have had on the lives of the hundreds of people they have helped through the charities they donated money to.

There are certainly smart planning strategies to execute your charitable giving intentions. These include making gifts of appreciated assets, establishing donor-advised funds, executing qualified charitable distributions from your IRAs, and implementing more complex strategies generally associated with those who have a net worth north of $10 million.

However, this chapter is not about the technical aspects of charitable giving. I trust you will use the combined efforts of your CFP and CPA to guide you toward the right strategies. These strategies will allow you to get the maximum tax benefits from your giving. This is extremely important, and I remind you that every dollar you save in taxes is a dollar you can spend or give away elsewhere.

I wanted to focus this chapter on having both the confidence to enjoy your best retirement life and the heart attitude to be generous with your surplus with those you love and with those less fortunate than you. Remember, you don't get extra points by crossing the finish line of life with more money. I have found that most of my clients would much rather be remembered for creating a legacy of generosity. It's a great way for clients to create their own wonderful lives!

So, there you have it. I have now laid out all 12 pieces you need to put together your own retirement puzzle. I have done this through the framework of great songs, movies, even a Broadway show, and some history. Now that all the pieces on the table have been assembled, we will conclude our journey by making certain that your completed puzzle resembles the picture you aspired to create on your puzzle box. Please come with me as we examine your unique puzzle.

Your Completed Retirement Puzzle: Does It Match the Picture on the Box?

We all know the deep satisfaction of completing a task and knowing we did it exceptionally well. *That joy is yours today!* The final piece of your puzzle has now been placed. As you step back and admire your completed masterpiece, does it reflect the picture on the box? You know, the vision you meticulously crafted for *your ideal retirement?* More importantly, after completing your journey through the 12 chapters of this book, you should feel more confident in your clearly defined vision for retirement and your ability to generate the income and assets necessary to achieve that vision. Because of the proactive steps you have taken, you are truly setting yourself apart from most Americans.

This is the point and the purpose of PopEnomics! I wanted us to explore what it takes to create retirement success in a unique and engaging way. This book isn't about spreadsheets and graphs—no financial calculators, slide rules, or pocket protectors required. Instead, the goal was to share the secrets of retirement success from both a quantitative and qualitative perspective. My ultimate hope is that, after you assemble the 12 pieces of your unique puzzle, you approach your future retirement with newfound confidence and excitement!

This stands in stark contrast to the approach that the majority of the U.S. population takes to retirement. Most working-age people have not created a clear vision of where they want to be when they retire. Therefore, they have no idea whether they are on the right track or building enough resources to get there. Once again, remember that Yogi Berra quote: "If you don't know where you're going, you might not get there."[245]

According to Wikipedia, "Can't Get There from Here" "is the first single released by R.E.M. from its third studio album *Fables of the Reconstruction* in 1985. The song peaked at number 10 on the *Billboard* Bubbling Under Hot 100 Singles, equaling to a position of approximately 110 on the main *Billboard* Hot 100 chart."[246]

Unfortunately, the song's title represents how many people today feel about their future retirements. They lack confidence in their current financial situations and their future prospects. It's completely normal to feel this way, especially since many economic and geopolitical events over the last few years have decreased what little confidence or hope many people had of reaching their retirement dreams. The results of a recent study seem to bear this out.

Are You Confident About Retirement?

When EBRI released its 2023 Retirement Confidence Survey, it gave us some sense of what American workers and future retirees were grappling with.[247] This report highlighted a couple of key findings.

The first was that retirement confidence dropped double digits in 2023. A decline of this magnitude had not been seen since the '07–'08 Global Financial Crisis. However, when we look at the markets' performance in 2023, we should not be surprised. One of the triggers for this decline was the stock market, as measured by the S&P 500 index, falling 26% from early January to mid-October 2023.

What was even more disconcerting for those looking toward retirement was that the bond market dropped 13% at the same time. This was the worst performance for the bond market in over 100 years. Over the previous 25 years, the Federal Reserve Bank had often cut interest rates during times of economic uncertainty. This caused bond prices to rise during times of stock market volatility and downturns. Many investors had not experienced a time when both the stock and bond markets dropped concurrently. The last time this had happened was during the high inflation days of the late '70s and early '80s.

The double-digit drops in both stocks and bonds caused many employees to see their 401(k) and IRA balances drop enough to make retirement dreams and goals seem less attainable. This comes on the heels of the COVID-19 pandemic-inspired shutdowns, stimulus, inflation, and global supply chain issues that had already caused many workers to feel like their retirement plans had been thrown off track.

A second key finding from the survey was that only half of U.S. workers believe they will have enough money to last throughout their retirement lives. Furthermore, nearly two-thirds of workers don't feel confident about how much money they can withdraw from their savings once they do retire.

Inflation rising to levels not seen in four decades also caused significant concerns. The combination of higher prices and higher interest rates on mortgages, cars, and other large-ticket items that people generally finance put a dent in household cash flow. This affected how much money was left over for people to save for the future.

From 2020 to 2023, the number of retirees who felt that their retirement lifestyles would be better than expected declined significantly. There was a corresponding rise in the number of people who thought their retirement lifestyles would be worse than they had hoped. Both working and retired people are expressing more concern about market volatility causing potential losses to their retirement account balances and inflation making it challenging to maintain the cost of living during their retirement years.

According to the EBRI 2023 Retirement Confidence Survey,

- Four in 10 workers and three in 10 retirees worry that their money won't keep up with inflation in retirement.[248]
- Seventy-three percent of workers and 58% of retirees are worried they will need to make substantial cuts to their spending because of inflation.[249]

Luckily, *you are not like most workers and retirees.* You have the knowledge and wisdom that come from reading and applying the lessons of PopEnomics! You have the tools to separate yourself from the crowd. You do not have to feel like the people in the study above or risk getting caught up with the herd in the latest economic news or investment fads trending on social media.

[250]

We certainly *do not* want to do what most other people are doing. There is great danger in following the herd. It certainly did not work out well for the buffalo out west. Remember, if the herd were generally right, the herd would be wealthy, and since, by and large, they are not, we do not want to do what they are doing. Sometimes it is difficult to take the path less traveled. However, you have the PopEnomics tools to guide you going forward! Let's briefly review each one.

We began with "Puzzle Piece #1: Determining Where You Are Financially." If you don't know where you are, it is hard to know what steps to take or which direction to go. Once we know where we are, we can start to envision what retirement life looks like. This is where the fun begins!

We examined this in detail in "Puzzle Piece #2: Retiring to Something vs. Retiring from Something." Getting away from the grind of daily work, especially if you are in a career you don't love, may sound fun. However, I can tell you from more than 35 years of experience that my clients who enjoy retirement the most are those who are looking forward to what comes next in life!

I promised I would only make you focus on math for one chapter. I kept my word. In "Puzzle Piece #3: Determining How Much You Need to Retire (What's Your Number?)," we reviewed how to determine your monthly income needs and understand the income and asset resources you are building to help create your ideal retirement.

A cornerstone of most people's retirement income plan is Social Security. "Puzzle Piece #4: Maximizing Your Benefits from an Underfunded Social Security System" helped you understand the factors you need to consider in order to get the most income during your retirement years from all the FICA taxes you paid while you were working.

We then moved from the concrete world of math and numbers to the more abstract world of managing your thoughts so you can pursue the behaviors that will help you build wealth over time. In "Puzzle Piece #5: Navigating the Negative 24-Hour News and Social Media Spin Cycle," we discussed that the media's primary goal is to get you to tune in or click. This can lead to troubling behavioral patterns such as chasing attractive improbability, herd mentality, anchoring, and FOMO.

"Puzzle Piece #6: Managing Your Beliefs and Behaviors" shared cautionary tales from investment history as well as several client stories to illustrate the importance of following sound financial principles and not letting your emotions lead to bad financial decisions.

We then turned the page to what most people assumed would be the meat of a book about planning for your successful retirement: exploring economic cycles and the role of various investment asset classes. To help put things in the right context, we began with "Puzzle Piece #7: Understanding Economic Cycles and Investment History." We then moved on to "Puzzle Piece #8: The Role of Bonds in Your Retirement Income Portfolio." While most people love talking about the ups and downs of the market and their favorite stocks, very few people know about or understand the bond market. We concluded this section of the book with an in-depth look at the history of the stock market and its role in helping you retire successfully in "Puzzle Piece #9: The Role of Stocks in Building Your Retirement Wealth."

As we neared the completion of our puzzle, we spent time trying to understand "Puzzle Piece #10: The Risk of Rising Prices During Your Retirement Years." We can use simple examples, such as the price of postage stamps or a cup of coffee to illustrate what the constant drip, drip, drip (intentional) of inflation can do to the cost of living over a 20-to-30-year retirement life expectancy.

[251]

You might have thought it unusual to see a chapter such as "Puzzle Piece #11: The Challenge of Aging Demographics and Low Birth Rates" in a book about retirement planning. However, we were able to explore the significant economic and societal challenges presented by these two factors. They could affect everything from GDP growth rates to Social Security funding and the allocation of scarce government resources.

We concluded our journey through the various puzzle pieces with a much more upbeat and fun topic, "Puzzle Piece #12: Permission to Spend—Enjoying Retirement Life." For some readers, it may be surprising to learn that many people struggle to spend money in their retirement years, finding it difficult to part with what they worked so hard to save. For others, this struggle is all too familiar, and you may see yourself reflected in the illustrations throughout the chapter. My goal was to help you balance these perspectives so that you feel empowered to live the retirement life you have always envisioned.

At the end of the day, applying the principles of PopEnomics should help give you the confidence to create a retirement life of meaning, significance, and joy. This stands in stark contrast to the study from EBRI discussed at the beginning of this chapter, which showed how many people are struggling with financial and retirement confidence. I trust that if you apply these principles diligently and persistently, the compounded effects of good habits over time will allow you to move toward a more successful retirement.

Life Lessons from Dr. Seuss

A few years ago, we celebrated the 60th anniversary of one of Dr. Seuss's most important and well-known books, *Green Eggs and Ham*. When you think of Dr. Seuss, what words come to mind? As you begin to unpack your adjectives, most people think of words like *creative* or *innovative*. Other descriptors I would like you to consider for the good doctor are *determined*, *success-minded*, and *willing to be challenged*.

Like many people who broke new ground before him, Dr. Seuss had to struggle through many challenges and setbacks. This includes being turned down by 27 different publishers before finally getting someone to publish his first book, *And to Think That I Saw It on Mulberry Street*, in 1937. These character traits show up in Sam in *Green Eggs and Ham*. Sam had to ask his friend 16 times before he finally tried the meal he believed he would detest but ultimately loved!

In 1957, Dr. Seuss released two of the most cherished children's books ever written, *The Cat in the Hat* and *How the Grinch Stole Christmas* (both of which can be recited from memory by this CFP and author). While the success and popularity of those books were great, it also caused Ted Geisel, a.k.a. Dr. Seuss, to wonder whether he would ever be able to write another book of such acclaim. It took a successful mindset and a commitment to his creative process for Dr. Seuss to overcome those fears and go on to write one of his most important and well-known books, *Green Eggs and Ham*.

Most people are not aware that *Green Eggs and Ham* started out as a $50 bet between Dr. Seuss and his publisher friend Bennett Cerf, who bet him that he could not write an entire book using just 50 words.[252] The challenge sparked Dr. Seuss's creativity, and he embarked on one of his most ambitious yet successful projects.

We all have challenges and struggles in life and things that we have to work hard to overcome for success. Many people see the success of celebrities and think that reaching that success was easy for them or that they had some unique ability that opened the door. Fred Astaire was known to say something along the lines that every time you see him glide across the dance floor with poise and grace, there were over 100 hours of practice that you did not see.

In the midst of everything we all deal with in life, I thought a brief lesson from somebody we all know from our childhood might give you a boost to keep working to overcome the struggles in your life with a smile on your face. I hope it helps give you the tenacity to move past whatever is holding you back as you try to create the retirement you want and deserve!

As I mentioned in the introduction of the book, in January 1990, Random House published the last book that was written and illustrated by Dr. Seuss during his lifetime. *Oh, the Places You'll Go!* follows the life journey of a young boy throughout his challenges and successes. One of the most famous passages from the book is:

> You'll be on your way up!
> You'll be seeing great sights!
> You'll join the high fliers
> Who soar to high heights.[253]

[254]

That is the goal! I wanted to guide you through a thorough but fun exploration of the steps you need to take to build your own significant retirement. I wanted to do this in a unique and entertaining way. The last thing the world needs is another dry, boring, and numbers-based book on investing and retirement success. There is no reason that something this important needs to be dull.

I have always found that the use of metaphors, relating important topics to things that people love and remember—like movies and classic rock songs—resonates and makes it easier to comprehend and retain important ideas. I have also found that my clients understand and apply the principles I relay to them more easily when they are shared through the lens of real-life stories and anecdotes from my more than 35 years of serving as a financial advisor. During my career, I have truly been blessed to work with and serve some of the nicest people I have ever met.

When reflecting on your PopEnomics journey, I hope you can say the same. I trust that this was an enjoyable and engaging way to learn the principles you need to apply to successfully transition from work life to a successful retirement. As Dr. Seuss would say…

> You're off to great places!
> Today is your day!
> Your mountain is waiting.
> So…get on your way![255]

Whether you feel confident in applying these principles on your own or enlist the help of a qualified CFP, I wish you much joy and success in the next steps on your journey! Your mountain is waiting. So…get on your way!

Acknowledgements

First and foremost, I would like to thank my beautiful wife, Rachel, who served as my proofreader, editor, and chart creator. She was among the first to encourage me to create a book based on the substantial body of work I had developed by writing blogs over the last dozen years. Writing PopEnomics took more than seven months. This means that she gave me space and encouragement over many nights and weekends. Once the writing was done, she spent countless hours over the next six months helping me work through multiple rounds of editing and layout to produce what you have just read. I simply could not have created this book, or for that matter, built my business, without her love, encouragement, and support.

I would never ask my clients or my readers to do something that I was not comfortable or confident doing myself. Rachel has collaborated with me, and we have been blessed to build a fantastic life together. Life can be hectic when you each build and run your own entrepreneurial, self-employed business. However, as I suggested throughout the book, we have tried to use the gift of time, the gift of health, and the gift of financial resources, which have been built utilizing the principles laid out in this book, to create shared memories and experiences, both together and with our amazing kids and family.

To that end, we are thrilled that each of our three children has been able to create lives and career paths that allow them to use their unique gifts and abilities. Having your children and their spouses or significant others spread all over the eastern half of the United States can create logistical challenges when trying to connect. I am delighted that we have been intentional as a family to schedule times to be in the same places together each year, even if it is only for a few days, due to trying to manage eight people's work and PTO schedules. I am very proud of Shane and Hunter, who live in Manchester, New Hampshire, Zach and Kayli, who live nearby in northeast Ohio, and Sedona and Mark, who recently moved from Atlanta to Charleston, South Carolina. I love and am proud of you, and we look forward to sharing life with you in the coming years.

It has been said, "You are the average of the five people you spend the most time with." Over the last 35 years, I have been blessed to have a significant number of friends and mentors who have shaped my outlook, my habits, my business acumen, and my success as an advisor, husband, and father. I want to take a moment to thank a few of the more notable ones here, understanding that this acknowledgement section is far too short to name everybody who could or should be included.

In 1994, when I was 29 years old, I was lucky enough to meet Larry Roth, the owner and CEO of Vestax Securities. He was trying to recruit me and my business associates from our current broker-dealer to his. In the process, he did some business coaching and future vision exercises with us. I had just finished my best year ever, grossing six figures for the first time. When Larry asked me what my goals for the future were, I shared numbers beyond anything anybody in my family had ever made. He looked at me directly and said, "I think you are significantly underselling your future potential. I think you are capable of much more than that." It was the first time anybody had given me encouragement and confidence that I could accomplish much more than I believed. I am happy to say that Larry was right. I am even happier to say that he is still a friend and a mentor that I reach out to and count on for wise counsel to this day. Thank you.

In 2006, I was asked to join a study group known as "The Hole in the Wall Gang." At the time, I was the youngest person in the group by nearly 10 years. This group of elite financial advisors included seven of our broker-dealers' top producers across the eastern half of the United States: Darla, Jim Bob, Steve, Dan, Jeff, John, and Scott. Over the next dozen years, the group eventually grew to 10 advisors. We met in person two times a year, three days each time, to share best ideas and best practices. It was peer-to-peer sharing at its best. This group helped to mentor my growth, and became some of my most trusted personal and professional friends.

All good things must come to an end, and as a number of the advisors in "The Hole in the Wall Gang" started moving toward their retirement years, we decided to disband in 2017. Eric, who was now the youngest person in the group, and I tried to catch lightning in a bottle a second time by forming a new study group. I am happy to report that the "Incite Planning Group" was created in 2018 with four initial members and has now grown to six of the top advisors within our broker-dealer. And, while I was the youngest person in the previous group, I am now the oldest person in this group. My, how things change.

Eric Pascarella, Clint Gault, Brian Toma, Pete Bush, and Trevor Wilde truly embody the idea of abundance mentality. I know that I could reach out to any of them, anytime, and they would be more than willing to help me or share their thoughts and wisdom whenever asked. They are not only five of the best advisors and business owners I know, but also five of the best people I know and friends I could ever ask for. My business and my life are better because of them. Thank you.

On April 13, 2025, I marked my 30th anniversary with my broker-dealer. Since Larry Roth recruited me there in 1995, I have gone through three names, six owners, and nine CEOs…so far. I have had the opportunity to serve on a number of committees and leadership councils during my tenure, and my journey has been positively impacted by more people than I can count. I want to thank some of the people who helped me grow, and who I am lucky to say are lifelong friends, including Pat McEvoy, Randy Ringer, Gene Goldman, Mimi Bock, CeCe Marshall, Nicole Summerlin,

Elisa del Valle, Adam Antoniades, and especially Brett Harrison and Erinn Ford, who provided invaluable amounts of both wisdom and friendship through the years.

The team at Impel Wealth Management is incredible, and I am lucky enough to work with them every day, serving our friends and clients. I have always believed that you hire for character and values. You can teach a smart person a job or a task, but you cannot teach somebody to be caring or empathetic. Over the years, clients have told me repeatedly what an incredible team we have here.

I want to give a special shout-out to Karen Johnson and Sarah Montgomery, who have helped me serve my clients with excellence for nearly 20 years. They know and treat our clients like family. I would also like to acknowledge Nathan Ollish, CFP, AIF. He took a chance by leaving another firm he had been part of for six years to join Impel Wealth as an Associate Advisor in 2018. He is now a Lead Advisor and my right-hand person and sounding board. Our firm's future is bright with him in the picture. Thanks to you all.

Finally, I would like to thank all the economists, strategists, and coaches who have helped me grow over the years. I genuinely believe in being a student of business. As Rachel can attest, I read 600 to 800 pages a month of economic and political commentary to try to stay on top of an ever-changing and more complex investment environment for the benefit of my clients. I have benefited from the collective wisdom of these leaders over the years.

As I stated in the book, I started in the business just before the stock market crash in October 1987. I also have more than 35 years of life experience and a whole cadre of economic and political crises to learn from. I was recently looking at a stock market chart from 1945, just after World War II, to 2024 with a close friend of mine who had been in the business since 1983. We looked at each other and realized we had been in the industry for roughly half that chart.

I guess there is no substitute for the combination of extreme curiosity, a quest for knowledge and wisdom, and life experience to help you grow. I am excited to see what the next decades bring, and I look forward to continuing this journey with all of you.

Your Narrator's Story

I began my career as a financial advisor in August 1987, just a few weeks before the Black Monday stock market crash in October of that year. In 1997, two other CFPs and I became the founding partners of Millennial Group. The firm focused on helping people successfully pursue their retirement goals and aspirations. With more than 35 years of experience in the financial planning industry, my purpose and goal is to leverage my industry and historical knowledge and skills to help my clients successfully navigate the areas of investment portfolio management, retirement income planning, and estate planning.

As both a CFP professional and an Accredited Investment Fiduciary, I focus on building meaningful relationships with my clients. I get to know their goals, desires, and financial histories. Then, I create a custom road map designed to help them reach their ideal financial futures.

I founded Impel Wealth Management in 2017 to help individuals and families "move life forward" through meaningful conversations, comprehensive planning, and sound financial advice. In addition to founding Impel Wealth, I developed a partnership with Horizon Advisor Network, a national enterprise group serving more than 60 advisors and responsible for managing over $4 billion in assets in more than 20 offices across the country. I have also led the network's Investylitics investment management committee since its inception.

In 2018, I was honored to be named a best-in-state wealth advisor for the state of Ohio by *Forbes*/SHOOK Research, and I have now been named to that annual list six times. In 2021, I was also named a Notable Wealth Manager by *Crain's Cleveland Business* for providing ethical, honest, and productive financial management and financial planning.

I was named an "All-Star Wealth Advisor" on the *Investment News* Hot List 2023, which celebrates 100 individuals redefining success in the financial planning industry. In June 2024, AdvisorHub named me to their 2024 "1,000 Advisors to Watch" list in the "100 Fast-Growing Advisors to Watch" category.

Additionally, I served as president of the Financial Planning Association's Northeast Ohio chapter and served on Cetera Advisors' President's Advisory Council from 2004 to 2022.

I have always believed that part of leadership is giving back. In the book of Luke, it is stated, "To whom much has been given, much will be required."[256] Or, as Uncle Ben told his nephew Peter Parker, also known as Spider-Man, "With great power comes great responsibility."[257]

As a result of this belief, I have been deeply involved in community service. Over the last 30 years, I have been on 14 community and industry boards. I have served as president of nine of those boards and have been an officer or member of the executive committee on all of them.

Since entering the financial planning field in 1987, I have been driven by a belief espoused by motivational speaker and author Zig Ziglar: "You can get everything in life you want if you will just help enough other people get what they want."[258] By the way, I was blessed to hear Zig Ziglar speak live two different times before his passing. He was an incredible man with an amazing and upbeat outlook on life. If you have never heard him speak or read his books, I highly encourage you to check out some of his books or videos. The videos can be found on YouTube.

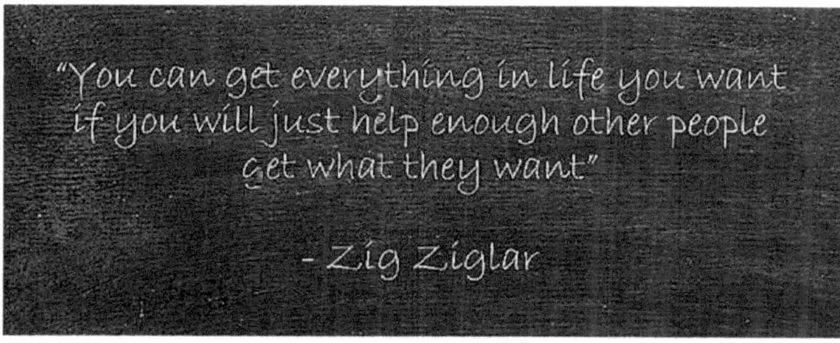

[259]

You may call this karma, what goes around comes around, or sowing and reaping. Whatever you call it, it has served me, my clients, and my business well for over 35 years.

Award Disclosures

Forbes: Best-in-State Wealth Advisors Award received by Jesse Hurst, Senior Wealth Advisor, (2018-2024). The Forbes ranking of Best-In-State Wealth Advisors, developed by SHOOK Research, is based on an algorithm of qualitative data, rating thousands of wealth advisors with a minimum of seven years' experience and weighing factors like revenue trends, assets under management, compliance records, industry experience, and best practices learned through telephone and in-person interviews. Portfolio performance is not a criteria due to varying client objectives and lack of audited data. Neither Forbes nor SHOOK receive a fee in exchange for rankings. Research summary as of April 2024: - 44,990 nominations received, based on thresholds - 23,876 invited to complete online survey - 20,412 telephone interviews - 4,926 in-person interviews at Advisor's location - 1,507 virtual interviews. Listing in this publication and/or award is not a guarantee of future investment success. This recognition should not be construed as an endorsement of the advisor by any client. No compensation was provided directly or indirectly by the recipient for participation or in connection with obtaining or using the third-party rating or award.

Crain's 2021 Notable Wealth Managers issued by Crain's Cleveland Business won by Jesse Hurst. The honorees do not pay to be included. Their profiles were drawn from the nomination materials submitted. This list is not comprehensive. It includes only individuals for whom nominations were submitted and accepted after a review by editors. To qualify for the list, nominees must be based in Northeast Ohio. They must be currently employed full time at a financial institution or company offering wealth management services and showcase professional achievements. They must have a minimum of three years' experience and oversee at least $10 million in assets under advisement. They must be active in the community and/or philanthropic activities, mentoring programs and/or diversity and inclusion initiatives. Listing in this publication and/or award is not a guarantee of future investment success. This recognition should not be construed as an endorsement of the advisor by any client. No compensation was provided directly or indirectly for participating or in connection with obtaining or using the third-party rating or award.

Investment News invited wealth professionals from across the country to nominate their most exceptional leaders for the Hot List. Investment News narrowed the list down to 100 whose contributions have helped shape the wealth industry and who support underserved groups and the next generation of wealth professionals over the past 12 months. Listing in this publication and/or award is not a guarantee of future investment success. This recognition should not be construed as an endorsement of the advisor by any client. No compensation was provided directly or indirectly by the recipient for participation or in connection with obtaining or using the third-party rating or award.

Book Disclosures

Securities and advisory services offered through Cetera Advisors LLC, member FINRA/SIPC, a broker/dealer and a Registered Investment Adviser. Cetera is under separate ownership from any other named entity. 2006 4th St, Cuyahoga Falls, OH 44221

Neither Cetera Advisors LLC nor any of its representatives may give legal or tax advice. This information is not intended as tax or legal advice. Please consult legal or tax professionals for specific information regarding your individual situation.

A diversified portfolio does not assure a profit or protect against loss in a declining market.

The hypothetical investment results are for illustrative purposes only and should not be deemed a representation of past or future results. Actual investment results may be more or less than those shown. This does not represent any specific product [and/or service].

Past performance is not an indication or guarantee of future results.

The return and principal value of bonds fluctuate with changes in market conditions. If bonds are not held to maturity, they may be worth more or less than their original value,

Generally, a donor advised fund is a separately identified fund or account that is maintained and operated by a section 501(c)(3) organization, which is called a *sponsoring organization*. Each account is composed of contributions made by individual donors. Once the donor makes the contribution, the organization has legal control over it. However, the donor, or the donor's representative, retains advisory privileges with respect to the distribution of funds and the investment of assets in the account. Donors take a tax deduction for all contributions at the time they are made, even though the money may not be dispersed to a charity until much later.

The cost and availability of life insurance depend on factors such as age, health, and the type and amount of insurance purchased. Before implementing a strategy involving life insurance, it would be prudent to make sure that you are insurable by having the policy approved. As with most financial decisions, there are expenses associated with the purchase of life insurance. Policies commonly have mortality and expense charges. In addition, if a policy is surrendered prematurely, there may be surrender charges and income tax implications.

Some IRA's have contribution limitations and tax consequences for early withdrawals. For complete details, consult your tax advisor or attorney. Retirement Plans: Distributions from traditional IRA's and employer sponsored retirement plans are taxed as ordinary income and, if taken prior to reaching age 59½, may be subject to an additional 10% IRS tax penalty.

Roth IRA: Converting from a traditional IRA to a Roth IRA is a taxable event. A Roth IRA offers tax free withdrawals on taxable contributions. To qualify for the tax-free and penalty-free withdrawal or earnings, a Roth IRA must be in place for at least five tax years, and the distribution must take place after age 59½ or due to death, disability, or a first time home purchase (up to a $10,000 lifetime maximum). Depending on state law, Roth IRA distributions may be subject to state taxes.

The U.S. Aggregate Bond Index is a benchmark that measures the performance of a broad range of investment-grade, fixed-rate US dollar bonds. It includes Treasuries, corporate securities, government-related securities, and mortgage-backed securities.

Investors cannot invest directly in indexes. The performance of any index is not indicative of the performance of any investment and does not take into account the effects of inflation and the fees and expenses associated with investing.

LET'S BUILD YOUR
RETIREMENT PUZZLE TOGETHER!

Find out more and get additional resources at
http://PopEnomics.com

For special discounts or bulk purchases,
contact **http://PopEnomics.com**

Book Jesse Hurst for speaking events by contacting
http://PopEnomics.com

CONNECT WITH JESSE AT

- Website: PopEnomics.com
- LinkedIn: jesse-hurst-author
- Facebook: JesseHurstAuthor
- Youtube: @jessehurstauthor
- Instagram: @jesse_hurst_author
- X: @jhurstauthor

THANK YOU FOR READING!

If you enjoyed *PopEnomics*, please leave a review on Goodreads or on the retailer site where you purchased this book.

Endnotes

1 Image generated by ChatGPT, response to "I need a black and white at least 300 dpi image of a jigsaw puzzle box and completed puzzle. I want the puzzle image to be a turntable with spins of albums in the image. No words on the images please," OpenAI, April 17, 2025, https://chatgpt.com/c/68014206-0d60-8004-850d-3fa3fa29bcbf.

2 iStock.com/bankrx, Stock illustration ID: 2154595222

3 *Seinfeld*, season 4, episode 14, "The Movie," written by Bill Masters, Steve Skrovan, and Jon Hayman, directed by Tom Cherones, aired January 6, 1993, on NBC.

4 Wikipedia, "*Oh, the Places You'll Go!*," last modified February 5, 2025, 9:57 (UTC), https://en.wikipedia.org/wiki/Oh,_the_Places_You%27ll_Go!.

5 Dr. Seuss, *Oh the Places You'll Go!* (Random House, 1990).

6 Quote from Dr. Seuss, *Oh the Places You'll Go!* (Random House, 1990).

7 iStock.com/Tatgynsy, Stock illustration ID:2188759196

8 Yogi Berra, *When You Come to a Fork in the Road, Take It!: Inspiration and Wisdom from One of Baseball's Greatest Heroes* (Hachette Books, 2001), 53.

9 "Four-in-Ten Participants Admit to Calculating Retirement Savings Goals Off the Top of Their Head," Escalent, September 20, 2023, https://escalent.co/news/four-in-ten-participants-admit-to-calculating-retirement-savings-goals-off-the-top-of-their-head.

10 Image generated by DALL-E, response to "Create image in BW at least 300 dpi that says 'The Survey Says,'" OpenAI, December 12, 2024, https://chatgpt.com/c/675b0ab4-adb8-8004-beac-74a4d8a52537.

11 "Four-in-Ten Participants."

12 "The Changing Generational Values," Johns Hopkins University, November 17, 2022, https://imagine.jhu.edu/blog/2022/11/17/the-changing-generational-values/; Megan Gerhardt, "About 'Those Millennials'…," LinkedIn, September 20, 2022, https://www.linkedin.com/pulse/those-millennials-megan-gerhardt-ph-d-/.

13 "Four-in-Ten Participants."

14 Berra, *Fork in the Road*, 53.

15 "The New Issue of Rolling Stone: The 100 Greatest Guitar Songs," *Rolling Stone*, May 28, 2008, https://www.rollingstone.com/music/music-news/the-new-issue-of-rolling-stone-the-100-greatest-guitar-songs-108589.

16 Interview with Curtis Mayfield, *Goldmine*, July 4, 1997.

17 "2021 RCS Fact Sheet #4: Age Comparisons Among Workers," Retirement Confidence Survey, 2021, https://www.ebri.org/docs/default-source/rcs/2021-rcs/rcs_21-fs-4_age.pdf?sfvrsn=69d83a2f_4.

18 "2021 RCS Fact Sheet #4."

19 "2021 RCS Fact Sheet #4."

20 "2021 RCS Fact Sheet #4."

21 "Economic Well-Being of U.S. Households in 2022," Board of Governors of the Federal Reserve System, May 2023, https://www.federalreserve.gov/publications/files/2022-report-economic-well-being-us-households-202305.pdf.

22 "2021 RCS Fact Sheet #4."

23 Chris Horymski, "Experian Study: Average U.S. Consumer Debt and Statistics," Experian, January 29, 2025, https://www.experian.com/blogs/ask-experian/research/consumer-debt-study/.

24 iStock.com/SilviaZecchin, Stock illustration ID: 1172793567

25 Wikipedia, "Follow That Dream (song)," last modified December 4, 2023, 8:31 (UTC), https://en.wikipedia.org/wiki/Follow_That_Dream_(song).

26 "Gen X Is the Most Stressed Generation Alive and Studies Reveal Why – Hint: They're $440,000 Short on Retirement, and It's Only Getting Worse," The American Institute of Stress, July 31, 2024, https://www.stress.org/news/gen-x-is-the-most-stressed-generation-alive-and-studies-reveal-why-hint-theyre-440000-short-on-retirement-and-its-only-getting-worse/; Derek Beres, "Why Is Gen X More Stressed than Other Generations?," Big Think, May 11, 2020, https://bigthink.com/neuropsych/gen-x-stress/.

27 Wikipedia, "*Going in Style*," last modified November 2, 2024, 23:50 (UTC), https://en.wikipedia.org/wiki/Going_in_Style.

28 "*Going in Style.*"

29 iStock.com/SilviaZecchin, Stock illustration ID: 1081391472

30 "*Going in Style.*"

31 "New York Life Wealth Watch Survey Finds Key Financial Differences Among American Families," New York Life, April 19, 2023, https://www.newyorklife.com/newsroom/2023/wealth-watch-financial-differences-in-families.

32 "Survey Says: Gen Xers Most Worried About Finances, Retirement Preparedness," New York Life, accessed December 12, 2024, https://www.newyorklife.com/newsroom/wealth-watch-2023-genx-financial-health-sb.

33 "To Spend or Not to Spend?," BlackRock, December 2023, https://www.blackrock.com/us/individual/literature/whitepaper/spending-retirement-assets-final-whitepaper.pdf.

34 "Spend or Not."

35 "Spend or Not."

36 Image from Microsoft Word, text added.

37 MP Dunleavey, "How Gen X Could Reinvent Retirement," Kiplinger, January 24, 2025, https://www.kiplinger.com/retirement/retirement-planning/how-gen-x-could-reinvent-retirement; Richard Fry and Dana Braga, "The Growth of the Older

Workforce," Pew Research Center, December 14, 2023, https://www.pewresearch.org/social-trends/2023/12/14/the-growth-of-the-older-workforce/.

38 "58% of Americans Say They'd Consider Post-Retirement Employment to Seek Personal Fulfillment: New Empower Research," Empower, September 21, 2023, https://www.empower.com/press-center/americans-say-theyd-consider-post-retirement-employment.

39 "My Hero Zero," School House Rock Wiki, accessed December 10, 2024, https://schoolhouserock.fandom.com/wiki/My_Hero_Zero.

40 iStock.com/NataliaKononova, Stock illustration ID: 2207630729

41 Image generated by ChatGPT, response to "Create a black and white image of a man in his 40s sitting on a couch, talking to his psychiatrist (show both figures). The man has slightly messy hair and appears unshaven," OpenAI, March 10, 2025, https://chatgpt.com/c/67cee2b8-b6b8-8004-a81e-e980adc20bc9.

42 iStock.com/Mirikiteki, Stock illustration ID: 2175576884

43 Wikipedia, "*The Sound of Music* (film)," last modified December 16, 2024, 1:07 (UTC), https://en.wikipedia.org/wiki/The_Sound_of_Music_(film).

44 Image generated by DALL-E, response to "Create a black-and-white illustration of a serene mountain top scene. A woman sits gracefully, playing a guitar and singing to seven children who are seated around her," OpenAI, December 18, 2024, https://chatgpt.com/c/67632dd2-4bb8-8004-9a84-9495cfabfbb6.

45 David Floyd, "What Is the Tax Cuts and Jobs Act (TCJA)?," Investopedia, last updated November 4, 2024, https://www.investopedia.com/taxes/trumps-tax-reform-plan-explained.

46 Wikipedia, "Take the Money and Run (Steve Miller Band Song)," November 26, 2024, 1:10 (UTC), https://en.wikipedia.org/wiki/Take_the_Money_and_Run_(Steve_Miller_Band_song).

47 William P. Bengen, "Determining Withdrawal Rates Using Historical Data," *Journal of Financial Planning* 7, no. 4 (October 1994): 171.

48 Alexandra Twin, "Dow Fights Back," CNN Money, last updated March 6, 2009, archived from https://web.archive.org/web/20090307121018/https://money.cnn.com/2009/03/06/markets/markets_newyork/index.htm.

49 "Historical Background and Development of Social Security," Social Security Online, accessed December 9, 2024, https://www.ssa.gov/history/briefhistory3.html.

50 "Historical Background and Development."

51 *The 2021 OASDI Trustees Report*, (Social Security Administration, 2021), https://www.ssa.gov/OACT/TR/2021/trTOC.html.

52 *The 2021 OASDI Trustees Report.*

53 "The 2005 OASDI Trustees Report," Social Security Online, last updated March 23, 2005, https://www.ssa.gov/OACT/TR/TR05.

54 "Report of the National Commission on Social Security Reform – January 1983," Social Security Online, accessed December 9, 2024, https://www.ssa.gov/history/reports/gspan.html.

55 Benjamin Plackett, "How Many French Revolutions Were There?," Live Science, January 17, 2021, https://www.livescience.com/how-many-french-revolutions.html.

56 Wikipedia, "Political History of France," last modified November 11, 2024, 12:20 (UTC), https://en.wikipedia.org/wiki/Political_history_of_France.

57 *Encyclopedia Britannica*, "French Revolution 1787-1799," last updated November 13, 2024, https://www.britannica.com/event/French-Revolution.

58 *Encyclopedia Britannica*, "Revolutions of 1830," last updated July 20, 2023, https://www.britannica.com/event/Revolutions-of-1830.

59 *Encyclopedia Britannica*, "Revolutions of 1848," last updated November 12, 2024, https://www.britannica.com/event/Revolutions-of-1848.

60 Wikipedia, "Yellow Vests Protests," last modified December 8, 2024, 11:18 (UTC), https://en.wikipedia.org/wiki/Yellow_vests_protests.

61 iStock.com/AGaeta, Stock illustration ID: 492968579

62 Frank Holmes, "From France to The U.S.: Pension Reforms And The Retirement Age Debate," *Forbes*, March 20, 2023, https://www.forbes.com/sites/greatspeculations/2023/03/20/from-france-to-the-us-pension-reforms-and-the-retirement-age-debate.

63 Recreated image in Excel – Source Eurostat and Statistica

64 "Social Security Beneficiary Statistics," Social Security Online, accessed December 9, 2024, https://www-origin.ssa.gov/OACT/STATS/OASDIbenies.html.

65 "Is Inflation High Compared to Years Past? Breaking Down Inflation Rates by Year," *Forbes*, January 2, 2023, https://www.forbes.com/sites/qai/2023/01/02/is-inflation-high-compared-to-years-past-breaking-down-inflation-rates-by-year.

66 Image generated by ChatGPT, response to "Please create a black-and-white image at least 300 dpi of a Caucasian child holding a bowl, looking hungry and sad with dirty clothing and a light background," OpenAI, March 9, 2025, https://chatgpt.com/c/67ce0c8b-bbc0-8004-8f30-8b29c176dd17.

67 Charles Dickens, *Oliver Twist* (E.P. Dutton & Co., 1920), 12.

68 "Consumer Price Index – June 2022," Bureau of Labor Statistics, U.S. Department of Labor, July 13, 2022, https://www.dol.gov/newsroom/economicdata/cpi_07132022.pdf.

69 Data from "Cost-Of-Living Adjustments," Social Security Administration, accessed February 26, 2025, https://www.ssa.gov/oact/cola/colaseries.html.

70 "Consumer Price Index - September 2023," Bureau of Labor Statistics, U.S. Department of Labor, October 12, 2023, https:/www.bls.gov/news.release/archives/cpi_10122023.pdf.

71 "80 Percent of Retirees Want Better Inflation Protection," Senior Citizens League, October 13, 2023, https://seniorsleague.org/80-percent-of-retirees-want-better-inflation-protection.

72 "80 Percent of Retirees."

73 Wikipedia, "*Airplane!*," last modified November 28, 2024, 11:45 (UTC), https://en.wikipedia.org/wiki/Airplane!.

74 "*Airplane!*"

75 *Airplane!*, directed by Jim Abrahams, David Zucker, and Jerry Zucker (Paramount Pictures, 1980).

76 Image generated by ChatGPT, response to "Create a black and white image of a man dressed as a pilot, splashing a glass of water in his face," OpenAI, April 19, 2025, https://chatgpt.com/c/6803e2bb-4b20-8004-a40a-14f1c2f00aa3.

77 Amy C. Arnott, Christine Benz, and Jason Kephart, "Morningstar's Retirement Income Research: Reevaluating the 4% Withdrawal Rule," Morningstar, February 11, 2025, https://www.morningstar.com/retirement/morningstars-retirement-income-research-reevaluating-4-withdrawal-rule; Julia Kagan, "What Is the 4% Rule for Withdrawals in Retirement?," Investopedia, last updated June 11, 2024, https://www.investopedia.com/terms/f/four-percent-rule.asp; David Rodeck, "The 4% Rule for Retirement Withdrawals Gets a Closer Look," Kiplinger, last updated December 16, 2024, https://www.kiplinger.com/retirement/retirement-planning/the-4-rule-gets-a-closer-look.

78 Becca Wallis, "20 Top Finance News Publications," Digital Marketing News, February 2, 2025, https://www.dmnews.com/20-top-finance-news-publications/.

79 John Kellerman et al., "The Mental Health Impact of Daily News Exposure During the COVID-19 Pandemic: Ecological Momentary Assessment Study," *JMIR Mental Health* 9, no. 5 (2022): e36966, https://doi.org/10.2196/36966.

80 John Templeton, "16 Rules for Investment Success," StockSastra, archived November 11, 2011, at https://web.archive.org/web/20111111031943/http://www.stocksastra.com/sir-john-templeton/.

81 Image generated by ChatGPT, response to "Chart showing the growth of a $100 investment in the S&P 500 from 1936 to 2021. This version uses more realistic historical average returns and variability, reflecting the exponential growth typically seen in the stock market. Then add historical events that affected the market 1942 WW2 Price Controls, 1962 Cuban Missile Crisis, 1973 Oil Embargo, 1987 Black Monday, 2000 Tech Bubble, 2007 Global Financial Crisis and 2020 Coronavirus Outbreak," OpenAI, December 29, 2024, https://chatgpt.com/c/677157ed-08d0-8004-94bd-44726a01f5db.

82 "Faith, Patience Discipline," Nick Murray Interactive, accessed December 10, 2024, https://www.nickmurraynewsletters.com/members/login.cfm?hpage=Faithpatienceanddiscipline%2Ecfm&loggedout=y.

83 Jess Romeo, "Sharks Before and After Jaws," JSTOR Daily, August 14, 2020, https://daily.jstor.org/sharks-before-and-after-jaws/.

84 "International Shark Attack File," Florida Museum, accessed December 16, 2024, https://www.floridamuseum.ufl.edu/shark-attacks.

85 "Newly Released Estimates Show Traffic Fatalities Reached a 16-Year High in 2021," National Highway Traffic Safety Administration, May 17, 2022, https://www.nhtsa.gov/press-releases/early-estimate-2021-traffic-fatalities.

86 "Introduction," National Safety Council, accessed December 16, 2024, https://injuryfacts.nsc.org/motor-vehicle/overview/introduction.

87 "Tobacco-Related Mortality," Centers for Disease Control and Prevention, last updated April 28, 2020, https://archive.cdc.gov/www_cdc_gov/tobacco/data_statistics/fact_sheets/health_effects/tobacco_related_mortality/index.htm.

88 Jeff John Roberts, "Exclusive: Thirty-Year-Old Billionaire Sam Bankman-Fried Has Been Called the Next Warren Buffett. His Counterintuitive Investment Strategy Will Either Build Him An Empire—Or End in Disaster," *Fortune*, August 1, 2022, https://fortune.com/2022/08/01/ftx-crypto-sam-bankman-fried-interview.

89 MacKenzie Sigalos, "Sam Bankman-Fried Steps Down as FTX CEO As His Crypto Exchange Files for Bankruptcy," CNBC, November 11, 2022, https://www.cnbc.com/2022/11/11/sam-bankman-frieds-cryptocurrency-exchange-ftx-files-for-bankruptcy.html.

90 Cointelegraph, CC BY 3.0 <https://creativecommons.org/licenses/by/3.0>, via Wikimedia Commons (link: https://commons.wikimedia.org/wiki/File:Sam_Bankman-Fried.png)

91 Peter Coy, "It's Been Forty Years Since Our Cover Story Declared 'The Death of Equities,'" *Bloomberg*, August 13, 2019, https://www.bloomberg.com/news/articles/2019-08-13/it-s-been-40-years-since-our-cover-story-declared-the-death-of-equities?embedded-checkout=true.

92 Image generated by ChatGPT, response to "Using Yahoo Finance as the data source, chart the ending balance of the S&P500 from 1982–2000," OpenAI, December 19, 2024, https://chatgpt.com/c/676436c7-3ba8-8004-b785-44105cbae9a6. Data from "S&P 500 (^GSPC) Dec. 31, 1980–Dec. 31 2022," Yahoo Finance, accessed December 19, 2024, https://finance.yahoo.com/quote/%5EGSPC/history/?frequency=1mo&period1=347068800&period2=1672444800.

93 Peter Coy, "Did Capitalism Kill Inflation?" *Bloomberg*, April 17, 2019, https://www.bloomberg.com/magazine/businessweek/19_18.

94 Data from "Wall Street Year-End 2023 Targets for S&P 500," Evensky & Katz/Foldes, Newsletter 17, no. 1 (February 2024), https://19611460.fs1.hubspotusercontent-na1.net/hubfs/19611460/HRE%20NewsLetter/Newsletter%20Vol%2017%20%231%2C%20Feb.%202024_Web.pdf.

95 Image generated by ChatGPT, response to "Create a black and white chart using the data provided from Evensky & Katz/Foldes, Newsletter Volume 17, #1," OpenAI, March 10, 2025, https://chatgpt.com/c/67cef1ee-647c-8004-917a-4ee65930aeb4, numbers added manually. Data from Evensky & Katz/Foldes, Newsletter 17, no. 1 (February 2024), https://19611460.fs1.hubspotusercontent-na1.net/hubfs/19611460/HRE%20NewsLetter/Newsletter%20Vol%2017%20%231%2C%20Feb.%202024_Web.pdf.

96 Wikipedia, "*Hare-Way to the Stars*," last modified December 3, 2024, 00:59 (UTC), https://en.wikipedia.org/wiki/Hare-Way_to_the_Stars.

97 "Business Cycle Dating Committee Announcement January 7, 2008," National Bureau of Economic Research, January 7, 2008, https://www.nber.org/news/business-cycle-dating-committee-announcement-january-7-2008.

98 Data from Edward Yardeni, Joe Abbott, and Mali Quintana, "Stock Market Historical Tables: Bull and Bear Markets," Yardeni Research, Inc., January 21, 2024, https://yardeni.com/wp-content/uploads/BullBearTables.pdf.

99 "S&P 500 Index - 90 Year Historical Chart," Macrotrends, accessed December 12, 2024, https://www.macrotrends.net/2324/sp-500-historical-chart-data.

100 Nick Murray, "The Sixty-Two Year Scorecard," Nick Murray Interactive, February 2024, https://www.nickmurraynewsletters.com/public/TheSixtyTwoYearScorecard-3.cfm.

101 Murray, "The Sixty-Two Year Scorecard."

102 Steven Horn, "An Interview with Arnold Schwarzenegger," IGN, last updated May 20, 2012, https://www.ign.com/articles/2003/06/27/an-interview-with-arnold-schwarzenegger.

103 Data from "What You'll Be Tested On," Certified Financial Planner Board of Standards, accessed February 26, 2025, https://www.cfp.net/get-certified/certification-process/exam-requirement/about-the-cfp-exam/what-youll-be-tested-on.

104 Image generated by ChatGPT, response to "Create a linear chart showing the montly closing prices of the S&P500 from 2018 – 2023 from the data provided from Yahoo! Finance," OpenAI, March 10, 2025, https://chatgpt.com/c/67cf03d2-b2b4-8004-b0b8-e572efbc4b2e. Data from "S&P 500 (^GSPC) Jan. 1 2018–Jan. 1 2024," Yahoo Finance, accessed March 10, 2025, https://finance.yahoo.com/quote/%5EGSPC/history/?frequency=1mo&period1=1514764800&period2=1704067200.

105 "TED: The Economics Daily," U.S. Bureau of Labor Statistics, March 6, 2024, https://www.bls.gov/opub/ted/2024/annual-average-unemployment-rates-decreased-in-6-states-in-2023.htm.

106 Brett Eversole, "This Stock Market Decline Has a Silver Lining," Stansberry Research, May 24, 2022, https://stansberryresearch.com/articles/this-stock-market-decline-has-a-silver-lining.

107 Warren Buffett, "Buy American. I Am," *New York Times*, October 16, 2008, https://www.nytimes.com/2008/10/17/opinion/17buffett.html.

108 *2024 Investment Company Fact Book* (Investment Company Institute, 2024), https://www.ici.org/system/files/2024-05/2024-factbook.pdf.

109 *Guide to the Markets* (J. P. Morgan Asset Management, 2022), https://www.financialplanningassociation.org/sites/default/files/2022-05/DL%20SLides_Fishers_13May2022.pdf.

110 Data from *Guide to the Markets U.S. | 2Q 2022* (J. P. Morgan Asset Management, 2022), 16, https://www.financialplanningassociation.org/sites/default/files/2022-05/DL%20SLides_Fishers_13May2022.pdf.

111 Templeton, "16 Rules for Investment Success."

112 Data from Morningstar Fund Flow Data as of 12/31/22. Stocks represented by the S&P 500 Total Return Index.

113 Morningstar as of 12/31/22 S&P 500 TR Index.

114 Blackrock and Morningstar as of 12/31/22. U.S. stocks are represented by the S&P 500 from 1/1/89–12/31/22.

115 Image generated by ChatGPT, response to "Please analyze the data provided in this chart and create a black and white that is easy to read, and add the section about the returns over 3 and 5 years," OpenAI, December 29, 2024. Data from Morningstar data as of December 31, 2022. Emerging Markets stocks are represented by the FTSE Emerging Markets Index from January 1, 1994, to December 31, 2000, and the MSCI Emerging Markets Index from January 1, 2001, to December 31, 2022.

116 Data from "S&P 500 Index - 90 Year Historical Chart," Macrotrends, accessed February 26, 2025, https://www.macrotrends.net/2324/sp-500-historical0chart-data.

117 Paul Sexton, "Time Was On His Side: The Street-Smart Soul of Jerry Ragovoy," UDiscoverMusic, September 4, 2024, https://www.udiscovermusic.com/stories/time-side-street-smart-soul-jerry-ragovoy.

118 Image generated by ChatGPT, response to "Create a chart with the provided data and asked it to create a chart with the percentages," OpenAI, December 30, 2024. Data from "Time, Not Timing, Is What Matters," American Funds, Capital Group, accessed February 26, 2025, https://www.capitalgroup.com/individual/planning/investing-fundamentals/time-not-timing-is-what-matters.html.

119 "Time, Not Timing, Is What Matters," American Funds, Capital Group, accessed February 26, 2025, https://www.capitalgroup.com/individual/planning/investing-fundamentals/time-not-timing-is-what-matters.html.

120 Warren Buffett, "To the Shareholders of Berkshire Hathaway Inc.," Berkshire Hathaway, February 28, 1989, https://www.berkshirehathaway.com/letters/1988.html.

121 Quote from Warren Buffett, "To the Shareholders of Berkshire Hathaway Inc.," Berkshire Hathaway, February 28, 1989, https://www.berkshirehathaway.com/letters/1988.html.

122 Wikipedia, "(Your Love Keeps Lifting Me) Higher and Higher," last modified November 20, 2024, 1:14 (UTC), https://en.wikipedia.org/wiki/(Your_Love_Keeps_Lifting_Me)_Higher_and_Higher.

123 "(Your Love Keeps Lifting Me) Higher and Higher by Jackie Wilson," SecondHandSongs, accessed December 17, 2024, https://secondhandsongs.com/performance/5008/versions.

124 Adam Hayes, "Recency (Availability) Bias: What It Is, How It Works," Investopedia, last updated August 15, 2024, https://www.investopedia.com/recency-availability-bias-5206686.

125 Image generated by Claude, response to "Create a linear chart showing the montly closing prices of the S&P500 from 2018 – 2023 from the data provided from Yahoo! Finance," Anthropic, January 5, 2025. Data from "S&P 500 (^GSPC) Jan. 1 2018–Jan. 1 2024," Yahoo Finance, accessed January 5, 2025, https://finance.yahoo.com/quote/%5EGSPC/history/?frequency=1mo&period1=1514764800&period2=1704067200.

126 Image generated by DALL-E, response to "Create an image of three teddy bears, line sketch type drawing, simple in black and white," OpenAI, December 30, 2024, https://chatgpt.com/c/6772c49c-9eb0-8004-8387-2d85ee8852b7, text added using Designer.

[127] Wikipedia, "Spinning Wheel (song)," last modified September 14, 2024, 20:14 (UTC), https://en.wikipedia.org/wiki/Spinning_Wheel_(song).

[128] Image generated by ChatGPT, response to "Using data from Yahoo Finance create a chart showing the volatility of the S&P 500 from June 2021–June 2023," OpenAI, December 20, 2024. Data from "S&P 500 (^GSPC) May 16, 2024–May 16, 2025," Yahoo Finance, accessed December 20, 2024, https://finance.yahoo.com/quote/%5EGSPC/history/.

[129] Image generated by DALL-E, response to "Create a chart in black and white that represents an investment that goes up 20% and down 20% over and over," OpenAI, December 20, 2024.

[130] Image generated by DALL-E, response to "Using RIMES, Standards & Poor and Capital Group Data create a chart in black and white that shows the cumulative returns for each bear and bull market from 1950 – 2020," OpenAI, December 19, 2024. Data from "Guide to Stock Market Recoveries," American Funds, Capital Group, July 19, 2023, https://www.capitalgroup.com/individual/ca/en/insights/articles/guide-to-market-recoveries.html.

[131] "Case Study: LTCM," C.T. Bauer College of Business, University of Houston, accessed December 12, 2024, https://www.bauer.uh.edu/rsusmel/7386/ltcm-2.htm.

[132] Image generated by DALL-E, response to "Using When Genius Falls as a reference create a black and white chart of how $1 investment in long term capital management grew up to 1997," OpenAI, December 19, 2024. Data from Roger Lowenstein, *When Genius Failed: The Rise and Fall of Long-Term Capital Management* (Random House, 2001).

[133] Roger Lowenstein, *When Genius Failed: The Rise and Fall of Long-Term Capital Management* (Random House, 2000), 191.

[134] Image generated by DALL-E, response to "Using When Genius Falls as a reference please show how $1 investment in the long term capital management fund would rise and fall," OpenAI, December 30, 2024. Data from Roger Lowenstein, *When Genius Failed: The Rise and Fall of Long-Term Capital Management* (Random House, 2001).

[135] "Yellow Submarine," The Beatles Bible, accessed December 12, 2024, https://www.beatlesbible.com/albums/yellow-submarine.

[136] Templeton, "16 Rules for Investment Success."

[137] Image generated by DALL-E, response to "Create a black and white image of a baby in a suit with money around him, in a highchair," OpenAI, December 18, 2024, https://chatgpt.com/c/67c1c1a5-aa68-8004-a498-8c5f398450b2.

[138] Image generated by DALL-E, response to "Create a black and white image of a trucker in his cab with a picture or reference to a beach," OpenAI, December 19, 2024, https://chatgpt.com/c/67dc1561-c978-8004-8616-ad661036a2e1.

[139] "Bernanke Was Wrong," posted May 22, 2009, by Alan Fox, YouTube, 5 min., 7 sec., https://youtu.be/INmqvibv4UU?si=CRzIhR2txX-73-XF.

[140] *Merriam-Webster*, "herd mentality," accessed December 12, 2024, https://www.merriam-webster.com/dictionary/herd%20mentality.

141 George Santayana, *The Life of Reason, or the Phases of Human Progress* (Charles Scribner's Books, 1905), 82.

142 Re-creation of "Stocks and Bonds: Risk Versus Return 1970-2019" from "Investor Biases: Naïve or Apparent Diversification," Investorpolis, September 26, 2020, https://investorpolis.com/managing-our-behavioural-biases-naive-or-apparent-diversification/.

143 "M2 Definition and Meaning in the Money Supply," Investopedia, last updated March 2, 2024, https://www.investopedia.com/terms/m/m2.asp.

144 iStock.com/EkaterinaKorzh, Stock illustration ID: 1454324788

145 Image generated by DALL-E, response to "Create a minimalist image in black and white of the side view of a seesaw with no people," OpenAI, December 31, 2024, https://chatgpt.com/c/6773fa56-4408-8004-a476-3247cdcd044f, text added in Designer.

146 Up My Interest, accessed December 12, 2024, www.upmyinterest.com.

147 Jeff Cox, "Federal Reserve Points to Interest Rate Hike Coming in March," CNBC, January 26, 2022, https://www.cnbc.com/2022/01/26/fed-decision-january-2022-.html.

148 Morningstar as of 11/30/21. U.S. Bonds are represented by the U.S. Aggregate Bond TR Index from 1/3/89–11/30/21 and the U.S. Government IT Index from 1/1/1926–11/89.

149 Michael Adams, "Federal Funds Rate History 1990 to 2024," *Forbes*, last updated September 18, 2024, https://www.forbes.com/advisor/investing/fed-funds-rate-history; Up My Interest, accessed December 12, 2024, https://www.upmyinterest.com/bloomberg-us-aggregate-bonds.

150 "Ten Year Treasury Rate – 54 Year Historical Chart," Macrotrends, accessed December 12, 2024, https://www.macrotrends.net/2016/10-year-treasury-bond-rate-yield-chart.

151 Image courtesy of Maulden Economics, used with permission.

152 Wikipedia, "*Young Frankenstein*," last modified November 28, 2024, 2:23 (UTC), https://en.wikipedia.org/wiki/Young_Frankenstein.

153 *Young Frankenstein*, directed by Mel Brooks (1974; 20th Century Fox).

154 Re-creation of "1926–2022," in Ron Surz, "2022 Stock and Bond Returns in a 97-Year Perspective," VettaFi, January 3, 2023, https://www.advisorperspectives.com/articles/2023/01/03/2022-stock-and-bond-returns-in-a-97-year-perspective.

155 "Ten Year Treasury Rate – 54 Year Historical Chart," Macrotrends, accessed December 12, 2024, https://www.macrotrends.net/2016/10-year-treasury-bond-rate-yield-chart.

156 Image generated by ChatGPT, response to "Create a black and white image of a gentleman serving as federal reserve chairman, gray hair/suit, maybe a building behind him and a flag? Add glasses," OpenAI, March 20, 2025, https://chatgpt.com/c/67dc2599-7180-8004-830e-c7fcc11eacd7.

157 iStock.com/Aluna1, Stock illustration ID: 1323457906

158 Image generated by ChatGPT, response to "Create a black and white bar chart using data from up my interest to chart the Bloomberg Aggregate Bond Index Calendar Returns from 1976 – 2022," OpenAI, January 1, 2025, https://chatgpt.

com/c/67754f66-3160-8004-ba2e-270d24645eb9. Data from "Annual Returns," Capital Group, accessed January 1, 2025, https://www.capitalgroup.com/individual/investments/fund/bfafx/chartmodalfullscreen?initialchart=returns.

159 Image generated by ChatGPT, response to "Using WSJ data create a black and white line chart of the daily close of the Core US Aggregate Bond ETF," OpenAI, January 1, 2025, https://chatgpt.com/c/67755a8b-b944-8004-84a4-a0526f1db74c. Data from AGG US Aggregate Bond Index 1/1/22–12/31/23.

160 Image generated by ChatGPT, response to "Using data from Yahoo Finance and WSJ focusing on May (-1.1%), June (-.4%), July (-.1%), August (-.6%), September (-2.5%), October (-1.6%) and November (+4.5%) of 2023 please create a bar chart in black and white showing the returns," OpenAI, January 4, 2025. Data from Morningstar as of November 30, 2023. US bonds represented by the IA SBBI US Government Index from January 1, 1926, to January 3, 1989, and the Bloomberg US Aggregate Bond TR Index from January 3, 1989, to December 31, 2022.

161 *Ferris Bueller's Day Off*, directed by John Hughes (1986; Paramount Pictures).

162 Image generated by ChatGPT, response to "https://skloff.com/growth-of-1-investment-1926-2022/ - using the data on this website, please create a chart showing how much $1 invested in 1926 through 2022 would grow to in small stocks (11.8% or $49052), large stocks (10.1% or $11535), government bonds (5.2% or $131), Treasury bills (3.2% or $22) and inflation (2.9% or $17). Showing market fluctuations with the volatility of various economic crises like the stock market crash/depression, Pearl Harbor, the Sputnik launch, the JFK assassination, the Arab oil embargo, the stock market crash in the 1980s, the Gulf War, 9/11 and the Global Financial Crisis," OpenAI, March 23, 2025, https://chatgpt.com/c/67e01937-e0fc-8004-8edf-35bf540cf957, labels and colors edited in Designer.

163 Wikipedia, "You Better You Bet," October 5, 2024, 20:56 (UTC), https://en.wikipedia.org/wiki/You_Better_You_Bet.

164 "Record 68 Million Americans to Wager $23.1B on Super Bowl LVIII," American Gaming Association, February 6, 2024, https://www.americangaming.org/new/record-68-million-americans-to-wager-23-1b-on-super-bowl-lviii.

165 Adam Liptak and Kevin Draper, "Supreme Court Ruling Favors Sports Betting," *New York Times*, May 14, 2018, https://www.nytimes.com/2018/05/14/us/politics/supreme-court-sports-betting-new-jersey.html.

166 Re-created from "Time, Diversification and the Volatility of Returns," J.P. Morgan, accessed May 16, 2025, https://am.jpmorgan.com/us/en/asset-management/institutional/insights/market-insights/guide-to-the-markets/guide-to-the-markets-slides-us/investing-principles/gtm-histreturns/.

167 Gregory L. Taylor, "Macroeconomic Conditions in 2018," United States International Trade Commission, accessed December 12, 2024, https://www.usitc.gov/research_and_analysis/trade_shifts_2018/macroeconomic_conditions.htm.

168 "U.S. GDP Growth Rate 1961-2024," Macrotrends, accessed December 12, 2024, https://www.macrotrends.net/global-metrics/countries/USA/united-states/gdp-growth-rate.

169 "Composite Index of Leading Indicators: Definition and Uses," Investopedia, last updated January 26, 2023, https://www.investopedia.com/terms/c/cili.asp.

170 Data from "Annual Growth of Real GDP in the United States of America from 1930 to 2022," Statista, December 2023, https://www.statista.com/statistics/996758/rea-gdp-growth-united-states-1930-2019/.

171 Michael LeBoeuf, *How to Win Customers and Keep Them for Life* (Putnam's Sons, 1987), 181.

172 Image generated by DALL-E, response to "Create a picture of a sticky note that I can add text to easily," OpenAI, March 20, 2025, https://chatgpt.com/c/67dc5825-60ec-8004-905c-1033f440549d, text added in Designer.

173 "Complete Historical Data," in "Sentiment Survey Historical Data," American Association of Individual Investors, accessed May 16, 2025, https://www.aaii.com/sentimentsurvey/sent_results.

174 Morningstar and Gallup as of 3/31/22. Stock market represented by the S&P 500 index. Note: Gallup "Satisfaction Level" polling data was recorded every month after April 2000. Prior to April 2000, Gallus "satisfaction level" polling data was recorded on an ad hoc basis.

175 Data from "1980 Full List," CNN Money, accessed May 16, 2025, https://money.cnn.com/magazines/fortune/fortune500_archive/full/1980/; "2000 Full List," CNN Money, accessed May 16, 2025, https://money.cnn.com/magazines/fortune/fortune500_archive/full/2000/; The 100 largest companies in the world by market capitalization in 2024, Statista, June 2024, https://www.statista.com/statistics/263264/top-companies-in-the-world-by-market-capitalization/.

176 iStock.com/photokozyr, Stock illustration ID: 1091645028

177 "Bernanke Was Wrong."

178 Re-created from "S&P 500 Intra-Year Declines Vs. Calendar Year Returns," in "How Does the Volatility of the Stock Market Affect Your Investment?", X and Y Advisors, December 12, 2017, https://www.xandyadvisors.com/blog/how-does-the-volatility-of-the-stock-market-affect-your-investment.

179 "How Old Is the Grand Canyon? The Real Age of the Grand Canyon," Grand Canyon Visitor Center, last updated April 9, 2021, https://explorethecanyon.com/the-real-age-of-the-grand-canyon.

180 Image generated by ChatGPT, response to "Using the data provided in an excel spreadsheet showing the value of the dollar over time create a visual to represent the decline," OpenAI, December 21, 2024, edited in Designer. Data from Govind Bhutada, "Purchasing Power of the U.S. Dollar Over Time," Visual Capitalist, April 6, 2021, https://www.visualcapitalist.com/purchasing-power-of-the-u-s-dollar-over-time/.

181 Wikipedia, "Maginot Line," last modified December 14, 2024, 14:59 (UTC), https://en.wikipedia.org/wiki/Maginot_Line.

182 Photo by John C. Watkins V.

183 "Maginot Line."

184 Map by Goran tek-en (Wikimedia Commons, CC BY-SA 4.0).

185 Wayne Duggan, "A History of U.S. Bear Markets, 1957 to 2022," *Forbes*, last updated August 21, 2023, https://www.forbes.com/advisor/investing/bear-market-history.

186 Alexandra Twin, "Dow Fights Back," CNN Money, last updated March 6, 2009, archived from https://web.archive.org/web/20090307121018/https://money.cnn.com/2009/03/06/markets/markets_newyork/index.htm.

187 Nick Murray, "Client's Corner: How Do You Feel About Money?" Nick Murray Interactive, accessed December 16, 2024, https://www.nickmurraynewsletters.com/members/login.cfm?hpage=Clients%5FCorner%5FHow%5FDo%5FYou%5FFeel%5FAbout%5FMoney%2Ecfm&loggedout=y.

188 Photo by Jesse Hurst.

189 Eric Rosenbaum, "As Inflation Bites and America's Mood Darkens, Higher-income Consumers Are Cutting Back, Too," CNBC, April 8, 2022, https://www.cnbc.com/2022/04/08/as-inflation-bites-higher-income-consumers-are-cutting-back-too.html.

190 Rosenbaum, "Inflation Bites."

191 Rosenbaum, "Inflation Bites."

192 "How Does Consumer Spending Impact the Health of the Economy?," U.S. Bank, December 12, 2024, https://www.usbank.com/investing/financial-perspectives/market-news/consumer-spending.html.

193 "Chart Book: Tracking the Recovery from the Pandemic Recession," Center on Budget and Policy Priorities, last updated April 3, 2024, https://www.cbpp.org/research/economy/tracking-the-recovery-from-the-pandemic-recession.

194 Image generated by ChatGPT, response to "Please create a black and white image of a game show scene with a female contestant and a male host, she is winning a car and the price was $4125," OpenAI, April 20, 2025, https://chatgpt.com/c/67670c4c-66b0-8004-a70a-8ccbd5641f18.

195 "Average New-Vehicle Prices Continue to Surpass $40,000, Up More Than 5% in January 2021, According to Kelley Blue Book," Kelley Blue Book, February 15, 2021, https://mediaroom.kbb.com/2021-02-15-Average-New-Vehicle-Prices-Continue-to-Surpass-40-000-Up-More-Than-5-in-January-2021-According-to-Kelley-Blue-Book.

196 Image generated by DALL-E, response to "Create a black and white at least 300 dpi image of 3 grocery bags (the brown bag style), in the first bag (left) inside the bag, please put inside the bag a carton of milk and juice, vegetables, fruit, canned food and two loaves of bread. Make the bag look full of items. The second bag (middle) same brown bag, please put inside the bag a carton of milk, vegetables, canned food and fruit and one loaf of bread (image should represent less food than the first bag). In the last bag (right) same brown bag, please put inside the bag a carton of milk, canned food and one loaf of bread only. The image should reflect that each bag has less items than the one next to it," OpenAI, January 4, 2025, https://chatgpt.com/c/67794abd-88bc-8004-be98-570986e9ab17, text added.

197 Re-created from "How Much Debt Does the US Have – US Debt by Year," Kailash Concepts, July 16, 2021, https://kailashconcepts.com/how-much-debt-does-the-us-have-us-debt-by-year/.

198 Julia Kagan, "Owners' Equivalent Rent (OER): Definition and Relationship to CPI," Investopedia, last updated May 14, 2023, https://www.investopedia.com/terms/o/owners-equivalent-rent.asp.

199 Image from Bureau of Labor Statistics.

200 Chart created using macromicro.me.

201 "Metric Conversion Act of 1975," U.S. Metric Association, last updated November 17, 2015, https://usma.org/laws-and-bills/metric-conversion-act-of-1975.

202 Erin Blakemore, "Here's the Real Reason the U.S. Doesn't Use the Metric System," National Geographic, June 18, 2024, https://www.nationalgeographic.com/history/article/metric-system-imperial-measurement-history-us-america.

203 Data from Marc E. Fitch, "Inflation May Be Much Higher than Reported, and That Could Hurt Seniors and the Poor," Yankee Institute, December 15 , 2021, https://yankeeinstitute.org/2021/12/15/inflation-may-be-much-higher-than-reported-and-that-could-hurt-seniors-and-the-poor/.

204 Juliana Menasce Horowitz, Ruth Igielnik, and Rakesh Kochhar, "Trends in Income and Wealth Inequality," Pew Research Center, January 9, 2020, https://www.pewresearch.org/social-trends/2020/01/09/trends-in-income-and-wealth-inequality.

205 Richard Scammon and Ben Wattenberg, *The Real Majority: An Extraordinary Examination of the American Electorate* (Coward-McCann, 1970).

206 Image courtesy of Maulden Economics, used with permission.

207 Image courtesy of Maulden Economics, used with permission.

208 "How Much Will You Spend in Retirement?," Fidelity, accessed February 24, 2025, https://www.fidelity.com/viewpoints/retirement/spending-in-retirement.

209 "How Much Will You Spend?"

210 Data from "ACS Demographic and Housing Estimates," United States Census Bureau, accessed February 27, 2025, https://data.census.gov/table/ACSDP1Y2017.DP05?q=United%20States&table=DP05&g=010XX00US&lastDisplayedRow=29&vintage=2017&layer=state&cid=DP05_0001E&tid=ACSDP1Y2017.DP05.

211 Image generated by ChatGPT, response to "Using the data on the spreadsheet provided please chart the declining birthrates," OpenAI, March 15, 2025, https://chatgpt.com/c/67d6fe20-6ae8-8004-9654-1598834d307b, labels and colors edited. Data from "International Database," United States Census Bureau, accessed March 15, 2025, https://www.census.gov/data-tools/demo/idb/#/dashboard?dashboard_page=country&COUNTRY_YR_ANIM=2025.

212 Thomas William Dorsey, "The Impact of WTO Ascension," IMF eLibrary, February 24, 2003, https://www.elibrary.imf.org/display/book/9781589061781/ch012.xml.

213 By Larry Hachucka - Own work, CC BY-SA 4.0, https://commons.wikimedia.org/w/index.php?curid

214 "Estimates of the Population of the United States January 1, 1950 to February 1, 1967," *Population Estimates* 25, no. 363 (1967): 1–2, https://www2.census.gov/library/publications/1967/demographics/P25-363.pdf.

215 "U.S. and World Population Clock," United States Census Bureau, accessed February 25, 2025, https://www.census.gov/popclock/.

216 "What Will America's Population Look Like by 2100?," USAFacts, January 26, 2024, https://usafacts.org/articles/what-will-americas-population-look-like-by-2100/.

217 Image generated by ChatGPT, response to "Create a chart using the data provided in this spreadsheet from https://www.macrotrends.net/global-metrics/countries/CHN/china/birth-rate," OpenAI, March 15, 2025, https://chatgpt.com/c/674a0848-6898-8004-b750-f378fb332b8e. Data from "China Birth Rate 1950-2025," Macrotrends, accessed March 15, 2025, https://www.macrotrends.net/global-metrics/countries/CHN/china/birth-rate.

218 Albee Zhang and Farah Master, "China's First Population Drop in Six Decades Sounds Alarm on Demographic Crisis," Reuters, January 17, 2023, https://www.reuters.com/world/china/chinas-population-shrinks-first-time-since-1961-2023-01-17.

219 Ed Yardeni, "China: The World's Largest Nursing Home," Yardeni Quick Takes, November 27, 2023, https://www.yardeniquicktakes.com/china-the-worlds-largest-nursing-home.

220 Image generated by ChatGPT, response to "Using this spreadsheet chart the government mandatory vs discretionary spending – source - https://www.usgovernmentspending.com/spending_chart_1962_2024USp_26s2li011t-gnc_F0f_Mandatory_and_Discretionary_Spending_Since_1962," OpenAI, March 15, 2025, https://chatgpt.com/c/67d6f9c5-a80c-8004-b2c6-80c5a994ab80. Data from Christopher Chantrill, "Mandatory And Discretionary Spending Since 1962," USGovernmentSpending.com, accessed March 15, 2025, https://www.usgovernmentspending.com/spending_chart_1962_2024USp_26s2li011t-gnc_F0f_Mandatory_and_Discretionary_Spending_Since_1962.

221 Alicia Wallace, "Fed Chair Jerome Powell Says 'Some Pain' Is on the Horizon. Here's What That Means," CNN, last updated August 30, 2022, https://www.cnn.com/2022/08/30/economy/fed-jerome-powell-pain-economy/index.html.

222 Image generated by ChatGPT, response to "Using the data downloaded from FRED, using this data, create a chart showing employment native vs. foreign born (cumulative change) – Data source - https://fredblog.stlouisfed.org/2022/12/native-and-immigrant-employment-during-the-pandemic/?utm_source=series_page&utm_medium=related_content&utm_term=related_resources&utm_campaign=fredblog," OpenAI, March 16, 2025, https://chatgpt.com/c/67d6d6d1-f5e4-8004-b6e1-4b0f2649ff98. Data from "Native and Immigrant Employment During the Pandemic," *Federal Reserve Bank of St. Louis Blog*, December 15, 2022, https://fredblog.stlouisfed.org/2022/12/native-and-immigrant-employment-during-the-pandemic/.

223 Wikipedia, "My Back Pages," last modified September 22, 2024, 10:39 (UTC), https://en.wikipedia.org/wiki/My_Back_Pages.

224 "My Back Pages."

225 Chris Duderstadt, "Peak 65: Nearly 4.4 Million Americans Projected to Turn 65 in 2024," Modern Wealth Management, January 3, 2024, https://www.modwm.com/peak-65-nearly-4-4-million-americans-projected-to-turn-65-in-2024.

226 Image from the Bureau of Labor Statistics.

227 Image generated by ChatGPT, response to "Using the following data source https://www.genworth.com/aging-and-you/finances/cost-of-care/cost-of-care-trends-and-insights can you create a chart from 2011-2023 showing the Assisted Living Costs (last chart)," OpenAI, January 2, 2025, https://chatgpt.com/c/6776f1f2-d2a8-8004-85d0-2458f6b84b43. Data from "Calculate the Cost of Long-term Care Near You," CareScout, accessed January 2, 2025, https://www.genworth.com/aging-and-you/finances/cost-of-care/cost-of-care-trends-and-insights

228 Wikipedia, "Things That Make You Go Hmmm…," last modified November 22, 2024, 23:57 (UTC), https://en.wikipedia.org/wiki/Things_That_Make_You_Go_Hmmm….

229 Image generated by ChatGPT, response to "Create a black and white sign that says Things that make you go hmmm...," OpenAI, April 20, 2025, https://chatgpt.com/c/6805049c-a23c-8004-987d-721340ecc285.

230 "Spend or Not."

231 "Spend or Not."

232 "Spend or Not."

233 Wikipedia, "The Beat (British band)," last modified December 4, 2024, 3:24 (UTC), https://en.wikipedia.org/wiki/The_Beat_(British_band).

234 Wikipedia, "Livin' on the Edge," last modified July 13, 2024, 2:57 (UTC), https://en.wikipedia.org/wiki/Livin%27_on_the_Edge.

235 Aerosmith and Stephen Davis, *Walk This Way: The Autobiography of Aerosmith* (Dey Street Books, 2003), 475.

236 Image generated by ChatGPT, response to "Using data pulled from the WSJ please chart the price of the S&P 500 from January 1 2010 through December 31, 2019 in a line chart black and white," OpenAI, January 2, 2025. Data from "S&P 500 Index Jan. 1 2010–Dec. 31, 2019," *Wall Street Journal*, accessed January 2, 2025, https://www.wsj.com/market-data/quotes/index/SPX/historical-prices

237 Wikipedia, "The Gold Diggers' Song (We're in the Money)," last modified August 28, 2024, 21:35 (UTC), https://en.wikipedia.org/wiki/The_Gold_Diggers%27_Song_(We%27re_in_the_Money).

238 Wikipedia, "*42nd Street* (musical)," last modified December 14, 2024, 9:38 (UTC), https://en.wikipedia.org/wiki/42nd_Street_(musical).

239 iStock.com/Evgenb, Stock illustration ID: 96244905

240 Wikipedia, "*National Lampoon's Vacation*," last modified December 11, 2024, 6:11 (UTC), https://en.wikipedia.org/wiki/National_Lampoon%27s_Vacation.

241 Image generated by ChatGPT, response to "Create a black and white image of a station wagon from the 80s with wood panels with luggage on top representing a family going on vacation," OpenAI, April 20, 2025, https://chatgpt.com/c/680506a8-eb2c-8004-b615-601be76cd783.

242 Wikipedia, "*It's a Wonderful Life*," December 15, 2024, 20:20 (UTC), https://en.wikipedia.org/wiki/It%27s_a_Wonderful_Life.

243 "*It's a Wonderful Life*."

244 Stephen Cox, "On a Wing and a Prayer," *LA Times*, December 23, 2006, https://www.latimes.com/archives/la-xpm-2006-dec-23-et-wonderful23-story.html.

245 Berra, *Fork in the Road*, 53.

246 Wikipedia, "Can't Get There from Here," last modified May 29, 2024, 1:41 (UTC), https://en.wikipedia.org/wiki/Cant_Get_There_from_Here.

247 "2023 Retirement Confidence Survey," Employee Benefit Research Institute, 2023, https://www.ebri.org/docs/default-source/rcs/2023-rcs/2023-rcs-short-report.pdf.

248 "2023 Retirement Confidence Survey," 5.

249 "2023 Retirement Confidence Survey," 5.

250 Image generated by DALL-E, response to "Create an image of sheep on a mountain following the leader who has fallen off the cliff – like a follow the leader type image," OpenAI, December 22, 2024, https://chatgpt.com/c/67d59c73-cb40-8004-a095-041b9047993c.

251 Image generated by DALL-E, response to "Create a black and white image of a to go coffee cup with a lid, blank no writing or markings on the cup," OpenAI, December 22, 2024, https://chatgpt.com/c/67683b59-1f34-8004-ac41-dd8c33188ee3, text added using Designer.

252 Rachel Chang, "Dr. Seuss Wrote 'Green Eggs and Ham' on a Bet," Biography, March 2, 2020, https://www.biography.com/authors-writers/dr-seuss-green-eggs-and-ham-bet.

253 Dr. Seuss, *Oh the Places You'll Go!*.

254 Quote from Dr. Seuss, *Oh the Places You'll Go!* (Random House, 1990). Photo from pixabay.com by chriskeller. Text added using Designer.

255 Dr. Seuss, *Oh the Places You'll Go!*.

256 Luke 12:48 (New Revised Standard Version).

257 Jim Owsley, M. D. Bright, and Al Williamson, *Spider-Man vs. Wolverine #1* (Marvel Comics, 1987).

258 Zig Ziglar, *Secrets of Closing the Sale* (Berkley, 1984), 22.

259 Quote from Zig Ziglar, *Secrets of Closing the Sale* (Berkley, 1984), 22.

www.ingramcontent.com/pod-product-compliance
Lightning Source LLC
LaVergne TN
LVHW052256200926
848481LV00002B/380

* 9 7 9 8 9 9 8 7 3 1 4 0 2 *